BREAKING THE BONDS

Making Peace in Northern Ireland

FIONNUALA O CONNOR

MAINSTREAM PUBLISHING

EDINBURGH AND LONDON

First published in Great Britain in 2002 by
MAINSTREAM PUBLISHING COMPANY (EDINBURGH) LTD
7 Albany Street
Edinburgh EH1 3UG

ISBN 1 84018 610 0

A catalogue record for this book is available from the British Library

Typeset in Garamond and TradeGothic
Printed and bound in Great Britain by
Mackays of Chatham Ltd

CONTENTS

ACKNOWLEDGMENTS

ACKNOWLEDGEMENTS

The Joseph Rowntree Charitable Trust generously supported the preparation of this book, as they did the writing and publication of *In Search of a State*. It may not be the study originally planned, but at one point it looked as though there might not be a further process to record. To Trust Secretary Stephen Pittam and the tribe of Quakerdom in York and in Ireland, sincere thanks. The good-hearted and sparky discussions they offered were, as always, a bonus.

My thanks to many perceptive colleagues over the years for their views; some might be more alarmed by acknowledgement than appreciative. *The Economist* has been forgiving towards an occasionally distracted Belfast correspondent. To my husband, David McVea; and my friends and colleagues David McKittrick and Póilín Ní Chiaráin, who read the text at various stages so patiently and offered so many suggestions, I am indebted for their charity as much as for their professionalism. The imperfections are all mine. Deborah Kilpatrick in Mainstream has given the book consideration beyond the call of duty.

To Emer and Karen, a big thank you for the laughter and encouragement at trying moments; to Caitriona and my parents Frances and Liam, thank you all three for forgiving the neglect of family; Syd, Fiona, Ruth and Rosie, I hope we're still friends. And to David, who advised, cooked, comforted and read some more: I couldn't have done it without you.

INTRODUCTION

Ten years on from writing a book, *In Search of a State,* which tracked how northern Catholics had changed politically, it seemed a good time to look again at developments. Then, the nationalist community looked ready for considerable movement. In fact, although few knew it, the two very different nationalist leaders, John Hume of the Social Democratic and Labour Party (SDLP) and Gerry Adams of Sinn Féin, had just begun to talk out the first steps of a peace process, and emissaries from the British government were secretly meeting the IRA.

Talking to a wide range of Catholics for *In Search of a State,* including Hume and Adams, I kept glimpsing the potential for a breakthrough. The title selected itself: this was a community never comfortable in a unionist and British Northern Ireland, now at last confident and well enough led to begin setting terms for a new arrangement. A senior SDLP man told me: 'People will not accept an arrangement which doesn't recognise their Irishness, in exactly the same way as the Britishness of unionists.' There was a wish to be done with the violence, to re-examine relationships with Britain and the south, and with Protestants and unionists.

By the time negotiations began, nationalists were already half-prepared for the Good Friday Agreement. Unionists were not, and the gap between the expectations and moods of the two political groups remain painfully wide. The personalities of those who lead have mattered more, perhaps, than they ought. Northern Ireland is a small place, its political society smaller again because in reality it splits in two. Politicians growl at each other, at least in public, across deeply incised boundaries. In the heat of constant battle, personality makes a disproportionate impact, for good and ill. But the hope now is that verbal battle alone will carry the burden of bitterness and mistrust, that the next few years might see only the dregs of violence.

This has been a testing time for many politicians, disastrous for some, a walk in warm sunshine for others. Their profiles vary accordingly. They are sketched here from close observation, my own and that of others, from years spent reporting their behaviour, trying to understand what makes them tick and how they relate to the wider political context. The cartoons by Ian Knox are part of the book; I hope at least some readers will judge it by its cover, and buy it on the strength of Ian's work.

Few opinions in this book are attributed to named sources, a working method of particular use in a small and divided society. Those in the political world who spoke frankly, occasionally fondly, of their peers over many years did so in the knowledge that they would not be identified, that their identities would be disguised. There are only so many synonyms for 'veteran' and 'observer', a limited number of ways to fudge the gender of a source. Where those become tiresome, I apologise to the reader. Political and religious background is given where relevant, unaltered. Once or twice the first effort at a deft cover-up so thoroughly protected one person that it pointed to another instead, an accidental double-bluff. Let no one suppose that any identity is obvious. If it appears obvious, I promise, it is not so.

1

THE DAY THE LANDSCAPE CHANGED

For Britain the general election result of 2001 was unsurprising and undramatic, confirming as it did that Tony Blair's Labour government would continue to be in charge with a huge majority: business as before. Across the Irish Sea in Northern Ireland, however, the earth shuddered.

There ageing faces sagged under trial and in defeat as they faced involuntary redundancy, as line-ups in the television studios tested tempers. The election had always promised to be a key test for all the parties and for the underpinnings of the Good Friday Agreement. Would it shake the accord? Who would it leave in charge of unionism, who would be predominant in nationalism?

In the event, Sinn Féin bypassed the SDLP by a narrow margin to become possessor of most nationalist votes. Ian Paisley's Democratic Unionists made much headway at the expense of David Trimble's Ulster Unionists. It was the day the landscape changed, a watershed in Northern Ireland's political geography which observers and many participants needed months to absorb.

The hope had been that politics might in time focus on power-sharing at Stormont in Belfast's devolved assembly, with moderation making steady headway and the divisive headcounts of general elections becoming steadily less significant and central. If peace beds down, that might still happen. But in that crucial summer of 2001 the poll for the 18 Westminster seats was a gauge of electoral strengths inside both main communities, the best available measurement of where unionists and nationalists thought 'the peace process' had taken them. The results were a triumph for the extremes.

Paisley's party won three new seats, Sinn Féin two. The Democratic Unionist Party's (DUP) advance surprised no one, but Sinn Féin overtook the SDLP ahead of expectations. The old order faded amid the cruellest of sound bites, and the creak of disconcerted media. 'You'll just have to get used to this new dispensation,' Gerry Adams told one anchorman with steel in his smile, while Sinn Féin's spokespeople cruised the studios like basking sharks, huge grins revealing several rows of teeth. The biggest DUP smile came from the pioneer of the shark grin, party leader Ian Paisley, all his old menace channelled into pantomime satisfaction.

But, though David Trimble's authority took yet another knock, the Ulster Unionists held their position as biggest party and stayed ahead of Paisley's DUP. Nationalism was a different proposition. The lasting image of the day was that of a disoriented John Hume denying reality. 'Sinn Féin will not overtake the SDLP,' he told a reporter at his own Derry count. 'It has not happened and it will not happen.' Next day, with the conviction he once brought to his credo that nationalists and unionists must share power to find a common purpose, he called the result 'a blip', eyes blank behind more than usually smeary glasses.

It was a dismaying glimpse of a shaken political giant, the man who had lifted the problems of Northern Ireland's once passive and hopeless nationalists on to the world stage through unrelenting positiveness, helping to transform them into a confident people in the process. His groundbreaking thinking had helped bring comparative peace, and the Nobel Peace Prize for himself and Trimble. Suddenly, all that seemed the stuff of history rather than news and current affairs.

In a day of telling images, a procession of Paisley's people thanked God for their victories, bowed their heads to sing remorselessly grim old-fashioned hymns and laid into the media for downplaying their chances. Other shaken SDLP figures completed the picture of an ageing party falling in on itself. Ulster Unionists presented a characteristic mishmash of attitudes, from the inconsequential cheeriness of the newly retired and ennobled Lord Maginnis, previously Ken, ricocheting round the television studios, to a rattled candidate beaten in Maginnis' former Fermanagh-South Tyrone by a much younger Sinn Féin woman with a margin of 53 votes. Defeated Ulster Unionist James Cooper immediately explained the result by claiming that republican intimidation forced a polling station to stay open late. He said he would challenge the result in court. It made no difference to the mood.

This was the moment when a crashing Sinn Féin tide hit unionists and moderate nationalists west of the Bann, always the most Catholic part of Northern Ireland. Cooper, a middle-aged country solicitor, had struggled to succeed Ken Maginnis and hold a seat with an inbuilt Catholic majority, safe for unionism only when a single unionist competes against divided nationalists. Unionists called on their different parties to unite, to stop republicans 'greening the west'. Local infighting threw up a challenger for Protestant votes. A youthful Sinn Féin machine read the signs and pounded the doorsteps for 31-year-old Michelle Gildernew, tailor-made to represent republicans at a time of transition: no IRA record, a recent graduate, a family pedigree that boasted the first squatters of the civil rights movement.

Next door in West Tyrone, the SDLP tried to block another Sinn Féin candidate by replacing a low-profile local man with the well-known Brid Rodgers, the SDLP's surprise star performer as a Stormont minister. They pitched scarce resources behind her, a gamble in itself. They also risked leaving the seat in the hands of the anti-Agreement Ulster Unionist MP Willie Thompson by giving nationalists a choice of candidates. In the language of Northern Ireland's unforgiving headcounts, they 'split the vote'. The nationalist voters chose Sinn Féin.

A crisp veteran of civil rights days, a sharp and fluent broadcaster who looks remarkably young for 66, Rodgers had done well as agriculture minister during the foot-and-mouth outbreak by sounding more in control than her counterparts in Britain. She was presented to the conservative nationalist voters of West Tyrone as the candidate for sense and sentiment, born in nearby Donegal, native Irish-speaker, mother and grandmother, with just a hint of gallant woman fighting what might be her last election. Sinn Féin's Pat Doherty, also from Donegal but with a Scottish accent from a childhood in Glasgow, looked homely by contrast with the smoothly dressed Rodgers and more middle aged, a humorous uncle with twinkling eyes. His IRA connections were background material that needed no advertisement – a brother who served 21 years for bombing offences in England, long years of republican activism.

When Doherty reminded interviewers that he had been cultivating the constituency since the previous election, most dismissed it as campaign hype and failed to register his squad of workers, few over 30. Media opinion during the campaign plumped for Rodgers. Or they said it would be too close to call between her and the unionist Willie Thompson, with Sinn Féin in third place. The SDLP campaign mocked Doherty's claims, though their own local supporters looked increasingly stretched. It was as if the prospect of Sinn Féin advances in the west had robbed the SDLP of judgement and stunned observers into believing party spin instead of their eyes and ears. A win for Sinn Féin in West Tyrone would put them level with the SDLP at Westminster, with three seats each. Even though republicans would refuse to take their seats, the SDLP could not contemplate the comedown. Nor, it seemed, could most of the media.

A Gildernew win in Fermanagh-South Tyrone had failed to even cross the horizon as a possibility. West Tyrone became the battleground which would uplift the SDLP elsewhere, 'our Stalingrad', as Rodgers' election manager ineptly dubbed it. Wishful thinking supplanted reporting. A feeling common to many journalists north and south, voiced out of print during the campaign and shared by the SDLP and unionists, was that republicans were 'getting beyond themselves, too big for their boots'. But SDLP workers drafted in from Belfast for a last canvass to make up what had been a permanent local shortfall were aghast at the strength of the Sinn Féin campaign. One told a reporter: 'Doherty had about 400 of them out round Omagh the whole weekend!'

West Tyrone was no contest on the night. While the Gildernew win in next-door Fermanagh-South Tyrone came out of the blue – partly because of the unpredictable split between the Ulster Unionist and a maverick anti-Agreement candidate – the signs in West Tyrone had been deliberately ignored. The Sinn Féin man beat the Ulster Unionist into second place, Rodgers trailed in third. Doherty beat Willie Thompson by a healthy 5,000 votes, hammering SDLP pretensions into the ground. Rodgers lost with a worse result than the local man she replaced had won four years earlier. On the platform as the result was read and republicans cheered, her face lost colour. As a tricolour-waving crowd yelled in triumph, defeat wiped out the last trace of public acclaim for her ministerial performance. Shoulders sagging, she left the hall with her agent to a vindictive chant of 'foot-and-mouth, foot-and-mouth'.

In nearby Mid-Ulster, Martin McGuinness, former IRA leader and now Stormont Education Minister, easily held his seat as predicted, making it a hat-trick for Sinn Féin in the west. Watched by SDLP and unionist supporters, equally disconsolate, the Sinn Féin victors in Mid-Ulster and West Tyrone seized a hand apiece of the new Fermanagh-South Tyrone MP and raised arms high. The three west of the Bann republican MPs were hoisted on willing shoulders, young Michelle Gildernew blinking happily between Doherty and McGuinness. Around the winners, election workers, many of whom who had served long jail sentences, whooped with delight. This was coming in from the cold with a vengeance.

In Newry-Armagh, Ulster Unionists and the SDLP took simultaneous blows. SDLP deputy leader Seamus Mallon watched a once-massive lead cut away by Sinn Féin. Though he held his seat it was a personal blow and another warning that the party's easy pre-eminence in nationalism had gone. Worse, it made clear that Stormont had given an extra boost to Sinn Féin, who had scorned it for so long, but did the SDLP no favours, though they had spent decades working towards power-sharing. Why had their ministers not improved the party's standing further in the Catholic community? Apart from Brid Rodgers, Mallon was the highest-profile SDLP figure in the Executive, indeed one of the most prominent figures in Northern Ireland. As veteran deputy leader of the party, MP since 1986 and most significantly, as Deputy First Minister to David Trimble, he had made almost daily TV appearances, exposure that election experts usually deem unbeatable.

'My vote is holding up well,' Mallon said an hour or so before the result, the effort at reassurance contradicted by a glaze of mournfulness on his deeply lined face. His vote dropped by more than 6 per cent. The 32-year-old Sinn Féin newcomer Conor Murphy upped the republican tally by nearly 6,000, teeing up the seat for the next election when Mallon will be almost 70. The tally seemed to wind him.

An eloquent man on form, his speech aimed high but rambled. He thanked the centre's staff, his manager, his party workers 'and the parish priest for the lend of the hall'. In the Church of Ireland building lent for the count, the quip struck the wrong note, a self-mocking joke in all-Catholic political gatherings, from the unionist-dominated days when ineffectual nationalists needed the approval of priests, and parochial halls for their meetings. As the SDLP lost their position as prime representative of nationalism perhaps for ever, the victory speech for a shrivelled triumph held only melancholy echoes of the flair that characterised a younger Mallon.

The youngest SDLP big name of the night was the biggest loser, and the sorest. For 41-year-old party chairman, Alex Attwood, there was crushing disappointment. He had worked for Rodgers in West Tyrone, at the cost of his own uphill campaign in the West Belfast fiefdom of Gerry Adams. The SDLP's failure to organise has always been most conspicuous in Belfast. Attwood's vote dropped by 60 per cent, leaving Adams nearly 20,000 ahead. Grey in the face, the loser made a sour little speech, wondering how the Sinn Féin president would represent his Protestant constituents, since Sinn Féin MPs refuse to swear the oath of allegiance to take their Westminster seats. 'Good luck in the British House of Commons,' he finished, lip curled on the 'British', surely misjudged given that he had been trying to get there himself.

Adams swanned off to a series of television appearances bedecked with 66 per cent of the West Belfast vote, the biggest vote of the day. Would the increased support for his party while the IRA still held their guns not make unionists more fearful? He told the interviewer to 'get used' to it. His huge majority crowned the republican triumph, the 'new dispensation', almost incidentally defining the SDLP's future in Belfast as nationalist also-ran while the city steadily becomes more Catholic than Protestant. As the hours went by and the results piled up, the scale of Adams' win pointed up the contrast with SDLP slippage. Hume's own lead over Sinn Féin in his home town of Derry was safe from the embarrassment visited on his colleagues, but still diminished.

Over a drink later that night a loyal SDLP worker said sadly: 'I idolised Hume. I always have. But there I was working hard for Brid Rodgers in West Tyrone thinking if she wins, and I wanted her to win, we'll have four MPs, every one of them well past 60. They've all gone on too long. And yet who's to compare with them . . .' He was admitting, if only tacitly, that the next rung down looks puny beside the founding figures, Hume above all.

For unionists, republican success was the occasionally intrusive backdrop to their own internal contest. As the night went on, DUP victory speeches blurred into each other, the after-effect more enigmatic than joyous. The winners kept the party's options open. During the election campaign DUP emphasis changed, and lambasting the Agreement and the traitor David Trimble was reduced to simply bashing Trimble. Clearly the message from the doorsteps was that Paisley's party should stay in the game at Stormont, in spite of the hated power-sharing.

Paisley loves a count, wallows in his victories. As always he steamrollered the election officer's objections to sing 'Oh God Our Help in Ages Past' verse after verse, 'the entire hymn', as a London newspaper sketch-writer bemusedly noted next day. Then came a speech beginning with thanks to the Lord and the crowd bowed heads for the prayer, roared 'traitor' for each ritualistic tongue-lash of Trimble. Connoisseurs of Paisley count performances heard pique behind the bombast. The once mighty vote is slipping, only fourth highest in Northern Ireland this time, well behind the accursed Adams.

A little later Paisley was questioned from the count by BBC NI's leading anchorman, Noel Thompson, who tastelessly mentioned the slippage before posing an equally unwelcome question on the DUP's secretive plans for an alternative to the Agreement. Instead of answering, Paisley gave the camera one of his gleaming, head-shaking smiles, leaning into the camera for maximum intimidating effect: 'If you were a fly, Mr Thompson, [pause] I'd swat you [smack of lips] against the wall.'

When the DUP took East Londonderry from the Ulster Unionist who had held it for 27 years, the normally cheery, freckle-faced victor, Gregory Campbell, closed his eyes with fervour and held out his arms. 'There is a God in heaven, there is a God in heaven,' his speech began, 'this is God's will.' Once on worldly matters, Campbell lashed into Trimble, but he made no promises to 'smash' the Agreement, damned initially by Paisley as a lie and abomination.

In North Belfast, the DUP's general secretary Nigel Dodds won another new seat and showed less piety. A dark-jowled brooding man, he gave the camera his most pugnacious glare: 'This is one in the eye for David Trimble and the pan-nationalist front.' But early next morning with David Frost he was decidedly milder. The DUP wanted movement on IRA decommissioning, and a way to preserve the power-sharing executive, he said.

Television producers, delighted to have a husband-and-wife MP team on camera, swiftly linked first-time MP Iris Robinson to husband Peter, Paisley's deputy leader, who had just retained East Belfast. Robinson, with Dodds, is the party's organising talent, a clever and calculating mind. His own vote had slipped, however, thanks to the showing of a loyalist paramilitary fringe party, the pro-Agreement Progressive Unionists. Iris had carved up a weak and last-minute Ulster Unionist candidate after Trimble's deputy leader declined to defend the seat. Expensively dressed and groomed in a party that likes its women homely, she pairs tireless efficiency with much cooing in public over her husband. This time it was 'Congratulations, darling' about 'Peter's feat in East Belfast'. While the couple made a stagey arrangement to meet for dinner in Iris' new constituency, Robinson's pale face reddened. Pleasure for his wife was hard to detect. Asked how the DUP would use their enhanced mandate, he reinstated the supercilious expression he reserves for journalists and deflected the question.

Reports came in throughout the day that Trimble might lose his Upper Bann seat, a rather wild assessment that nonetheless caught the sense of a dangerous moment, certainties gone. Trimble's DUP challenger, able youngish businessman and political newcomer David Simpson, flustered officials into holding a recount then held impromptu press conferences in the car park to claim that he might yet topple the First Minister. Cameras recorded him watching happily as a Paisleyite crowd gathered, increasingly loud and excitable.

When David and Daphne Trimble arrived as the recount ended, the crowd surged round them, shouting 'traitor'. There were only two or three extra police to help the First Minister's personal police guard steer the couple safely inside. Trimble won by a margin of over 2,000. He made a defiant, angry victory speech, shouting to be heard against jeers and heckling. Inexplicably, on his way out of the count, there was still no protective police shield. The crowd closed in, kicking and punching. Daphne Trimble looked small and increasingly terrified. Her husband reached futilely for her hand but was reduced to being half-carried to his car by his guards, forearms squeezed together in a pose that looked helpless in next day's papers.

It was standard Paisleyite roughhousing, meted out over decades to other unionists, ecumenical Protestant clergy, British ministers and delegations from Dublin. Daphne Trimble's presence changed the chemistry and increased the offence. Sweet-natured and universally regarded as the 'nice one' of the couple, her natural smile is a welcome contrast to the slightly robotic grimace with which Trimble shows mirth. She is touchingly loyal to her snappish husband, big spectacles magnifying innocent wide eyes upturned to his face during his awkward speeches.

A prominent anti-Agreement female unionist from Trimble's own famously disloyal party, followed the coverage with a younger male assistant while waiting to join the on-screen television discussion. They kept up a loud running commentary which made it clear that contrary opinions would not be welcome. As the mob surrounded the Trimbles, they voiced heavy mock-sympathy: 'Look at that, can't even go to his own count. Och, the poor things. Ah dear. There you go, David, serves you right. Ooh, poor Daphne.'

But non-political, normally indifferent Protestants were disproportionately offended by the scene in the car park, the marks on Daphne Trimble's neck where the police guard or someone in the crowd had grabbed her. She laughed it off a few days later to the *Belfast Telegraph*, house organ of the unpolitical Protestant, then confessed: 'Actually, it was absolutely awful. I'm not a tall person and my greatest fear was that I'd get knocked down and what sort of state I'd be in if I ever got back up. I was badly pushed, though I didn't feel the kick to the back of my left leg at the time. I noticed the bruise later. But once I was in the car I just felt like bursting into tears. It was the shock I suppose.

'Then I saw the TV cameras and I thought, "Oh no, I'm not crying in front of everyone." David did pat my hand and tell me we were all right now. And then everyone in the car, including the police officers, began comparing injuries. David can cope with that sort of thing up to a point, but does anyone really cope particularly well with being given a kicking? He has quite a few bruises. He was limping next day.'

The *Telegraph*, clearly very sympathetic, noted in uncharacteristically racy style that Daphne had been instructed to 'stand behind a burly policeman and grasp him around the waist. Like a kind of grotesque Conga? "Oh, stop it!" the modest Mrs Trimble giggled.'

The Daphne business registered in the public mind. So did the confidence of Gerry Adams. He sat perfectly still beside Ken Maginnis in election day programmes, a professional performer now on live television, more commentator than participant. Maginnis fidgets, tugs at his jacket. Ulster Unionists sat uncomplainingly side by side with Sinn Féin representatives all day in studios where once they refused to, a measure of how some attitudes have changed. The proximity of Adams no longer bothers Maginnis, but the republican insistence that theirs is the moral high ground obliges him to demonstrate distaste. He does it by crash-landing on every allusion Adams makes to human rights or equality, contrasting his professions of concern sarcastically with the IRA's record of murder. When he looked past Adams to the cameras on results night and was scathing about the IRA's failure to decommission, Adams scarcely reacted.

This was the first day of a new era for republicans, and he intended to enjoy it. For him, as for most northern Catholics, John Hume's SDLP has been the foremost voice of nationalism for a generation, the entire Troubles. In most people's minds, republicanism until recent times principally meant the violence of the IRA. A scrubby little party called Sinn Féin tagged on behind. They have been serious political contenders only for the past decade, still well behind Hume's party as spokespeople for the community they share – to Irish governments, for example, and until Bill Clinton's presidency, in Washington.

But the decline of the SDLP has been coming for a long time. The final slump was on the cards. In advance of the results Adams had taken to saying breezily that he looked forward to Sinn Féin becoming the biggest party in Northern Ireland, never mind nationalism. It turned out that he meant they would canter past the SDLP in the next election, perhaps for the Assembly in 2003 or in the next contest for Westminster seats. Even republicans did not expect what happened on 7 June 2001.

At the end of an evening television session Adams came off the set smiling, bending down to untangle the handbag of a woman panellist from a chair leg, joking easily with journalists and the waiting republican staffers. A psephologist billeted on the other side of the studio came over to him clutching a notebook, face set with what might have been tension, or distress at the end of an era. Many academic political experts in Northern Ireland are local people. They have as much difficulty as other politics-watchers transcending their communal origins and being objective. Like others in his trade, the electoral expert might not always have rated the SDLP highly, but their rivals for nationalist votes fell into a different category. While the IRA kept on killing, Sinn Féin were essentially creatures from the underworld.

The academic looked a little as a defeated officer might, surrendering to the enemy. '175,914 Sinn Féin to 169,944 SDLP,' he announced with dogged professionalism. 'That's what we're making the total votes when we get the graphics ready.' Adams smoothed out a scrap of paper to show the same figures scribbled in biro. He'd been passed it during the programme for use on air by Sinn Féin's veteran press officer Richard McAuley, but, he smiled, 'I can't read Richard's writing.'

A gaggle of aides and minders closed in, and off they went into the night.

2

A PROFILE OF NATIONALISM – THE ADVANCE

JOHN HUME: THE MAN WITH THE PLAN

There was a moment in New York in January 1994, a meeting organised by Irish-Americans to push the process on, when all eyes were on Gerry Adams while John Hume sat by disregarded. It was Hume's clout in America that helped get Adams a visa against strong British opposition, helped produce the invitation to make speeches and meet opinion-formers. The cameras and microphones wanted only the novelty of gunman turned peacemaker. A knowledgeable onlooker who has worked with both men but knows Hume much better, saw the older leader upstaged and read emotion on his face for which he could not find the words: 'You'd need Tolstoy for that.'

As the smoke clears after three awful decades, there is really no doubt as to who has been the towering figure of the Troubles. The wonder is that Hume's remarkable abilities and acute political judgement survived at such a pitch for so long. Elements of classic tragedy leap from the picture of the last few years: the hero exhausted by an epic struggle, the younger rival with a dark side befriended then edging past to take the applause, and perhaps the allegiance, of some who once followed the older man.

The tragedy is that this outcome was predicted, by his enemies but also by some of his friends. Hume's greatness may lie principally in his awareness of the risk and his determination to keep going. In a heated meeting with party colleagues, in the early stages of what most eventually acknowledged was a 'peace process', he told them: 'If it's a choice between the party and peace, do you think I give a fuck for the party?' Some took the point better than others. Almost a decade on, it

John Hume

is plain that the sweep of history will leave no shadow on Hume's choice. The future of his party is not so clear-cut, and that may be its tragedy.

Only after the IRA called their first 'cessation of military operations' in 1994 did Sinn Féin seriously challenge the SDLP's position as the prime voice of nationalism. It took the ceasefire to win republican votes outside the circle of the faithful, who blinked at or always actively supported the gun and the bomb.

It took much bloodshed and grief before republicans 'sued for peace', in the phrase Adams sometimes uses. The IRA were responsible for more deaths than loyalist paramilitaries, British soldiers and police combined; a total of almost 1,800 over 24 years. It took Hume to get Adams through hoops to achieve that ceasefire, and it drained the last of Hume's reserves. He had done much more than help Adams bring republicans in from the cold, the hazardous and punishing business which brought him such abuse from foes and agonising among friends. During two decades he first dreamed of, and then helped assemble, international backing for inclusive government in Northern Ireland. Much of the concept that underpins the still-fragile institutions set up by the Good Friday Agreement came from Hume. He deserves honour, rest and imitation.

The trouble for the party he helped found is that over recent years republicans skilfully adopted his most successful techniques, while the SDLP drifted as if becalmed. Victory by a margin of 6,000 votes does not allow Sinn Féin to settle in as top dog, but it certainly poses a tough challenge to the new SDLP leader, the 41-year-old Mark Durkan, Hume's long-time heir apparent, who must revive the SDLP's fortunes. Essentially, this will come down to a judgement by the community that votes for both the SDLP and Sinn Féin as to what form of representation best suits them now, and whose is the face that fronts it.

Hume's party also have to shape up to a new and testing situation. 'For the last few years,' a Dublin observer noted, 'Hume has been more cosmic force than anything else.' It has been an opinion widely shared inside and outside the party, though discussed internally with diffidence, a degree of pain and a little shame.

'Many knew well but didn't like to say,' said one lifelong Hume admirer, 'that while John was turning into an icon, we effectively lacked leadership.' There was diffidence because party loyalists were the first to appreciate Hume's massive achievement, leadership that had played a major part in transforming a demoralised community. There was also pain in recognition of the cost to him, and shame at the realisation of how the drift had continued, how passive many were in anticipation of the next life, life after Hume. An expert on the SDLP watched with dismay: 'It's like when Jesus ascends into heaven, hallelujah, then the day after, the disciples are left looking at each other saying, right, that's that then, how do we carry on His legacy?'

The problem extended beyond an exhausted, ageing Hume, born in 1937, to most of the party's big names: Mallon, born in 1936, Eddie McGrady and Brid Rodgers in 1935. The election rammed home a cruel contrast with the front rank of republicanism. It was not a contrast that passed without unsparing and defensive internal SDLP comment. 'We have no local organisation worth talking about. We have local councillors, the sort of a guy who would have three-quarters of a quota on his own, but do you think he'd organise a branch? I'm bloody sure not, somebody else might get his seat. Whereas the Shinners . . . we have no organisation, they have their military organisation. It's "listen you, your country needs you".'

The comment blazed with the enduring suspicion and animosity in the SDLP towards republicans. It also said something about the state of the party, and perhaps more about the compensations of inspirational leadership and the primacy of belief. 'You could say we staggered through,' says a tired activist, one of the few apart from the founders who can remember the first days. 'And for years we didn't even pretend to be a proper party. There were the magnificent six, Gerry Fitt, Hume, Paddy O'Hanlon and the others, then we were the Assembly party in the time of the first power-sharing thing, then the convention party . . .' His voice tails off. 'And then we won seats at Westminster.' It was a slow and painful business.

Hume has many gifts, but organisation is not one of them. The other side of his passion, the advocacy that built networks and informed opinions halfway round the world, is a lack of interest in detail amounting almost to disdain. For years, people who praised him to the skies also complained that he was too often in them, flying back and forth. Given the worth to the party of his international profile, it sounded unreasonable. But the charge was that he refused to delegate,

that he agreed to appoint organisers then undercut them. 'If he isn't in
Washington or Strasbourg or Dublin or who knows where else, he's in
Derry,' an irritated party worker once snapped at a particularly tense
time, 'and don't expect me to know his movements.'

The Derry crack revealed considerable impatience. Hume's
attachment to his home town is standard for a Derry person, the tiny
city having a singular attraction for its natives. Party headquarters
might be in Belfast, but Hume has never liked Belfast and spends as
little time as possible in it. For years he ran office business primarily
from Derry, or rather his wife Pat did. Fellow Derry man Mark
Durkan's succession took shape years before Hume finally retired,
because Durkan also worked out of the Derry office.

Hume built a small team of draftsmen: Durkan, Denis Haughey,
who had been with him from civil rights days, and the academic Sean
Farren. 'A good praetorian guard,' says an equally long-standing
insider, having trouble visualising a Hume-less SDLP, 'good staff men
– will Mark keep them on?' Another wondered if Durkan would
'appeal to unionists who could never see past Hume, the civil rights
agitator who started the Troubles – I think he does. But they won't vote
for him. And appealing to unionists won't win him any votes from
nationalists.' The conclusion is that Hume tipped Durkan for the job,
but could not help him further. Durkan's period as heir apparent
coincided largely with Hume's own decline. When he announced his
candidacy, in the knowledge that he would be unopposed, some heard
an almost painful modesty in his opening words: 'I'm not John Hume.
I don't make any apology for the fact that I am not John Hume.'

Arguably the most difficult issue facing the SDLP is policing. When
controversy flared between the first police Ombudsman, Nuala
O'Loan, and the Chief Constable of the RUC, Sir Ronnie Flanagan, a
test for the SDLP, Durkan's response was awaited with some curiosity.
O'Loan might have expected support as she fielded scorn and ridicule
from Flanagan and from unionists. Durkan left it to his party
spokesman on policing. Was this a new leader trusting the person in
the job, onlookers wondered, or an inheritance of Hume's disposition
to avoid touchy issues and concentrate on the grand sweep? On the
day the row reached its peak, the SDLP issued a statement announcing
that Hume had won yet another peace prize, the Mahatma Gandhi
award, with an expression of gratitude from Hume. The coincidence

struck an unpromising note in some minds. The party needs new energy, not more reflection on past glory.

Hume could with justice say that for most of the past 30 years his individualistic leadership style served the party well. He might have argued, though he did not, that in the absence of a local political forum, what was the point of a local party? The SDLP gained a substantial and in later years steadily growing vote, much of it due to their inspirational leader. But he was the leader, and while he inspired he failed to organise. He stayed too long, many say now.

Yet over a prolonged period the SDLP had nonetheless enjoyed loyal and growing voter support, largely thanks to the quality of their front rank, and in particular to Hume and the message he so powerfully conveyed. The irony, of which some are uncomfortably aware, is that it was Hume's vision that pushed Catholics and nationalism away from passiveness and into practical politics. If the party is adrift, having achieved their mission, does it have a flavour of the passivity he set out to erase?

It was always his harshest judgement that many hoarded grievance instead of working for improvements. Instead of the dream of a united Ireland Hume focused the community on moderate nationalism, the reform of Northern Ireland. In the judgement of many commentators, both sympathetic and unsympathetic, that one 'right call', as one described it, had enormous significance.

No other Northern Ireland politician generates the same complex reaction. Hume has spent 30 years in the very front line of politics, surviving a string of failed initiatives, fears for his safety, years of sterile debate in the midst of bloodshed, buckets of criticism, oceans of adulation. He is worn physically and mentally, by the endless travel, by the twin corrosions of malice and flattery, by bitty communication with too many people, but chiefly by trying to master a stagnant and bloody situation. A commentator who says Hume has for years 'done the job of a senior diplomat and a leading politician rolled in one' wondered how he had gone on for so long. 'Wasn't that what made him different, and hard to stand sometimes?' he says. 'Hume didn't just try to cope with the Troubles and get by like the rest of us, he tried to fix it.'

He faced an IRA beyond rational argument for most of the time, politicians in London and Dublin with the attention span of a goldfish, and unionists who resolutely refused to put anyone up against him with either the ability or desire for accommodation. Hume was already the persuasive voice of a rational nationalism to the outside world, the first many had heard, while Martin McGuinness as a young IRA man was standing on a platform in the Bogside saying, 'It does not matter what Gerry Fitt says. It does not matter what John Hume says. The IRA will fight until the British leave and we get our united Ireland.' McGuinness is fond now of saying that he and Gerry Adams were 'only children' when they were flown to London in 1972 to parley with British ministers. Certainly, they had no programme other than a demand that 'the British leave', and no other mechanism for achieving it than gunfire.

Through the worst of the Troubles, Hume provided a more attractive image for Northern Ireland's nationalists than the apparently endless violence of the IRA. In itself, that would have been achievement enough for most. But for a whole generation, Hume's passion for political progress made him a major figure. People who had turned away from politics in almost total disgust made an exception for him. 'At least he tries,' they said. They could have added, and occasionally did, that whatever drove him was clearly not personal financial gain or easy gratification. It was no surprise that he gave his £286,000 Nobel Peace Prize to Northern Ireland's two main charities, the Salvation Army and the St Vincent de Paul Society – no one expected less.

Characteristic sightings of him for almost 30 years have been of a shapeless crumpled man in mid-argument, or mooching into a room to make a speech, hair sticking up and suit looking as though he had slept in it, notes, if any, crumpled in a back pocket. Or just off a plane from Washington, Strasbourg, Brussels; speaking to business groups, credit unions, in schools and universities.

It was determination to prevent an 'internal settlement', leaving northern nationalists in a purely British and unionist construct, that led Hume to criss-cross the world in the '70s and '80s, almost incidentally attracting inward investment for an unemployment black spot where deprivation and violence fed off each other. His vision included the rest of Ireland, politicians from the US, and most controversially Britain, with the help of finance from the European Union. He made it real. Business leaders have a refrain that dismisses local politicians for their lack of interest in the connection between politics and the economy. Do they include John Hume? 'Oh, Hume's different,' the more thoughtful say instantly, 'Hume sees the connections between the economy and politics.' But they refuse to be quoted, because Hume is the leader of nationalism, and unionists would object.

His exhaustion has been visible for years, accentuated by recurrent depression about which he talks with considerable honesty. To some degree, this combination damaged a rare quality of concentration. The strain on him was already a problem in the gruelling marathon talks that eventually brought the 1998 Agreement. The talks were held in what one official described as 'the original sick building; colours specially chosen to sedate, all sludge and heat and artificial light, without a corner anywhere to encourage private deal-making'. One sympathetic onlooker thought the SDLP leader looked abstracted from the start, in the testing time when the first ceasefire had ended, when unionist voices demanded that Sinn Féin be permanently excluded. Ian Paisley and the UK Unionist Robert McCartney made long, hectoring speeches; many others wilted, not Hume alone. But perhaps it was a trial too far.

'He's there physically but not mentally,' said one. Another thought there were 'hours, days and months when Hume might as well have been somewhere else. Head down on his arms while the discussion went on. Or he'd be in the room for a while and then missing for days. You'd meet him on the corridor and he was miles away.' This person added sadly: 'If he'd been inside the room any longer, mind you, he'd have been swinging from the curtains.' There was a moment, recalled by several, when a flash of the old Hume talent appeared – a session stuck for a phrase which would meet both sides' requirements. Hume reached for a pen, wrote a few words and handed them over; the phrase satisfied both sides. But people in the other parties and several note-takers realised early that the burden of the nationalist case rested squarely on the SDLP deputy leader, Seamus Mallon. In the absence of Sinn Féin, and with Hume below par, it was a thankless task.

In that session of talks, the measure of a great leader's decline became painfully obvious. With him present but not participating, Mallon's role as stand-in for a once masterful player was almost unplayable. 'Hume's hardly in evidence. Mallon carries almost 40 per cent of the electorate but he's almost lost in the crowd,' said one non-SDLP bystander at the time. 'Everything on the unionist side is raised to the power of three because you get it in three versions and Mallon is the one nationalist voice. There's a lot of pressure but he's doing extremely well, like a sort of tireless full-back.'

For many who have watched Hume's travels for years, the wonder is not that he eventually frayed but that his power of concentration and argument lasted so long. The former SDLP figure Brian Feeney, now an acid-tongued newspaper columnist, recalled with uncharacteristic respectfulness when Hume retired how he had set out to 'transcend' the narrow confines of a unionist Northern Ireland. In pursuit of his vision, it seemed Hume was in the air more often than he was at home. More typically, Feeney relayed a joke of the '80s, originally nationalist but taken up with glee by unionists who resented the SDLP leader's growing stature abroad: 'What's the difference between John Hume and God? Answer: God is everywhere. John Hume is everywhere but Derry.'

Nancy Soderberg, a Ted Kennedy aide who went on to work in the Clinton White House, gave a vivid glimpse in the year 2000 of the reach and effectiveness of Hume's networking over decades, and the remorseless persistence it required. She recalled the multiple efforts to convince Washington that republicans were now on the march away from violence, and to enlist official support for the first stumbling steps towards peace. She cited the Irish-American congressman Bruce Morrison, who had first intrigued Bill Clinton, then described how Hume's clout crucially reinforced the message from Morrison and others.

'The foreign policy establishment, the British, others, dismissed any change and we would get briefings to say, "Nothing's changed. You know, it's one IRA, there's no difference among these people and there's no movement and do not engage them, it will only leave egg on your face." Bruce would say you have no idea how difficult it is to convince a movement like the IRA to stop its tactics of using violence. I remember having lunch with John Hume in the White House mess some time later that year, and I said, "Should I pay attention to this now?" And he said, "This is the time to do it."'

She believed him because he had told her earlier 'it's not ripe yet', and because 'he was the first one to move the non-violent nationalist agenda forward. For many years he was our eyes and ears onto what was happening on the ground there. John would come and talk to me while I was in Kennedy's office, and that relationship continued when I worked for President Clinton. He was in the United States quite regularly and would drop by and just brief me on what was happening.'

Younger nationalists often voted for the SDLP out of dislike for Sinn Féin, closing their eyes to the rest of the lacklustre party, won solely by awareness of Hume's unique contribution. Against tremendous odds, he gave his party influence abroad and in Dublin that was unbeatable for years. Northern nationalists today are buoyant, well led and confident of a better future: much of the credit goes to Hume.

When he finally stepped down, one of his earliest journalistic allies and the sanest and most committed of commentators, the Dublin-based Mary Holland, sketched one of his essential qualities. 'At bad times, when it seemed the British could only reach for more security and this state just wished the whole ghastly mess would go away, one would meet John obviously preoccupied and he'd say, "I've got an idea, what do you think?" Sometimes they would seem like crazy dreams, that the Secretary of State should make a speech declaring that the British had no long-term political interest in Northern Ireland, or the Irish government should set up a conference for all nationalist parties on the island to look at possible political options . . .'

Both happened, of course, and were significant moves in triggering other developments. It was a glimpse of better days for many who have only known the latter-day Hume. The almost irrecoverable sense for those under 30 is of a politician from a small benighted corner of Ireland, with no local political forum for much of his career, who nonetheless managed to develop the power of influence and walked with more useful people than princes. So much that Hume said first now sounds boring, banal or hackneyed, but only because he began saying it so long ago and because so much has taken root and is now regarded as given.

He has occasionally admitted the frustration of making the case over and over again, that more 'security' and repressive legislation was not the answer, that violence would never be sidelined unless the two major traditions accommodated each other, that stability could be found in the British and Irish governments working together and that there might be salvation in creating a wider context, and that violence should stop. Terms he coined passed into common usage: inclusiveness, the three essential relationships, the need to unite people before uniting territory. 'Humespeak,' unionists and some others mocked.

As he tired, he became steadily more irritable, head inclined intensely, arguments laid out methodically, repeated over and over again in sentences with no full stops. Hume became a gruelling interviewee. At its best his was a voice that began calmly, a patient teacher's voice with an abiding quality of stating common sense, a mind that dealt in practicalities rather than emotive slogans. Hume prefers low-key language which is also deliberately vague, with no sharp edges to snag on. But where once he sounded like a dedicated teacher pounding a lesson home, at his lowest points, it has now become a mechanical recital.

At his best, the quality of Hume's advocacy was anything but mechanical. About ten years ago a Yorkshire TV crew waited for Hume through a series of hitches: a missed connection between Strasbourg and London, hours sitting on the runway. He phoned several times to explain. He had been in Washington two days before. Filming started about four hours late, interviewee grey in the face and bedraggled. It was a schools programme and they wanted him to trace the start of the Troubles; the interviewer knew some of it, the crew nothing. Hume was so vivid the cameraman nearly forgot to change film-reels. 'I've never heard anyone so convincing,' he said later. 'Tell me about him.'

Those who heard Hume on form, urging lateral thinking on the most intractable questions, tended to come away with a sense above all of a powerful theorist, genuinely open-minded about possible solutions and happy to think unconventionally to reach them. In 1992 he said he imagined Britain would remain in Northern Ireland for the foreseeable future, but that some form of new all-Ireland arrangement would evolve. 'Unity I've always defined as agreement, not a takeover bid. And the form of unity? I don't mind what it is . . . Once people start working together you grow into a completely new Ireland – and two or three generations down the road, you create new structures that give expression to what has happened.'

For the old Utopia of a united Ireland, Hume long ago substituted an 'agreed Ireland', whatever that might be. The phrases that he made his own were often fuzzy, deliberately undefined. It is a quality that infuriates many unionists, and exasperates others. 'Figuring out what he means is like trying to pin down blancmange,' a non-political liberal once said. From another perspective, that of a commentator from a Protestant but anti-unionist background, it was the unionist irritation that seemed worth criticising. 'Unionists got so annoyed about that phrase, "an agreed Ireland". They thought it was just a euphemism for Irish unity, didn't they? They couldn't ever imagine Ireland being agreed.'

The Hume precepts were patently full of virtue and maddened many, especially the less virtuous – 'spilling sweat not blood . . . working out differences . . . diversity threatens no one'. He grew testy in the end because people wanted him to explain what he could not influence and perhaps did not himself understand, for example, why the IRA refused to decommission.

Maybe the stories about his health – accounts of his being rushed to hospital, repeated tests – say most about how he affects those who know him well. A much-polished anecdote had him visiting SDLP deputy leader Seamus Mallon in hospital in Dublin with a suspected heart attack, asking Mallon anxiously where exactly he had first felt pain. In his left arm, said Mallon. 'Oh God,' says Hume, 'mine's killing me,' and they had to get a doctor to come and see him.

'The way he's lived for years has been the opposite of healthy, no doubt about it, and he's been badly stressed,' said another. 'I wonder sometimes how come he's not a basket case. But he isn't. A grade A hypochondriac, maybe.' But that was the year before Hume's constant complaints became an unpleasantly real and serious medical emergency, when he suffered a perforated bowel and had repeated emergency surgery. The jokes stopped overnight; his hypochondria was now vindicated as well as his political strategies, one of the jokers said ruefully.

The striking thing about the people who told such stories is that when they stopped laughing they were liable to state, with evident pride, the list of concepts that underpinned the peace process but which Hume had voiced in the course of interview after interview. 'That was John, too,' they say. The strongest mitigation of Hume's undoubted irritableness in the public mind for a long time was that many across the divide accepted his gospel that there could be no equality in employment unless there were more jobs, that violence would only deepen divisions, that the two communities would learn to trust each other by working together for the common good. He preached jobs, a future for 'our young people'. One section of the population visibly responded to Hume's lesson as though it were fresh. A poll early in 2000 supported an impression shared by several observers that a considerable number of young people in both communities approved of Hume.

On the day it was announced that he and Trimble were to share the Nobel Peace Prize, in late 1998, he arrived by prior arrangement to speak at a girls' school in affluent South Belfast, Victoria College. The school is mainly Protestant, though increasingly popular for its academic achievements with upwardly mobile Catholics, who until recently saw Hume as the prophet and agent alike of their stake in a changed society. A Catholic school sent a group. Hume gave his talk, with interruptions for phone calls from Stockholm and the White House. When the photographers flocked in, he got spontaneous hugs. 'The school was delighted he was there when the news came,' said one bystander, 'and though the buzz impressed the girls, I think he impressed them first.' A teacher in another school found this easy to understand. 'I think kids respond because he sounds reasonable and practical. They hear the words "together" and "shared" and "partnership", he talks about Europe and progress and a better future. They're not turned off by an ideology that shuts anyone out. He makes links with the world outside. Young people in a small place like that sort of talk. Maybe what they like most is that he talks about hope. They've not heard much of that until recently.'

But when the results of the June 2001 election were analysed, it emerged that more first-time nationalist voters were opting for Sinn Féin than for Hume's party. He reacted badly to post-election suggestions, more or less unanimous from within and without the party, that the results were a verdict on an ageing leadership as well as on disastrous organisation. They must nonetheless have registered. He retired as leader within the year, promising to maintain an international role. The party will soon find out if without him they can regenerate enthusiasm and support, or if the ageing leadership still had an irreplaceable appeal.

People needed hope. At the lowest points of the Troubles, the signs were that they welcomed Hume's positivism. It was the least effective of unionist criticisms of Hume, that he prematurely raised hopes of peace. Back in 1993 when the SDLP man looked momentarily abandoned by Taoiseach Albert Reynolds, briefly doubtful of his ability to persuade republicans towards an IRA ceasefire, the Ulster Unionist Ken Maginnis mocked that it was time for 'another dose of verbal Humus'. This was typically derogatory, and soon shown to be completely wrong – Hume's visions began to come true. By a 70 per cent vote in the referendum on the Good Friday Agreement, the electorate went on to approve at least the spirit of a message originally and very largely his creation.

In the early days of the peace process, Sinn Féin leaders attracted unionist loathing as IRA front-men who had dared to muscle into politics. But Hume took much of the flak from those who were threatened by the very possibility of a political place for Sinn Féin, and from those who had always resented him. In the gruelling months before the first IRA ceasefire, and during the renewed bloodshed and prolonged frustration of its breakdown, he faced a barrage of abuse and near-hatred from unionists, Conservative politicians and British officials, and from some of Dublin's political and media elite. Characterisation of Hume as a terrorist 'mouthpiece' was predictable enough from unionists, many of whom had always been ambivalent in their own reactions to loyalist violence. David Trimble's predecessor Jim Molyneaux, usually a circumspect, even taciturn man, accused him of 'supping with the devil' in maintaining contact with Adams.

The attacks from Dublin hurt most. A stream of invective seeped from a sizeable number, many with a distinct political agenda. Hume's tactic had been to keep the meetings with Adams largely to himself, liaising erratically with the Irish government. In Dublin there were frazzled nerves as the SDLP leader grew ever more strained and impatient. Seamus Mallon as deputy leader was told the minimum, and at key moments found himself besieged by reporters asking questions to which he genuinely did not know the answers, an intolerable position. One Dublin paper, the *Sunday Independent*, mounted a sustained campaign of vilification against Hume. When he collapsed with strain and went into hospital in Derry, it was clear that overwork, constant travel and unremitting anxiety were largely responsible. But his collapse coincided with a peak in the campaign against him.

Clearly some officials and leading politicians thought Hume was deluded about the possibility of peace, gulled by republicans while they continued to bomb and shoot. A number claimed that he had sided with Adams and aggrandised the IRA, at the expense of coming to an accommodation with unionism. Many northern nationalists were disgusted, but not surprised. The anti-Hume sentiment was unrepresentative of wider opinion in the Republic, and swiftly retreated to the margins.

Appreciation of a peace process of which Hume is still seen as prime mover has since washed away all but the dregs of the argument that the SDLP leader was the principal obstacle in the way of an emergent moderate unionism. The spectacle of an anti-Agreement unionism in which Ian Paisley was the loudest voice did the rest. Hume has regularly topped polls as the most popular, most trusted political figure in the whole island. It is a fair bet that some of those who put him there do so simply because he went on insisting that peace was possible, and sounded as though he had some idea of how to achieve it. Others clearly make a judgement that this is a politician more genuine than leading party figures in Dublin, more serious, more committed and less venal than those with egos just as huge, but no matching achievement – their mission office and power, while his was to stop the deaths and bring peace. Northern observers bemused by Dublin venom towards Hume conclude that his real offence was to make southern politicians look bad, and petty, that he did not leave Ireland's unfinished political business to be taken care of by the independent part of the island, and its intelligentsia, in their own sweet time.

Southern wariness of northern nationalists is about to enter another phase, as Sinn Féin gears up for further electoral advance south of the border. A veteran observer of the shifts in attitudes eyes the new order in the north and has misgivings, especially about the slowness with which the IRA has decommissioned its weapons. 'If effectively the average punter in the south says the only package you can buy in terms of northern nationalism is one that has weapons and the IRA folded in, I think the long-term consequences of that are serious.' From this perspective, how Hume came across in the Republic had been vital to an entire generation's disposition towards building any kind of new and practical relationship. 'There's a lesson to be learned from Hume, which is if you represent northern nationalism, you need to be very careful to shape it in a way that doesn't drive the southern constituency off the reservation.'

As the republic deals with ascendant republicans in the future, those who sniped at Hume may come to realise, with some anguish, how skilfully and with what restraint he handled relations with Dublin. After the 2001 election, the narrow ground shared by unionist and nationalist suffered tremor after tremor as the implications sank in of the new threat from Ian Paisley's Democratic Unionists to the bigger Ulster Unionists, and of the Sinn Féin advance. Fresh SDLP leadership and internal reorganisation might tip the balance back, but there is a new mood in nationalism and the Paisley rise will only harden it.

If Paisley is at last to be the avowed champion of mainstream unionism, then even nationalists who might otherwise have hesitated about supporting the IRA's political wing may well choose the tougher and younger party over the SDLP. It was arguably Hume's greatest strength that he represented eloquently and reasonably what the majority of Catholics wanted for so long, in a style that fitted their image of themselves. Now many look to Gerry Adams and Martin McGuinness to put their case most forcefully, to Britain, to Dublin and to the unionists. While Hume's ability waned, the dominant self-image among Catholics changed and, with it, their demands.

A small but growing nationalist middle class is now larger and more self-confident, increasingly indistinguishable from a new establishment. What was once a hopeless underclass, then a resentful and aggressive group on the move, has also developed a considerable and increasingly almost relaxed self-confidence. They are not disposed primarily to see the difficulties for any unionist in power-sharing with republicans; what they see is people who clearly still dislike sharing power with any nationalist. They may have turned away from violence but these are different nationalists, less intent on preaching accommodation and mutual respect, more determined to have their Irishness recognised and reflected, and more flinty about their entitlement to equality than the people Hume once spoke for so perfectly. If unionists cannot accept that, too bad, is the underlying message; that's their problem.

In his last election as leader, Hume used the term 'post-nationalism' sparingly, but Sinn Féin scented voter alienation and swooped in. Hume meant to invoke the idea of wider allegiances, of European unity neutralising old quarrels by providing a wider and healing context. But republicans claimed to find a doorstep reaction against ditching an old label. 'People have been hearing from John,' said a senior republican, careful to at least sound respectful before putting the boot in, 'that we're in a post-nationalist situation, it's all about Europe now. The border doesn't matter, the British presence doesn't matter. People are tired of listening to John saying it isn't about uniting the land, it's about uniting people. Well, people want it to be about uniting the land.' A mocking columnist on a republican website noted that soon after the results Seamus Mallon had redeclared his allegiance to nationalism; 'post-post-nationalism', he joked.

Republicans kept the argument largely off the record and on the doorsteps, but probably scored points nonetheless. 'Would their new methods of achieving unity bear public scrutiny?' a political writer asks sarcastically. 'Martin and Bairbre in cross-border bodies? We might get there some day but you wouldn't want to have to spell it out.'

New SDLP leader Mark Durkan is no more an old-style nationalist than Hume, but the 'post' prefix has already gone. Durkan's preferred term is 'a new nationalism'. He now has to row against a current of conviction that the SDLP sat back when the Good Friday Agreement was concluded, in the belief that now it was reward time, the bulk of their work done. With the benefit of hindsight, it was naive to imagine that their community's highest aspiration would be satisfied by sharing power with unionists in a Stormont administration, especially when unionists were intent on denying equal public recognition of both political identities. If there is even a hint that more is possible, more is what nationalists will demand. It may be that it was not the age of the SDLP's front rank that damaged them, much less any diminution in Hume's appeal, so much as a degree of self-satisfaction in the party's public face. As one insider put it dourly after the vote, personally winded by Adams' usurpation of Hume's position, 'Let's face it, the SDLP of late has exuded complacency, while the Shinners continue to look hungry. Maybe we all have to face it – it's the Shinners who are closer now to the midpoint of nationalist opinion.'

Mallon, Durkan and Hume

Belatedly it became apparent that the party had relied too much on their presence in Stormont. There was scant intrinsic attraction for any kind of nationalist in watching an SDLP man, first Hume's deputy and fellow-veteran Seamus Mallon and then Durkan, performing as Deputy First Minister. First Mallon and then Durkan have watched and listened while Ulster Unionist leader David Trimble makes the crudest of party political statements under his First Minister title. Trimble has been apt to forget that he is not the prime minister in a standard cabinet. In the eyes of many nationalists, one of the main tests of the new SDLP leader will be whether Durkan can 'put manners on Trimble'.

One senior Dublin civil servant suggested early on that it was precisely this kind of scenario that decided Hume against sharing the post with Trimble himself. Others never thought it likely for a moment. 'He would have swung for him,' said a Belfast official. 'It was only Mallon's determination to make something of the biggest job he'd ever had that kept his hands off Trimble's throat.' While Mallon was struggling with the job, he also struggled to provide leadership to the party in Stormont. Hume stayed in the leader's post, but it was increasingly a virtual position. Between them they offered a pale shadow of what had once been a striking double act, Mallon the rhetorical nationalist playing to an old-fashioned gallery while Hume hit new shores. Awkward dual press conferences demeaned both men.

At one time, John Hume reflected his community perfectly by wording their aspirations in the vaguest and most flexible terms, a stratagem that made it possible for Catholics, nationalists, across a wide spectrum to support him, and annoyed unionists. The most superficially damaging denigration of Hume, at least to those at a distance from Northern Ireland, has always been that he has not 'reached out' to Protestants, not reconciled unionists and nationalists, that he turned away from accommodation with unionists towards Sinn Féin and the IRA. In effect, the argument is that having failed to work a miracle, the man is clearly not a saint.

The suggestion that unionist dislike makes Hume a lesser figure is surely fundamentally absurd. Can he be credibly blamed for failing to accommodate politicians for whom compromise is still forbidden? Admiration of Hume among Catholics – supporters of the SDLP, Sinn Féin, or of neither – was largely built on appreciation of how well he judged opinion and support for possible Northern Ireland outcomes in the Republic, in Britain and internationally, and the doggedness with which he pursued a settlement that, in his oft-repeated words, would bring stability and humiliate no one.

But admiration for the politician most responsible for launching, maintaining and giving a terminology to the peace process was hardly going to come from those who saw only a nationalist plot that would require fundamental change inside Northern Ireland, and leave open the possibility of further developments. A broad consensus on Hume's effectiveness is confirmed by the observant and acute broadcaster David Dunseith, anchor of the long-running *Radio Ulster Talkback* phone-in programme, widely regarded as a gauge of unionist opinion in particular. During the Nobel Prize day programme, Dunseith commented that over the years unionists had repeatedly told him how Hume irked them, in the main because he'd won so much for nationalists: 'They always add, "I wish he was ours."'

Hume's analysis of unionism long ago convinced him of the need to widen the parameters of political developments, his assessment of republicanism that nothing short of an all-inclusive settlement would work. In 1992, involved in talks with unionist leaders who complained at his refusal to contemplate their proposals for an extremely modest Stormont administration, he commented on the then new confirmation from census studies that Catholics were no longer a mere third of the population, but constituted at least 42 per cent, perhaps more. 'The census figures might underline to unionists the generosity of what we're offering. If they don't accept it, what's going to emerge in the end could only be worse for them and their people, and therefore for all of us.' The census currently being counted will almost certainly show a 'minority' of over 45 per cent, perhaps several points higher.

Hume helped pioneer and champion the power-sharing idea. He also saw the first experiment destroyed in 1974 by an alliance between unionist politicians and loyalist paramilitaries, complete with intimidation on the streets. Since then the world has been his oyster, Stormont a deeply unattractive option. Like Hume himself, a friend and ageing colleague always saw the likely drawbacks of a restored devolved assembly; the risk of Northern Ireland closing in around it, stifling a broader sense of Irishness and heightening sectarian tensions. 'But I didn't see the Shinner rise taking the feet from under us,' he said, 'though the state the party's in, it wasn't that hard.'

After yet another in the interminable series of crisis talks about the Stormont institutions, this time at the rural English mansion of Weston Park, Hume made a statement thanking Tony Blair and the Taoiseach Bertie Ahern for their efforts: 'I want to express my appreciation to the two governments for the enormous amount of energy they have invested.' Compared to the invariable Sinn Féin response at such moments of 'we have made the smallest of advances, more is needed' and to ears acclimatised to Sinn Féin's political aggression, Hume sounded over-grateful, too humble by half. He is not a humble man, but the old touch may have finally gone. Viewed from outside, and with the evidence of voter restlessness, it seems likely enough that the jolt of June 2001 will not be the last for the SDLP. A skilled Dublin-based reader of northern politics says: 'All right, this was only one test – but looks like the beginning of a graph that will go up hugely in the next election that's held.'

Seamus Mallon had announced his own retirement as deputy leader immediately after Hume's exit. In November 2001 civil servants and politicians came north to the SDLP's annual conference to pay homage as one era ended and another began. No one challenged Hume's protégé, Durkan, for the position of leader. With typical understatement, tact and perhaps more than a touch of realism, Durkan yielded the conference's prime time of Saturday afternoon to the outgoing senior figures. The hotel in the little County Down seaside town of Newcastle filled up with whole families of supporters, more young faces in the audience than usual – teenage children, one observer thought, brought along because they showed some interest in a historic moment.

Chief among the guests of honour was Mo Mowlam, the first of Tony Blair's Northern Ireland Secretaries, sent to see in the peace process and therefore an immediate hit with nationalists. John Reid, the incumbent, arrived later and was the humorous hit of the day, telling stylish jokes. A specially commissioned video tribute combined clips of the young, sideburned Hume and Mallon, leading civil rights marches and holding press conferences outside Downing Street, with filmed tributes from Bill Clinton, Tony Blair, Bertie Ahern, Ted Kennedy and others. Hume and Mallon, the old firm, the founder generation, might be on the way out but the SDLP's long pre-eminence as political operators came true again for the afternoon, thanks to international approval. Unionists watching television coverage later must have grimaced at the spectacle.

Hume made a lengthy, not very good speech, kicking off with: 'You stand with me today as you have stood for 31 years.' Later he appealed stodgily to the next generation: 'This is your time, young people, and this is your challenge.' In the lobby just before the speech he was visibly shaking with nerves. Another founder-figure, Paddy O'Hanlon, paid eloquent tribute. The audience cheered and clapped, standing up repeatedly to applaud the outgoing leaders. For Mallon there was warmth, for Hume a great surge of affection and pride, and tears, even a few at the press table, where political reporters had aged with the SDLP. When at last the new leader stood up to take his bow, to great applause, a glance at Hume showed that he was watching his protégé with an unfathomable expression.

Critics as well as admirers pointed to the irony that Hume and the SDLP had been pushed aside at the moment when they should have been celebrating the fruits of 30 years' labour. What does it say about the peace process that the man who was its major inspiration is relegated in its aftermath? Like every development in history, making a path towards a settlement was the work of many, a conjunction of accident, luck and evolution. Hume's was the front-man role, Hume's the language that clothed new possibilities. He did the thinking for a generation of moderate nationalists, and fresh energy if not fresh thought is needed for a new era.

Northern Catholics have for the moment made Gerry Adams their principal spokesman in Hume's place, by the narrowest of margins. In the next few years, nationalist voters will decide whether to permanently relegate the SDLP. Their decision will be shaped as much by the changing political climate as by the ability of Hume's successor. The SDLP may struggle for some time to find a new momentum, but they have the richest of legacies. The manner of Hume's departure depressed many, but the considered judgement since has been warm and affirmative.

Hume's followers can confound any lingering begrudger with a litany that is as simple as it is irrefutable. He was right to throw his weight into the civil rights movement, as a matter of justice, not political tactics. He was right to crusade against violence, stubbornly and often eloquently. Because he saw the risk of mayhem, he was right to urge people to stay away on Bloody Sunday. He was right to help form a new nationalist party as the vehicle for a confused but resurgent people. He was right to opt for the 1974 power-sharing, and right when it collapsed to draw the conclusion that unionists would never choose power-sharing voluntarily. He was right not to give up after the Loyalist Workers' Strike that brought down the power-sharing experiment, when many despaired, right to broaden the context, to go for Anglo-Irish agreement and right to bring republicans into politics, the boldest course of all.

An insider, irked by what he hears as 'moaning' about Hume from lesser political animals, says: 'Blaming him for the party's current travails is like saying, well Matt Busby was a great manager okay, but after he left Manchester United started to lose matches. It's like saying he was the guy who put the trophies on the sideboard, but after he stepped down there weren't as many.'

To this loyal and defensive eye, it is not a clinching argument that the SDLP failed to organise during Hume's leadership, or that the decline came during Hume's watch. Like many others he can see the weakness of Hume the party leader, the ravages of time and stress, but thinks his achievements negate his flaws. To this way of thinking, then criticism from lesser political figures at home, in Dublin and in London was entirely predictable. 'Look what he started from, the most nebulous of positions, leader of the SDLP, with no Dail seats and only a couple at Westminster, no real position except a self-created one, and one which strikes at the basis of their power and position and status. They'd have just loved him to be wrong. But he tended to be infuriatingly right.'

For the SDLP the road ahead may be bumpy and poorly lit, but for northern nationalism the wider perspective reflects back some of the optimism Hume generated in once-fatalistic souls. David Trimble is a convert, or a semi-convert, to the idea of accommodating political opponents. On the other side are the Provos (members and supporters of the IRA), the people who said almost literally that the way ahead was through death. Gerry Adams and Martin McGuinness have plotted their own political path ahead, not Hume's. But they are inside the political tent, thanks to his unsparing, painful effort, and show no disposition to leave it. History looks set to record that Hume was right, finally, to put peace before party.

GERRY ADAMS: FROM WAR TO PEACE

In 2001 republicans captured one prize after another, including two new seats at Westminster and the head of John Hume. 'Can they do nothing wrong?' an exhausted middle-aged SDLP canvasser asked after the June election. Shortly afterwards three republicans were picked up in Colombia after prolonged, unexplained contact with FARC (*Fuerzos Armadas Revolucionares de Colombia*/Revolutionary Armed Forces of Colombia) guerrillas. It seemed a sizeable and mystifying mistake, with what might have been considered disastrous overtones of the past. Yet the republicans paid no serious penalty. To the dismay of the SDLP and dawning alarm in Dublin at the prospect of Sinn Féin making electoral strides south of the border, Gerry Adams continued his stately and almost unbroken progress towards acceptance as the new leader of northern nationalism – and perhaps a wider role.

'Some talk about Sinn Féin's alluring whiff of cordite,' said one observer. 'I don't think that's what people like in them at all. The

Gerry Adams

SDLP recently exuded the whiff of wanting closure, sitting back in their armchairs saying, "This is it, we've done it." Whereas Sinn Féin are projecting that this is just the start.' He was speaking after a poll in the Republic named Gerry Adams as second most popular party leader, only a few points behind the leader of the largest party, Fianna Fail, perennially popular Taoiseach Bertie Ahern. For the republican, head of a party with only one Dail representative, it was a huge boost. Dublin's political class displayed dismay, shock and considerable anxiety about the electorate's overly forgiving disposition. There was some sniffiness about the glamour of cordite. More considered analysis thought Sinn Féin was becoming the anti-establishment party of choice, benefiting from a vote too young to appreciate the implications of their origin as the voice of the IRA. One of the most acute commentators on the remarkable developments of recent years is the Taoiseach who largely negotiated the 1985 Anglo-Irish Agreement on behalf of the Republic, Garret FitzGerald. That arrangement long pre-dated the strategy of bringing republicans into politics, indeed it was meant to dry up their support in the wider nationalist community. In August 2001, FitzGerald concluded that republican strategy might 'of course, contain further elements that we cannot at present guess at. It gives me no pleasure to say so, but hitherto Sinn Féin/IRA has consistently out-marted its unionist opponents, and has seriously tested the diplomatic skills of two sovereign governments.'

The increasingly presidential bearing of Adams is a major attribute, and a residue of mystery does him no harm. Like the organisation he leads, he is knowable to outsiders only so far as he and they deem useful. The personality demonstrated to the world is not necessarily the Adams known to friends and close colleagues. But the biggest riddle about republicans, and Adams, has probably been solved. It was a niggle that ate away at optimism and arguably kept Ulster Unionist leader David Trimble off-balance. Were the Provos for real, some people worried, or would they worm their way inside official politics while continuing to kneecap and mutilate in their own districts, occasionally killing disaffected republicans or suspected drug-dealers, then use their concealed weaponry to mount some kind of coup?

Few believed the blackest part of that scenario, even among their most stringent opponents. The term 'the Provos' had itself begun to sound a little dated, with its implications of an organisation dominated by ruthless militarists. Off the record officials and ministers on all sides may still use the term, almost as often as they do the more proper 'Sinn Féin' or the less proper 'Shinners'. But the British and Irish governments, with backing from America and on the advice of John Hume, clearly made the decision several years ago to accept the commitment to politics of the Adams leadership, and their intent to end violence. Doubts, though, were bound to linger, since this was a party with not just political power but continuing control over large quantities of guns, ammunition and explosives.

When the IRA began decommissioning in an unfilmed 'event' in October 2001, witnessed by the former head of the Canadian armed forces, John de Chastelain, and his commission, the relief was enormous, though still not total. The verdict from an experienced observer immediately afterwards far exceeded the reaction of unionists who had for so long demanded decommissioning: 'I think it means they're serious and we're effectively book-ending the Troubles at the right end – we'd be very unlucky now to go back. It's fantastic.' The observer's hope that unionists would take this as vindication was disappointed. Nonetheless, within a month signs began to suggest that the move had lessened pressure on David Trimble, and might indeed help produce stability. As the hopeful observer said: 'If a conventional army was disarming you'd say that was a pretty fundamental reflection. The weapons issue goes so deep with them . . . It would be impossible to go back, psychologically, having taken that step. Decommissioning is a kind of formal confirmation that a phase has been left behind.'

Many share the conclusion that for the history-drenched IRA to begin taking their weapons out of commission signified an end to their war, that it did indeed mean there was no going back. In the traditional republican mind-set 'holding arms' was the IRA's legitimacy. Making them unusable, to the satisfaction of an outsider with military expertise like the former general de Chastelain, was indeed significant, and a remarkable statement. Adams' triumph has been to present this process to his own people as both inevitable and beneficial. Students of his progress think that ending the IRA's war on terms far distant from their original goals has taken ingenuity and skill of a high order.

'It isn't unionists who've made the big moves,' says a journalist closer than most to the republican world. 'Republicans have made the biggest sacrifices of all.' This opinion is only unusual because the speaker wholly disapproves of the Adams strategy, and also believes the media have assisted the Sinn Féin leadership to 'con' grass-roots republicans. Most other observers think that republicans were more than ready to be told a comforting tale, no matter where it left the old legends. Cynics claimed originally that the leadership had fooled their supporters. The contrary view, borne out by developments, is that the people as well as the leaders saw the necessity of movement. It only needed a front-man to present the shift with dignity to a previously hostile world, and a ready audience in Dublin, America and London. That front-man has been Adams, ably supported by Martin McGuinness and others.

A measure of how far republicans have come is the anger among some of those most hostile to them, both nationalist and unionist. For them, the most debilitating aspect is the sense that the Adams leadership is on an inside track, that republicans have a particular licence and approval from the authorities.

For a full five months in 2001, from June to October, the mood was one of constant crisis. At several points republicans looked damaged, or likely to be damaged. Much of the crisis had to do with the IRA's refusal to begin decommissioning. Yet the tally in December showed considerable republican gain, at yet another point when they distanced themselves from a former point of principle. As the year ended, Sinn Féin won access to offices in Westminster for their four MPs, despite their refusal to take their seats because of the oath of allegiance to the Queen. It was a blatant example of a nod from Downing Street.

When Gerry Adams claimed his desk in the Palace of Westminster he looked sombre and matter of fact. He was there because Tony Blair's government overrode the always zealous guardians of parliamentary independence, and considerable distaste among many MPs and London opinion-formers. Offices are at a premium, and those allocated to Adams and Martin McGuinness were among the best available. Access to Westminster comes with approximately £400,000 in administration allowances, and provides, as Adams said with characteristic poker-faced cheek and less than tasteful wording, 'a beach-head for republicanism' at the heart of the British system. An organisation still professing opposition to British government in Ireland, which less than four years earlier had killed two police officers in Lurgan, County Armagh, had been enabled to send its front-men into the House of Commons. No more than republicanism's due, Adams said.

The tone, with reserves of command and control, may be exactly what many in the wider nationalist community, beyond the circle of republican support, want to hear. In its second stage, when it should have been settling in and stabilising, the peace process has spent too long stumbling from crisis to crisis.

The first assumption among many now is that Sinn Féin fully intend to take their Westminster seats, all the more because Adams and his colleagues stoutly deny they will do any such thing. These are people, say literal minds, who deny Westminster's competence as a parliament over any part of Ireland. In the scale of recent developments, that piece of dogma has a quaint old-fashioned ring. Every step away from the old absolutism seems to have brought nothing but success. The few voices to cry foul sound what they are, bystanders at a time of historic and rapid change, insisting the emperor has no clothes when everyone else can see that in fact he is wearing a well-cut suit or at the very least a neat jacket and trousers. There were only the faintest of cries from the dissident republican wilderness.

'What do you bet they'll actually promise during the next Westminster election campaign that they'll take the seats,' says another clear-eyed analyst, adept in the ways of the new political dispensation. 'They'll be hoping to take another couple of seats and they'll look like good bets.' It feeds this assumption, that a move to change the oath has already been mooted for avowedly parliamentary reasons: modernisation, reshaping the Union to take account of devolution to the regions etc. 'They'll say it's so Gerry Adams can speak for West Belfast at the heart of Westminster. With a fair wind in the meantime they could beat the SDLP down to Hume's seat alone. And by that stage they might have become a power to be reckoned with in the Dail too. Taking the offices is just a first step.' It might well be true, but the next election is probably too soon for such a move.

After the spectacle of Weston Park in mid-2001, presided over by Blair and the Taoiseach Bertie Ahern, the Westminster move brought comparatively little comment. Held in an English stately home, the conclave for all the pro-Agreement parties was meant to put pressure on republicans by emphasising the danger Trimble's resignation as First

Minister posed to the process. Instead, it produced a list of gains for republicans.

'Trimble opened the door to them big-time,' said one insider. 'He focused the thing on decommissioning – it was his sole demand! And in came the Provos with a big list. They made the SDLP look bad as well. Weak, easily pleased.' As one observer remarked, 'They've certainly got the rhythm of it, but then it's not that hard. The more they keep at it, the more they get.'

The most striking nationalist demand was a demilitarisation scheme involving the demolition of army bases, with a hint of forthcoming legislation to remove the fear of prosecution from republican suspects on the run – and the promise of those offices. Clearly the governments hoped for a rapid IRA move to decommission. It did not happen quite like that.

Adams and other Sinn Féiners acknowledged the Weston Park list as always somewhat offhandedly, but they had worries. It coincided with repeated and serious rioting and sectarian violence in North Belfast, by most accounts largely generated by loyalists around the harassment begun in June of Catholic primary school girls and their parents at the Holy Cross school in Ardoyne. Adams and other republicans called on leading unionists to come to Holy Cross to show their revulsion. Sinn Féin was promptly accused by unionists of manipulating the protest, a charge generally dismissed. 'Holy Cross banjaxed everything,' said one British official disgustedly. Disgust about North Belfast eventually helped republicans to weather a stormy summer. It may also have made them postpone the start of decommissioning for some months.

Unionists and conservatives repeatedly declare that, though they have supposedly 'ceased all military operations', the IRA have not stopped killing and retain a considerable arsenal. Many nationalists, and it seems the Blair government, increasingly focus on the level of loyalist violence instead. Apparently unnoticed by the bulk of unionist opinion, loyalist groups, also supposed to be on ceasefire, have killed more people than the IRA in the past ten years. Between 1999 and 2001 they were responsible for thirty-one deaths, the IRA for nine. The community that the republican leadership looks to first overwhelmingly accepts, as do the governments, that those nine killings do not mean the IRA ceasefire has broken down or is likely to.

They are instead aware of a pattern many thinks pre-dates the peace process, of attacks on Catholics at random when Protestants see them prospering, politically and economically. It is at least possible that Adams and those around him looked at the loyalist violence, and dithered about decommissioning.

Among those who thought that republicans had long ago decided decommissioning was inevitable, some began to wonder about the state of the Adams leadership as nothing happened. The best guess was that political success ahead of time in the elections had made republicans overconfident. Was it simply outrage among their people about loyalist attacks? Or did they think that since everything they touched turned to gold, perhaps they could delay what none of them relished? 'There was a lot of messing,' said an official who has worked closely with all the pro-Agreement parties. 'I think after the elections the Shinners lost the run of themselves.'

A number of well-placed sources have occasionally argued that the republican leadership pretends to more coherence and long-sightedness than it actually possesses. 'It's a wing and a prayer a damn sight more often than people realise,' a figure on the fringes of the leadership once confessed. Until and unless a leading republican tells the story of the peace process truthfully, a considerable proportion of analysis will be flawed because vital information is missing. The wait might be a long one.

In the end loyalists helped republicans yet again, at a moment when the limits of their cleverness became embarrassingly obvious. The Colombian arrests came in August. When the news broke, leading Sinn Féiners stalled and then lied. The purpose of the visit to Colombia remains a mystery. The one captured man without an IRA record was described in Colombia as Sinn Féin's accredited agent in Cuba. Gerry Adams said flatly that he was not, to be contradicted swiftly and apparently unwittingly by the Cuban foreign minister.

But from the Colombian end the story failed to develop legs. A promised surveillance video of the three in the jungle coaching the FARC guerrillas in bomb-making never materialised; a witness disappeared; the three were solicitously moved from a high-security jail 'for their own security'. A Sinn Féin meeting in Belfast with the new Washington administration's 'point-man' on the Northern Ireland peace process, Richard Haass, was said to have involved harsh language from Haass on the subject of Colombia, and on the need for the IRA to begin decommissioning swiftly. The attacks of 11 September on the US came during Haass' visit. The World Trade Center and Pentagon atrocities and the subsequent 'war on terrorism' and attacks on Afghanistan made decommissioning inevitable, conventional wisdom agreed, and a return to violence under the same republican leadership impossible.

There was another way to look at it. Adams seized a busy moment to admit that he had been mistaken and that Sinn Féin's Cuban representative was indeed one of the arrested threesome. It got scant notice, even from those most galled by how completely and swiftly the original denial had been turned around. But then Adams made the admission as a brisk preliminary to announcing that he and Martin McGuinness had advised the IRA that a start to decommissioning might be necessary to save the structures set up by the Good Friday Agreement from collapse.

The announcement came within weeks of 11 September, which Adams condemned as an example of terrorism, to unionist nausea and derision for his brazenness from many others. 'The rest of us might have thought 11 September made it impossible for the IRA to go back,' said an unshaken student of contemporary republicanism. 'The other way to look at it is that it actually made it easier for Adams to get agreement to move on arms, because he could say well, the loyalists are a worry. But since there's no going back this time, we might as well start on the guns and get the credit.' When it comes to modern republican self-presentation, scoffing tends to be briskly supplanted by grudging admiration.

Adams came through it all still looking statesmanlike. At the end of a year in which for a while republicans looked winded by events a long way from Ireland, he visited Fidel Castro's Cuba. It made for bizarre photographs, particularly a shot of an elaborately, stagily respectful Sinn Féin president listening to the septuagenarian Castro allegedly telling a joke, and a report of a five-hour dinner during which Castro quizzed Adams on education in Ireland and took copious notes, or so Adams told the dutiful reporters from Belfast newspapers who waited for briefings after each function. After the Colombian arrests, one remarkable aspect of the Cuban visit was that it took place at all and with so little sign of real disapproval from Washington.

Some wondered why it was so important for the Sinn Féin president to visit Castro. Few were satisfied by Adams' claim that republicans owed Castro for the support he gave to the 1981 prison hunger-strikes. That was, after all, 20 years in the past. A more persuasive explanation had it that he needed to cater to the internationalist leftism still prevalent among republican activists south of the border, who had been shocked and dismayed by their leadership's glib denial of the Colombian Three, and that he realised a visit would shock few outside the US. It would surprise no one who has followed his career that, in visiting Cuba, Adams simultaneously managed an internal constituency, displayed a grasp of politics outside Ireland, and associated himself with a legendary revolutionary figure, all with little cost.

To this way of thinking, all bets were off when the IRA first called a 'complete cessation of military operations' in 1994 without a reciprocal British declaration of intent to withdraw. After that point, no assumptions could any longer be made about what centuries of republican theology allowed the Provos to do. By the time of the first cessation, Gerry Adams, the ruthless and implacable IRA leader, had already been semi-transformed, by association with John Hume, into a politician to be taken seriously.

In the minds of many who have watched the process unfold, it was absolutely implicit in the Hume–Adams relationship that the political growth of Adams would weaken Hume's standing and that Hume above all must have realised this. Thanks in the first place largely to Hume's almost superhuman advocacy, republicans became part of a process which set the stage for a settlement of conflict. 'God, when you think about it, it would make your blood boil,' says a faithful SDLP supporter. 'On and on about their bloody analysis, how superior it is. But it wasn't their analysis got them out of the war, it was Hume.'

Adams' partnership with Hume caused the older man endless trouble, and did nothing but good for the republican. A less flinty personality, from a different kind of background, might have felt some sympathy as the SDLP man faced attack from inside and outside his own party. Instead, the Sinn Féin president began writing the ailing Hume out of the process almost as soon as it left the launch-pad.

Adams behaved entirely in character, as many observers of his rise agree. His ruthlessness was smoothed over by a bow towards proper respect, excellent manners concealing a ravenous political appetite on behalf of his organisation, if not for himself. 'This peace process that myself and John Hume helped to kick-start back in 1993 . . .' is a favourite tack. In someone else that might seem an inelegant, slightly awkward formula with a hint of pushiness, but the controlled and unspontaneous Adams is always courteous. On the day that Hume announced his resignation as SDLP leader, the Sinn Féin man prefaced his tribute to him with: 'When I went to him for what later became the Hume–Adams talks or initiative . . .'

The community of which Adams is now the leading political representative needs to be told that Hume was less crucial to the peace process than the Sinn Féin leader. If the impetus is shown to have come from within, there can be less suggestion that republicans have been fooled, fobbed off with less than their just demands. So the senior nationalist figure gets erased or pushed well down the credits, his party elbowed sharply aside. The story Adams has been telling republicans for much of the past ten years has been compelling, and for the most part coherent. Often they must have had to choke back disbelief, cynicism, even rage. He tells it as though he is confident they will applaud, and they do.

Upgrading his own role and downplaying Hume's was a gentle tactic by Adams' standards. In an organisation which values the ability to suspend conscience and ignore guilt, the Sinn Féin president has been a subtle and ruthless operator since soon after the Troubles began.

Close observers of the closed world of republicanism say he reached the top by having the clearest and most long-sighted view of the way ahead. The journalistic observer who thinks Adams has lied all along to his supporters argues, with a characteristic edge, that he developed a reputation early for a chilly caution, and that he has stayed at the top by welding associates to his side, in some cases having first set them to trap and compromise overt opponents. 'I think Colombia is an example of his lies catching up with him,' he said shortly after the arrests. 'He could do the necessary on decommissioning now if he wanted with little kickback from his people. But he'll wait, and wait.' In fact, the wait was only a matter of months.

Like all conspiracies, republicanism has the inherited ability, in some a liability, to see the world solely in its own terms. At the head of a united team, Adams brings to a fine art the talent necessary to all successful leaders, for rewriting events to demonstrate consistency or continuity where none has existed. He has added a usually sharp assessment of official attitudes, with the help of what one American official once described, tongue only slightly in cheek, as 'good staff work'. Sinn Féin rarely over-estimates what the market will bear. Their brazen handling of the Colombian adventure was a good example.

When Adams went into the peace process in partnership with Hume, he had the wind behind him in the shape of a war-weary community wishing him on. He has also had help from advisers to the three governments of the UK, US and the Irish Republic, a fund of goodwill internationally and in some sections of the media. The icing has been the assistance rendered entirely unconsciously by the behaviour of unionists, and the continuing, increasingly unpolitical violence of loyalist paramilitaries. But it has been a more fundamental help that with each republican step further into the political fold, the fold has changed so dramatically.

The return of a devolved administration to Stormont should have pleased unionists, but the spectacle of republican ministers took the shine off the pleasure. Former IRA prisoners strolling through the gilded corridors with copies of *Hansard* under their arms spoiled it entirely. The abandonment of traditional aims, carried off with considerable swagger, is invisible to unionists behind the sustained display of apparent republican pleasure. Adams has convincingly presented a wholesale retreat to his people as victory, has turned it into a victory they never dreamed of and at one stage would have scorned, and with one voice they cheer him on.

Standing back to look at his achievement, the horror is what springs out first – the thousands of dead, the injuries that some will bear for life, pain and grief and trauma. Every assessment of the skills of Gerry Adams must initially consider how he employed them during many violent years. Republicans defend their record first by recalling how the Troubles began: it is still contested by unionists but the history books are indeed likely to record a version much closer to that on the Falls Road. Adams began his announcement that he and McGuinness had recommended a start to IRA decommissioning, by talking about those days, far off in 1969. The modern IRA had emerged as defenders of a battered people, he recalled.

An observer who was a witness then, not Catholic, nationalist, or republican, largely agrees with that account: 'I accept, privately, that's how the Provos happened. People going to Dublin pleading for help from the government there, for guns . . . there was real panic. I think the Falls Road was under very dangerous attack from loyalists and B Specials and the root purpose behind it was to keep the RCs caged in with lesser rights and inferior justice.'

It is a description remarkably like the republican version. But the difference between theirs and other versions becomes marked when considering the next phase of the Troubles, when defenders became aggressors and the IRA began to bomb and shoot with indiscriminate ferocity. 'What was absolutely disastrous was the key conceptual formulation of the '70s by Adams and the others, the long war, that it was okay to keep on doing it no matter what, that one day it would all be retrospectively sanctioned and history would grant absolution.'

There is often admiration as veteran observers of the Troubles regard Adams and those around him in these latter years. But admiration and a reluctant respect are darkened by memories, many of them truly awful. The Adams pedigree probably includes responsibility for the Bloody Friday bombs in Belfast in 1972, twenty-one explosions in little more than an hour that killed nine people and left scores with serious injuries, and seniority in the organisation during the years when the IRA picked off Protestant farmers, teachers and school bus-drivers along the border.

'Not for justice, but in the hope of one day defeating the entire Protestant/unionist community?' says the witness who saw the Troubles begin. His is the assessment many now share, that Adams gets credit for helping bring the Troubles to an end, a massive achievement sustained over years. 'But he and the lads sustained the war for such a long time before that, and God was that wrong.'

Internal dissent will probably continue to sustain groups with the potential for lethal violence for some time, but it is withering rather than growing. Success has a dynamic, like failure. It is easy with hindsight to represent dangers overcome as having always been open to easy resolution: all of this took republican skill and nerve. Hume risked the destruction of his reputation if the process had failed to emerge and suffered occasionally venomous verbal aggression. For Adams, the stakes were in one sense immeasurably higher.

In the first shaky months after the 1994 IRA ceasefire, when unionists and the Conservative government rubbished its genuineness, rumours flew that Adams and a few close associates might well be killed by internal enemies. One dispassionate insider noted danger signs, pointing first towards Adams: 'It's understandable that unionists are suspicious, but you have to see that Adams has taken the greatest risk of all. It's very dangerous for him if others confirm that once the heat is off they may start playing hardball again. There must be some people in the wings, the ones who always said the political path was a snare, greedily noting down this grist to their mill.'

When the Canary Wharf bomb in February 1996 ended the first ceasefire, the same insider assessed three 'threads in the republican movement'. He thought there were the 'diehards who never believed in politics', a fairly manageable minority, the people clustered round Adams who believed the 'armed struggle has had its day and want to just go for the politics and be done with it', and what he judged the biggest group, including many 'average activists'. The latter looked at the process in tactical terms, he thought, and would have said 'back to war as soon as decommissioning raised its head'.

He also thought these tactical supporters could be turned around in relatively short order, once the process began to pay dividends. When Tony Blair arrived in government in May 1997, that was what happened. Adams, and the process, has come a long way since the nervy early days, through the protracted breakdown of the ceasefire, frustrating negotiations and a stubbornly slow initial settling-in period repeatedly disrupted by the problems of the unionist leadership and the protracted wrangle over decommissioning.

Along the way, observers in London and Dublin saw the Adams leadership come under considerable internal pressure and noted that it was handled with equal intelligence. Though officials are loath to admit it, they must also have marked a degree of ruthlessness in the way republican dissent was contained. They choose to focus instead on the skill with which the process has been sold internally.

When in October 2001 the IRA began to 'put their arms beyond use', no voice of substance in government circles claimed that Adams had been forced to deliver under the duress of Colombia, 11 September or the need to save David Trimble from his own dissidents and Ian Paisley. Adams, said a senior British figure, 'probably did what he always does, waited until he was good and sure the bulk of the outfit would stay on board'.

From the observer's tone of voice, it was clear that whatever black thoughts the authorities still entertain about him and the people he leads, the Sinn Féin president is seen as the safest, most controlled of political operators in command of a disciplined force. For Tony Blair's government, Adams is, in effect, their boy. They may be convinced he has opted for politics and peace, but in the main they luxuriate in the confidence that he still controls his secret army, unlike David Trimble.

Republicans are still secretive, and yet they have become more readable by a long way, and more predictable. By 1990, 20 years of violence showed no signs of producing anything like victory. From this viewpoint, the best guess at the republican gameplan was that a process of managing defeat swiftly made unexpected headway and encouraged more fluidity. 'What's so heartening about this,' said one observer when the October 2001 decommissioning move happened, 'is that it confirms that whatever the Sinn Féin strategy, they see it going through the working of political institutions.'

The gains for Sinn Féin that have accompanied the process spur on what is unmistakably optimism among the leadership. Their behaviour suggests that the long war has become a long, rewarding path to peace. 'You can hear it in Adams when he gives journalists confidential briefings,' said one. 'Except the odd time, when things have gone pear-shaped. But often it's like listening to a political analyst, and a good one too – someone who likes what he does and knows he's good at it.'

The reconstruction of a secret army into a force with a highly visible and steadily developing external wing has been lengthy and painstaking. Once Adams led IRA units while simultaneously urging the politicisation of 'the movement' to create more support for 'the armed struggle'. Shortly after the Good Friday Agreement, a leading republican figure said privately: 'You know us, we'll do whatever we have to.' For the record, there was still insistence that there would be no decommissioning in any fashion. But a middle-ranking stalwart lent further reassurance: 'If it comes to walking away from the institutions or walking away from the arms, we'll walk away from the arms,' he said. It took longer than he forecast. 'Management problems,' he admitted months later. 'Didn't realise how difficult it would be.'

A month after the 2001 elections when David Trimble made good his threat to resign as First Minister of the Stormont administration and thus 'throw the process into crisis', the coolness of the republican leaders was striking. On the day when republicans realised that there was about to be a second suspension of Stormont because Trimble had resigned, a Sinn Féin press conference was arranged so that Martin McGuinness could tell the media that the unionist leader had made 'a major blunder'. With the entire political class frazzled as the crisis ate into traditional holiday time, it was a showy example of how the party rotates its major players, an almost arrogant display of calm under stress.

As McGuinness wound up and journalists left, Gerry Adams strolled in and leaned over the long table to shake McGuinness' hand. 'Have a good break,' Adams smiled. 'Fish.' He sounded almost paternal, though he is only a year and a half older than McGuinness. The little routine had an artificial but entirely familiar quality. Journalists much struck by the display at the time mused after the news of the Colombian arrests that it was a good example of pride going before a fall. Sinn Féin's major figures work at presenting the image of an impregnable team, playing to each other's strengths with easy camaraderie, at least in the public eye.

While McGuinness answered questions about the fallout from Trimble's resignation with all the subliminal clout of his double capacity as former IRA commander and present-day Stormont minister, Adams was about a mile away in the Culturlann, an Irish language centre. The Trimble resignation crisis coincided with the West Belfast Festival, a week's populist cum cultural jamboree dreamed up by Adams to replace the rioting around the anniversary of Internment Day, 9 August. The proud local MP who refuses to attend Westminster reinvents the job of representative as local cheerleader in a style many appear to like, though it leaves local SDLP supporters wholly uncharmed.

The role combines management, direction, diplomacy and inspiration. David Trimble tells reporters that Adams is 'the most appalling person he has ever met', which most imagine to be what Trimble thinks he *should* say. What Adams says about Trimble is more thoughtful. He said in 2001, 'If I handled the Sinn Féin leadership or the Sinn Féin party the way David Trimble handled his, I would long since have ceased to be president of Sinn Féin. You keep trying to build on a solid foundation and don't surprise anybody . . . For the IRA's position to have been released or made public without its grass-roots having had the opportunity to engage in whatever the issue was, and certainly without there being some sense of quid pro quo from others, would have been a total disaster.'

To an audience of the fluent in the Culturlann, he joked in his lamentable Irish that he'd been unlucky in jail; his fellow prisoners had included no one whose Irish was good. He had learned to speak it without knowing how the words should sound and was now stuck with his bad pronunciation. But he would use it regardless, he said, because the language was such an important part of identity. Short-sleeved and open-necked on a sultry day, he headed a few hundred yards across the road to an exhibition of photographs of local landmarks. A journalist following him remarked, 'He was so laid back it was maddening. It had to be deliberate.' The other possibility was that the festival was relaxation for him. Over the week photographs caught him at one event after another, on the podium for a formal lecture, in the audience for a debate. He never looked less than engaged, frequently delighted.

The ups and downs of the peace process have put Adams under a relentless spotlight, and at moments he has sagged. During the negotiations before the Agreement and in the meandering progress since, the controlled and authoritarian republican has seemed at a loss to know how to handle Trimble. When the two met alone for the first time at Stormont, the unionist famously wedged a chair against the door to keep it open, much as teachers are warned to do to avoid allegations by pupils of abuse. Others watched Adams sweep the chair away, angrily they thought, as he went in. Adams claimed later that Trimble then rushed around drawing all the blinds to block photographs of them together, hardly surprising given the depth of unionist fury at Trimble's dealings with Sinn Féin.

Adams might well express awareness that unionists approach the peace process very differently from republicans, but Trimble's difficulties are clearly beyond him. How could Ulster Unionists be so undisciplined, and how could their leader be so feeble? Trimble's response to this kind of story is untypically apt. The penalties for dissent available to the leaders of what until recently he religiously referred to as 'Sinn Féin/IRA' are not available to him, he says tartly.

The most memorable moments of stress had Adams threatening in public to 'take a sabbatical' and devote time to his writing, when the Blair minister in Belfast most sympathetic to Trimble, Peter Mandelson, was about to suspend the administration at Trimble's request. For a few weeks, there was a peevishness about the republican leader. The self-discipline he habitually displays was swiftly and surely re-established, and watchers could not say with confidence if they had glimpsed the man behind the mask, or a deliberate display of righteous indignation.

A more typical performance is as benign and wise father figure, a blend of sternness, affection and concern for constituents, supporters, grass-roots republicans. A recent photograph with his small granddaughter on his shoulders, watching a politically correct Gaelic game might indicate the start of a new and more soft-centred phase. There are few previous photographs of him as real-life patriarch, no public appearances with wife Colette. Their son, Gerard, their only child, turned up on a public occasion with his father once, in 1981 as a seven or eight year old, at the funeral in South Armagh of an IRA hunger striker. They went to communion together, the small boy in a tweedy jacket that matched the father's, large and small hands joined in matching piety.

The hunger striker's brother was a priest, celebrating the Mass, the family fiercely republican, Irish-speaking and devout. About 30 priests proceeded up the aisle to communion ahead of Adams. At a highly polarised period, the sight of republicanism's figurehead parading his own religious practice incensed many Protestants and offended some Catholics. Adams was always keen, however, to emphasise in the midst of the IRA's violent campaign that it was possible to be a good republican and simultaneously a Catholic in good standing. Taking communion with his small son in South Armagh to honour a dead hunger striker would have struck him as the perfect example to give his people. At a moment when the emotion of the hunger strikes had pulled many nationalists into a communal rage against Britain and prime minister Margaret Thatcher, Adams as the devout father on his way to the altar-rails might well have appealed to some Catholics who at other times heeded the Church's injunction to regard him as an evil influence. The picture is still in the communal memory, a frequently replenished storehouse in a tightly knit community. Some years ago, an intelligent elderly nationalist said confidingly out of the blue: 'Adams is a faithful Catholic, you know. Hume, now, I'm not so sure about . . .'

As the IRA begins at last to take itself out of commission, the pious and patriotic who would always have preferred to vote for Sinn Féin as a traditional, reliably anti-British party might be tugged towards it in part by a clean-living, tweedy and reliably devout Adams. He famously does not smoke, drinks sparingly, apparently rarely swears. Being a role model is clearly something he sees as his duty and takes seriously.

His writing is presumably also meant to serve the cause, but is a bit of a puzzle. Several of his books are largely the same one rewritten, a history of his own republicanism minus information on his IRA career, plus some folksy description and short stories about the Falls, too crudely designed to boost local pride to have literary merit. But he talks about wanting to write well, not having time to practise. It may be the tension between ambition, lack of polish, and duty that produces the most awful stuff, like some of his columns for the Irish-American *Irish Voice*. When the Colombian story broke, he wrote: 'This column is officially on holidays . . .' and went on to complain that the arrests had preoccupied the media to the exclusion of more important issues, like the SDLP agreeing to join the policing board, the IRA withdrawing its offer to begin decommissioning and a spate of loyalist attacks.

'The British secretary of state insists the UDA's ceasefire remains intact. He should try explaining that to their victims. "I couldn't leave youse for a minute." That's what my mother used to say to us . . . That's the way this column feels. And if holidays could talk that's the way it would express itself about current affairs. Apart from all of the above, this column is trying to have a wonderful time . . .'

His addiction to news spoiled things, however. 'If your head is tied into the media, your head is not on holiday with you. Your head is annoyed at the failure of the Irish government and the SDLP and others to stand by what is right . . . Your head is exploring ways to sort out the bind . . . Your head is preoccupied by the furore arising from the Colombian arrests . . . Your head is wondering whether or not you are going to Latin America next month . . .' Clearly, the man needed his holiday. The column finished: 'Incidentally, I am 30 years married this week. Me and my present wife were wed 30 years ago. Which is nice. Happy anniversary to us.'

When Martin McGuinness had gone off to fish and Adams to that night's events in the West Belfast Festival, an IRA squad went out about their business. Masked men broke into a house, dragged out a teenage boy and shot him in the legs and arms. In October 2000, when two gunmen shot the dissident republican Joe O'Connor in Ballymurphy outside his mother's door, a protest campaign of sorts began, with local republicans who have been outspokenly critical of the peace process weighing in to say this was patently suppression of dissent. Their houses were picketed and both they and their families were threatened, they said. Letters to the *Irish News* kept the issue going for weeks. The campaign fizzled out, though not before a number of unionist critics noticed and quoted it as an example of continuing IRA violence, a breach of their ceasefire.

If local people were ever massively concerned, the effect had faded long before the June 2001 elections, in which Adams' West Belfast vote was 27,096. The SDLP's Alex Attwood, whose tally was 7,754, campaigned on 'the arrogance of those who think they own West Belfast' and saw the party vote fall by 10,000. Attwood's bitterness at the count was self-defeating and ill-judged, but he spoke from a widely shared SDLP sense of injustice, that killers should have transformed themselves into a political machine with more money than anyone else, more status and now more votes. There was also the memory of how SDLP workers and their West Belfast offices had been attacked over the years.

Plainly, however, there is considerable tolerance, at least for the moment, of the proposition that inside strongly republican districts the IRA may with impunity occasionally shoot and kill people who fall into certain categories. In the three years from 1999 to 2001 they killed a total of 9 people; six with connections to drug-dealing; along with dissident republican Joseph O'Connor, North Belfast taxi-driver Charles Bennett, and probably, the prominent former IRA member then anti-republican campaigner Eamon Collins. None of the killings were admitted and none caused significant public outrage locally nor, as far as could be determined, much private revulsion either. Is it possible that republicans are tempted by the idea of maintaining the shadow of violence as guarantor, insurance, protector? Among the ministers and officials who have backed the Adams leadership as the best bet for a peaceful future, there is considerable unease about the lingering violence and a believable assertion that they expect more of republicans than they do of loyalists. But not perfection, or not yet.

Some officials deny the unspoken, because unspeakable, position that authority can afford to blink at occasional killings, especially when locals and police agree that the victims have records as drug-dealers. 'You can't ever get to the point of saying well, it doesn't really matter, because these were marginal and nasty people and that's the way things are. That's populist stuff and it's very bad law,' says a government apparatchik more clear-sighted than most. 'Once you start saying these guys are scum and they deserve a bullet, there's no end to it.'

Although he insisted that government could not blink at such killings, blink they have, as has much of the population. Unionists and Conservative politicians, plus a number of journalists, campaign against the continuing IRA attacks, often suggesting that these constitute a level of violence equal to that before the ceasefires. Most unionists and many nationalists scarcely notice. What ordinary republican supporters truly think is impossible to say. Many unionists believe places like Ballymurphy, the Bogside and Creggan have been no-go areas for the past 30 years. 'They seceded long ago to the Provos,' as one leading unionist said off the record in the '80s. Among anti-republican nationalists, a nagging worry that a brutal vigilantism will drag on competes with hope that in time this too will disappear.

Clearly, the largely unvoiced official understanding is that all examples of IRA violence will eventually cease, as demilitarisation in the widest sense removes the military aspect of policing, paramilitary weapons and eventually the structures of paramilitary organisation. It has required an icy official pragmatism to deal with the IRA's political wing while it steadily becomes the prime mover in republicanism, and now perhaps nationalism; to require and keep on requiring the Sinn Féin leaders to 'persuade' the IRA, while they insist there are two entirely separate organisations.

There might well be an official argument, perhaps never explicitly voiced, that Dublin, Liverpool, Manchester and Newcastle, to take only cities comparable to Belfast in size, see more drug-related killings each year than Belfast. More likely the case is made behind closed doors that there was never going to be a neat and clean ending to the Troubles, and that this pattern is inevitable. Officials with long memories and service might even recall that for many years British governments operated to the maxim of 'an acceptable level of violence'.

There are no illusions in Downing Street or in Dublin's Government Buildings about Gerry Adams and the rest of his collective leadership. These are people who have spent the best years of their adult lives taking part in or directing violence. Many also had violence directed at them. Several were foot soldiers, then generals – theirs was not a desk war. Gerry Adams, Martin McGuinness and others share incriminating, terrifying and shaming memories, and most people who meet them know that. In their present incarnations those memories must seem very remote. When Gerry Adams and Martin McGuinness walk into Number 10 Downing Street or Government Buildings in Dublin, or wait for a US president in a White House ante-chamber, how far away is a past that included sniping at soldiers from windows of houses in which frightened families were held with guns to their heads, lying in ditches attaching wires to explosives, firing a gun directly into someone's head, and ordering and planning shootings and bombings? The record suggests that Adams and some of those closest to him have themselves killed, or ordered others to kill, former comrades now deemed traitors. They no doubt recall moments of abject whimpering fear and degradation, of being hunted, having to live away from their families, being on the run. Some share experience of capture, courtrooms, jail sentences. Several have been shot, or had close relatives killed by loyalists or by British soldiers.

A press conference to introduce Sinn Féin candidates for Westminster seats in 1990 went through the then mechanical formula of questions about their attitude to IRA violence: would they condemn it? That got the ritual answer, that Sinn Féin did not advocate violence and so had no need to renounce it. But the occasion became memorable when the 14 candidates were asked how many had been to prison and how many had themselves been touched by violence – there had been many rumours that the party was having trouble finding candidates. The question produced a glimpse of the culture which produces people like modern republicans, and organisations like Sinn Féin.

Nine of the fourteen had been jailed and one was out on bail on a charge of false imprisonment. One was standing for election in place of her father, who had contested the previous election and had since been shot dead by loyalists. Another had been to jail and twice been injured in loyalist attacks. Five said they had been attacked by loyalists or had their families attacked. Adams said he had been shot at a number of times, injured once, and the British army had shot dead his brother-in-law and shot and seriously injured his brother. 'I had a cousin picked up, tortured and stabbed to death by loyalists, and most of my immediate family have been in prison. I've a brother in prison at the moment.' A reporter listening to the story made a disgusted face. The bit that struck him was Pauline Davey's history: her father John Joe shot in his car near the family home, not long after he was accused in the House of Commons by a DUP MP as having been an accomplice in an IRA murder. His family and republicans voiced suspicion that the killers were wearing the uniform of the part-time Ulster Defence Regiment (UDR). 'Yeah, so they suffered,' the reporter said. 'I know they did – that woman's father shot dead up his own lane. But I remember going out to another car up a lonely lane. A UDR man shot in the head bringing his wife and new-born baby home in the dark, after showing off the child to their friends. And the poor man didn't die – maybe he'd have been better off. The photographer got there first. He said, "Don't look at what's on this bush."'

Republicans are practised in handling outrage and anger about the IRA. Some listening to leading figures then and now hear only self-righteous patter and wonder if they manage to believe their own version of events, if they have successfully submerged any guilt they feel, and the horror of what the IRA is responsible for, under the weight of 'what was done to our people', and 'the responsibility of British governments'. Others are more cynical. 'I don't hear self-righteousness. They're chancers,' says a skilled watcher, a whole-hearted supporter of the peace process and admirer of Adams and what his leadership has done. 'They'll say whatever they have to say. They can't ever admit how much was just a waste; so many lives ruined, their own people's lives too. They're doing the best they can with it, and the bottom line is they're on the right road.'

The Adams republican leadership is a group which has reached middle age while transforming themselves and the organisation they serve. They have moved from spending most of their time directing or committing violence to directing a political organisation and running a media operation of considerable skill and subtlety. And at the centre of this history is the figure of Adams, republican figurehead and dynamo of the peace process. By this stage it is difficult to guess how much his behaviour owes to selfless commitment, how much to a growing awareness of his own status and significance.

An unfriendly onlooker studied him at a function in 2000 with a mainly republican audience, in West Belfast. 'I watched him walking round with a word for everyone, a pat on the shoulder for the old guys and a joke with the younger ones and I thought, "You've had 15 years of this, son, that's a long time to be Ho Chi Minh. I wonder what it's done to your vanity?"' The less cynical and probably more accurate view is that Adams as he appears to the world is at the service of the collective, that he is the way they need him to be.

In the course of the effort to build up Sinn Féin in the Republic's politics, some party workers recently deplored the media's 'undue emphasis on personalities'. They protest too much. In Northern Ireland personalities have been fashioned, frame by frame, as republicans move away from the sharp dichotomy of 'the armed struggle', the divide between secret army and subservient political voice. In plain view, the front line made themselves over for new roles. Where the media were originally offered naive young killers or inarticulate veterans, they could now choose between the comparatively polished and sure-footed Adams, the more informal and still gritty Martin McGuinness or the sinuous, almost silky Mitchel McLaughlin, devalued only by his lack of IRA background but occasionally used because of that to fly kites – and handle thankless propositions like Colombia, while McGuinness fished in Mayo and Adams scribbled in Donegal.

As time has gone on the choice has grown, with a second row wheeled on for training under the lights and in front of mikes. Adams and McGuinness have had time to refine their presentation. Endless meetings chew over the line to take, a collective leadership maps the way forward. These two are at the centre of that collective and arguably its joint driving force. Though McGuinness has emerged on an equal footing in media terms, having developed star quality as Stormont minister on top of his old status as IRA leader, Adams still has the edge. The presidential niche is one he looks born to fill.

In photographs with the Taoiseach, Prime Minister of Britain, and American President, Adams is at least as serious, significant and dignified as his companions. He chose not to take office at Stormont, a move that is not explained. But to the outsider, with hindsight, it was the right decision from a propagandist perspective. Nobody could have known how snugly McGuinness would fit in as minister and particularly as education minister. But the collective leadership was right to decide, if that was the reasoning, that Adams has a quality which should not be touched by the mundane requirements of office, that he should remain above and beyond the daily round. Irreverent onlookers occasionally suspect he might be thinking 'How would the legends of the past comport themselves at this point?' There are moments when he looks as though he models his bearing on the gravitas of Eamon De Valera, although De Valera holds a dubious place in the modern republican pantheon. It might be the glasses and beard, the straight back that makes him seem taller, the suggestion of austerity – the idealised personification of republicanism? Self-schooled, sometimes almost ponderous in how he chooses words, there is no self-indulgent public embarrassment if the wrong one emerges. The effect diminishes him not at all. '"Distractionary" isn't a word, you know,' a reporter told him flippantly as he left a press conference. 'Ah, words is words,' said Adams. Seriousness of purpose is the lasting impression. His dignity is innate; he looks like a leader. 'The bastard has charisma,' an SDLP man once said.

The American republican congressman Peter King, an Adams fan, once caught to perfection and explained the double effect that leading republicans often have, especially on a first appearance. He was describing Adams arriving at Kennedy airport on his first American visit: '[It was] packed with reporters, not just regular news reporters, but celebrity-type reporters, the type who would be out if it was reported that Elvis had come back from the dead, mixed in with serious diplomatic reporters. Every type of media person was there, literally standing on chairs, fighting for position, pushing each other out of the way.

'Suddenly this door opens, and Gerry Adams walks in. And you could hear the reaction, almost like some of the oxygen went out of the room when he walked through. He looked the way his pictures had him – he had the glasses, he had the beard, but he didn't have any guns, he didn't have any grenades, didn't have any mortar rounds, and I think some of the reporters were surprised by that. In many ways Gerry Adams is indebted to the British for this, because they made him out to be this madman, this absolutely horrible human being, and so they had set the expectations bar so low that it was easy for Gerry to show that basically he is a very intelligent guy, and a very thoughtful person.'

It is one of the greatest assets Adams has that just by walking into a room, among people who only a few years ago damned all republicans as bloody terrorists, he makes republican supporters proud. There is an insatiable market in his own community for this kind of attribute. It disgusts anti-republicans and, no doubt, a number of his internal enemies. But it may be that the Gerry Adams now driving the peace process has caught the mood of many nationalists, in the way John Hume once did. These are people not at all disposed to regard the Good Friday Agreement as the sum total of their aspirations.

As the confrontation began between the first Police Ombudsman Nuala O'Loan and Sir Ronnie Flanagan, Chief Constable of the new police service and old Royal Ulster Constabulary about the true commitment to reform in the new service, Adams held a press conference in January 2002. He made predictable points, that more and more evidence of past collusion had come out, that Sinn Féin could not support the new service as it stood, that there must be a thorough public inquiry. In the course of a lengthy answer he made a remark that escaped much attention, throwing it in as though casually. 'I'm not seeking necessarily for anyone to serve a day for any of this,' he said.

Some of his listeners, attuned now to the techniques of republican transformation, spotted an important marker another choreographed move – the steady lowering of expectations to bring them into line with reality. Adams, and republicans, will still make many demands. One that has been difficult for the Blair government is the question of an amnesty for 'OTRs', 'On the Runs', the people who have never been charged but are still 'wanted for questioning' about many offences. Republicans simultaneously insist that a long line of accusations against soldiers and police must be investigated. A senior figure cheerfully admitted once, off the record, that there was nothing fair about this practice: 'We're greedy,' he grinned. What modern republicans demand is what they think they can get, without causing themselves undue pain.

Some time ago Adams said that Northern Ireland was still a long way from a formal truth and reconciliation process. A commission on South African lines might have to wait: 'It happened after the settlement and was part of developing a process of closure, and a new beginning.' The settlement, to republican minds, is far from complete.

On the supposed transformation of the RUC, when Adams sounds unappeased, perhaps unappeasable, but at the same time dignified, it is possible that he speaks for people who have begun to believe that this process might eventually deliver the level playing-field they were promised, if not the united Ireland they fought and killed and suffered for. Perhaps they hope for something more ambitious – their leaders sound resolute and energetic, not ready for retirement like Hume or reasonable and sensibly satisfied like his successor.

Asking for add-ons to the Good Friday Agreement is the thing to give the decommissioned troops. Those who find the new order hard to take should be consoled by an observable fact: that the astuteness Gerry Adams once employed to plan a long and bitter war is now engaged in entirely political calculations. Adams may sound reasonable, but it is clear that he is nowhere near satisfied. After Weston Park, when republicans walked off with the bulk of what was on offer plus a number of items no one but them had imagined, access to Westminster among them, a weary Dublin civil servant sighed, 'Sinn Féin are great ones for the wish-lists.' It has been a republican experience of the peace process, in its second, bumpy but perhaps now more stable stage, that keeping up their demands keeps everyone else alert, if only with fury. If you don't ask, Adams would no doubt reply in his folksy way, you don't get.

MARTIN McGUINNESS: A LONG EDUCATION

After the slow-footed, hard-thinking Gerry Adams, Martin McGuinness' surprisingly cheery and deft way with the most varied people is almost light relief. Once monosyllabic in public, he has turned out to be more adept than Adams in dealing with non-republican circles, 'much better at making conversation,' said a member of one of the small parties in the pre-Good Friday talks. 'It isn't something I thought I'd ever say about Martin McGuinness, but you get the feeling of a warmer human being.'

Martin McGuinness

As the former IRA chief of staff, McGuinness once personified the will to fight until the British sued for peace, declared their intent to withdraw and left the road clear for a united Ireland. Now he is a minister in a Stormont government, and about to start using an office in the Palace of Westminster. It is an amazing turnaround after a long, bloody journey, during which the organisation that McGuinness once led caused 1,780 deaths. What were those deaths for? Not for a united Ireland; not for Britain to withdraw from Ireland. The unforgiving and the short-sighted say that all those people died violently, all those families were ruined, to make Martin McGuinness minister of education at Stormont.

But the story is not over. What some call failure for republicans does not look like that to many of their supporters, nor to McGuinness. This is not the end of the journey, and McGuinness is the republican leader who talks about journeys most. He marked Remembrance Sunday in 2001 by recognising the importance of the day for unionists, a day the IRA once marked by exploding a bomb at the Cenotaph in Enniskillen, killing 11 Protestants. 'They have been hurt. They have been hurt by me and by republicans down the years. It is time to bring all of that to an end. We have the blueprint to do it. We do have to put out the hand of friendship to one another . . . we have to travel on a journey.'

The 'blueprint' is the institutions and undertakings of the Good Friday Agreement, which enthuses few unionists. There was little unionist acknowledgement of what McGuinness said. Instead the remarks were picked up as a good omen by London ministers, increasingly impressed by the distance republicans have travelled. 'They're capable of big gestures, aren't they?' an associate of Tony Blair said of the republican leaders, soon after McGuinness' remarks. 'They can be big men when the moment calls for it.' The comparison was unspoken but obvious. His previous remarks had been about loyalist aggression in North Belfast against small Catholic schoolgirls and their parents, and the failure to realise how this damaged the whole unionist case.

Republicans, positive and on the move, have impressed British governments more than confused and negative unionists. The Blair government has clearly made its calculations on the basis that they give David Trimble and the unionists what comfort they can as the old order is dismantled, but they see political republicanism as the more credible engine for delivering a peaceful future. Ending IRA violence is the major enticement for London, and also for the Republic's government. The official position is to move ahead steadily to make a Northern Ireland still inside the union acceptable to nationalists as well as unionists, plus to meet specific, extra demands made by Sinn Féin, the IRA's increasingly assertive voice.

McGuinness, reflective traveller and assured leader, is the figure who makes it hardest for unionists to accept the new situation, in which republicans hold two ministries in Stormont, the old seat of Protestant, unionist power. Everything about it is difficult for many Protestants, but the sight of the man who once led the IRA now performing creditably as minister for education is impossible for some to stomach.

McGuinness does not make it easy, nor by his own standards does he make it more difficult. He delights openly in his new job and leaves it to unionists to note that he is helping to administer Northern Ireland as part of the United Kingdom – they should draw their own conclusions. Many, including the British, American and Irish governments, think that this is a major compromise by republicans. The new minister for education helped deliver the new deal, by being the hard man beside the more political Adams. McGuinness was the guarantor of integrity, the insurance against sell-out. He was also the chief negotiator in secret talks with the British government that began in 1990, even before the talks between Adams and John Hume.

It was not the first time McGuinness had secret talks with a British government. When he was flown to London with Adams in July 1972, they were there as incorruptible young fighters on the ground, leaders in the making. Years later, McGuinness said that the sole purpose of the talks was 'to demand the declaration of intent to withdraw'. It was a short meeting: there was no discussion. The full IRA demands, listed by the then chief of staff, Sean MacStiofáin, were that Britain recognise the right of the people of Ireland acting as a unit to decide the future of Ireland, declare intent to withdraw by 1 January 1975 and grant an amnesty for political prisoners. The killing went on for more than 20 years.

It is the big black shadow behind the smiles of today's pragmatic, reasonable Sinn Féin leadership. 'There was no real thinking, was there?' says an observer who supports the entire peace process. 'It was just keep on going, keep on killing and one day we'll win out.'

Supporting McGuinness and Adams now, he means, does not include whitewashing what they stood for, all those years. Many share the feeling of a great choking sadness and baffled rage that it took so long for such intelligent people, such clever leaders, to find a way out of continuing to cause such carnage and such grief.

The fact that Martin McGuinness looks as if he enjoys every minute of every day is what sticks in unionist throats. It is also the essence of modern republicanism to move away from tradition with a smile, as though this was triumph not compromise, much less failure. It is a long way, and yet a perfectly logical progression, from the initial phase when the role of McGuinness was to fireproof Adams. In the culture of violent republicanism he could not have shielded him without a reputation for ruthlessness. McGuinness had paid his dues, which means that he shares the responsibility for a considerable number of horrifyingly violent deaths and injuries, the devastation by high explosive of the centre of his home town of Derry and surroundings, where he was almost deified as a republican hero.

In 1990, the year those secret talks with the British government began, the IRA in Derry used a local man as a human bomb to kill soldiers. A 42-year-old father of three, Patsy Gillespie was a worker in an army base. His family was held captive, he was strapped into the driver's seat of a van loaded with primed explosives and ordered to drive to an army checkpoint on the border of Donegal. Then the bomb was detonated, killing five soldiers. Little of Patsy Gillespie's body was recovered. Asked now about Patsy Gillespie or other specific IRA killings, McGuinness talks at length and, if pushed hard enough, angrily, in the vein perfected by Adams and the rest of his group of leaders: 'We have caused suffering and we have suffered too . . . it is time to bring all of that to an end.'

The years of sending others out to maim, burn and bomb, losing friends to the bullet or to jail, gave McGuinness the significance that in the end helped start a process towards peace. 'Inside the movement when this thing started Adams was regarded as a slippery customer by a number of people. There was the feeling that Adams liked it too much, that he'd do anything to get them on the political road,' says one jaundiced but acute monitor of today's Sinn Féin leadership. 'Martin was reassurance to the hard men. His presence beside Adams was supposed to show them that it wouldn't go too far, too fast.'

Another perspective comes from someone who recalls a glimpse of Adams in awe of McGuinness, or certainly happy to give that impression. 'The first time I saw McGuinness,' says a Dublin-based reporter, 'was in 1981 at a hunger strike funeral – Francis Hughes'', when people walked out because the priest criticised republicans. I went out to the churchyard and was talking to Adams when up came Martin to give the oration. Adams was like a little boy looking at McGuinness. He introduced him as if he was a special person, with genuine admiration.'

At that point and for years afterwards McGuinness made few public statements. 'He barely acknowledged me,' the reporter recalls, 'wasn't that what he was like? The chilly blue eyes and silence. You'd meet him on the stairs in the wee scruffy Sinn Féin office in Derry on your way to talk to Mitchel McLaughlin and you got no more than a grunt. Now he gives off-the-record briefings!'

The emergence of the chatty McGuinness coincided with the peace process: 'Overnight there he was, fully-formed.' Those who remember the earliest speeches, especially that very first recital in the Bogside – 'It does not matter what John Hume says' – are still amazed. At that stage of republican thinking, men of few words were the style. A few years later, he was working on a new style. His was the voice that scalded the critics in 1986 when the leadership he is part of began its public march away from the old ways.

At the Dublin party conference where the County Roscommon old-timer Ruairi O Brádaigh and a few dozen others walked out rather than agree that the party should start taking seats won in the Dail, it was McGuinness' speech that mocked O Brádaigh, for claiming the end of abstentionism would inevitably lead republicans away from 'the armed struggle' and into the corruption and compromise of democratic politics. The knowledge of McGuinness' other role, his status in 'the Army', was what lent force and a veneer of credibility to somewhat wooden rhetoric and wholly bogus indignation. 'Shame, shame, shame,' he shouted, to much applause.

A close associate of McGuinness and Adams, Danny Morrison, then on his way to becoming Sinn Féin's new publicity director, soon afterwards described those who wanted to hang on to abstentionism as 'a small number who argue fiercely, almost theologically'. He and his

colleagues, on the other hand, took a 'pragmatic' approach, said
Morrison. Not long before, 'pragmatic' would have been a dirty word
in a republican mouth. O Brádaigh was right in his suspicions but
irrelevant then and now, his republican Sinn Féin a sad obsolete model
of the shining machine that ferries the Adams/McGuinness leadership.
They knew their people better than O Brádaigh did. A new generation
of republican activists south of the border are as enthusiastic about
ending the war and the apparently endless possibilities of the future, as
the northern republican strongholds of West Belfast, South Armagh,
East Tyrone and Derry city.

McGuinness' Derry, the slightly bitter internal joke goes, beat the
IRA to its first ceasefire by about a year. Unemployment in the Bogside
and Creggan is still high, but the old walled commercial city centre
became largely Catholic-owned – apart from branches of British high-
street chains – more than ten years ago, just ahead of Sinn Féin
becoming a power in local government. Local unionists jeered that it
was clear the IRA would not bomb 'their own'. Sinn Féin gained
council representation steadily from the late '80s, sitting with
considerable satisfaction in the old Guildhall, the centre of unionist
power in the decades when nationalists were gerrymandered into
subordination, bombed by one of the new councillors. At an early
meeting of the re-shaped council, a Sinn Féin worker standing proudly
in the ornate doorway greeted journalists memorably: 'Welcome to
Derry, we're the future.' The limits of violence and the potential of
politics became clear early in McGuinness' home town.

The past few years have taken him to Chequers and the White
House, to English mansions and Downing Street, but primarily to
Stormont, to the Department of Education he now heads with every
sign of having found his true mission in life. At every step what blazes
through is his delight at the new world opening out for him, and for
republicans. Adams, glorying in mixing with big names in posh places
would sound laborious: perhaps the easy Derry manner helps
McGuinness to sound more likeably wide-eyed.

There was Chequers in the spring of 2000: 'We spent most of the
time sitting outside on garden chairs, very close to the rose garden at
the back of the building,' he said in the documentary *Endgame*. When
he became a grandfather for the first time, he was in Hillsborough, the
formal residence of Northern Ireland Secretaries. 'I remember, in

1999, a meeting in a very small sitting-room with Gerry Adams and the Taoiseach and the British Prime Minister, and normally I don't bring my mobile . . . but I did on this occasion because my daughter was about to have a baby. The four of us were sitting there talking about hugely important issues in relation to the peace process in Ireland. And suddenly my mobile goes off and it's my wife, and you'd have thought that she'd won the lottery. Both the British Prime Minister and the Taoiseach wrote messages of support for my daughter, which I appreciated.'

Familiarity with Downing Street has bred a degree of boredom. 'On occasions we've been left wondering why we were there in the first place . . . it's a very familiar building to us by this stage . . .' Familiar to the IRA too, who in February 1991, a year after McGuinness started those secret talks with British emissaries, fired three mortars towards the building while John Major was holding a Cabinet meeting. They fell into the gardens at the rear and no one was hurt. The meeting resumed in a basement bunker.

Through the slow saga of ceasefires on and off, entry into talks delayed, much-interrupted negotiations and the Agreement, McGuinness stood in every photo-opportunity beside Adams, a more substantial public figure with every appearance. After the long, slow anti-climax of more obstruction and delay, he and Bairbre de Brún at last became Sinn Féin's two ministers. By then 'the base', as the republican leadership call their inner and outer circles of supporters, had come to regard a place in government as a goal, though it was government at Stormont of a Northern Ireland still inside the United Kingdom. Only a few years before, no republican, and not many nationalists, could even bring themselves to use the title 'Northern Ireland'.

But McGuinness and de Brún insisted that they were taking office on behalf of their republican voters, in what they once termed a partitionist assembly, a pseudo-parliament with no legitimacy. Time and adversity overcome worked some of the magic; the stung, stubborn nature of unionist opposition worked even more. The final touch was the stunned reaction when Adams, third in the queue of party leaders to take his pick of posts, called out his first nomination: McGuinness to be minister of education.

'A former leader of the IRA in charge of our children's education?'

responded Ulster Unionists, DUP and the unionist splinters with one horrified voice. McGuinness in charge of schools was a shock, except to him. The ear-to-ear grin as he arrived to take possession of his office carried all before him. The former IRA leader appeared effortlessly at home in a setting that once embodied Protestant privilege and the unionist monolith, and his people were pleased for him. The fact says as much about the transformation of a community as the significance of one individual. A group which once co-existed sulkily with a unionist Northern Ireland, cowed or mutinous, is now big enough and self-confident enough to believe that the public face of society must reflect them. What is still not clear is whether most want it to reflect Sinn Féin, or a more moderate party. The betting is on Sinn Féin.

Taking office had already come to seem like an entitlement for McGuinness before it happened. The sight of him advancing on a large leather chair in what was to be his ministerial office is an enduring image: the widest of smiles on the choirboy face under the receding curly hair, flanked at a slightly nervous distance by senior civil servants, also smiling. Initially the office was not in Stormont but at Rathgael, near the overwhelmingly Protestant North Down town of Bangor. McGuinness described that for the documentary record too, pressing all the image-making buttons. 'The biggest day was the first day I went to my department at Rathgael House . . . *Rathgael* is an Irish word, it means "the fort of the Irish".' But Stormont had always meant unionist dominance to republicans. How did he answer those who were horrified by the step?

There was pain in it for everybody, McGuinness said piously, but the aim was to ensure 'that the domination the unionists had of Stormont in the past would finally be broken and we would be there on an equal basis with everybody else'. He had been in Stormont before, after all: the pre-Agreement negotiations were held there. From the steps of the grandiose parliamentary building he had looked out over the spacious grounds and seen that Stormont could be his. 'Coming out of the first meeting that we had with British government civil servants in December of 1994, back onto the steps and looking down the avenue and that huge expanse of ground, it was almost like taking ownership of the place for me.'

He talked a lot about the shock value of his appointment, piling it on in social and educational terms, emphasising that the person now responsible for primary and secondary education was an early school-leaver whose first job was on the bacon counter in Doherty's butchers. But previous Stormont ministers had included many of little academic achievement and as many with expensive education whose stints in office benefited no one. The significance of McGuinness' arrival lay in his almost magical feat of erasing its negative symbolism in the minds of an entire section of the population.

He and Adams know that they are transforming republicanism and the face of Irish politics: these are icons thoroughly aware of their own power. They can make dreadful mistakes, as one unenthralled observer remarked soon after the Colombian affair; 'when they're good they're very good and when they're bad they're awful'. The enterprise is a collective effort, and keeps moving. 'It's one of their major attributes, that when something goes wrong they don't agonise,' says another spectator. 'It's the first thing unionists should learn from them.'

A worthwhile assessment of McGuinness as a minister will take time. The initial impressions were favourable, with the caveat that he brought no real radicalism to the post. In his first month, in spite of Paisleyite pupil walkouts, he was so relaxed in his new persona that he had a chat with a headmaster in a Derry Catholic primary in which he laughingly recalled a relative of the teacher's whose home was a 'safe house' when McGuinness was 'on the run'. The media were within earshot and the snippet made it into the papers. Unionists unsurprisingly expressed outrage at the bad example to young children. In short order a departmental spokesperson insisted that his private conversation had not been in earshot of pupils: if there was disquiet among civil servants, it failed to surface. McGuinness minded his tongue on subsequent visits.

Civil service reaction to the Sinn Féin ministers was well managed. Reports had it that before McGuinness arrived, the department's most senior officials agreed it should be best foot forward – no loitering in the lobby, let's meet him as he gets out of the car. It set the tone. If any rebelled in either Sinn Féin department they did so silently or managed discreet transfers. The machine showed the public a neutral and professional face. 'We haven't had any malicious leaks from Education,' says a specialist reporter. 'No stories that reflect badly on Martin when he's off camera, no embarrassing memos. Remember what they did to Mo Mowlam?'

During the period when Tony Blair's first Northern Ireland Secretary unsettled unionists and many other establishment-type males, already reeling from the onslaught of a peace process, repeated leaks brought an unwelcome focus on civil service attitudes. The civil service has had its own internal upheavals in the course of the Troubles. A Protestant-dominated bureaucracy needed several doses of increasingly severe monitoring and assessment before it made radical changes. Top-level appointments put Catholics into a few key positions, and they have gradually reached proportionate representation at middle and some upper levels.

When the power-sharing executive was established, anecdotal evidence suggested that there were as many Catholics unnerved at the notion of working with David Trimble and Peter Robinson as Protestants repelled by the thought of taking orders from Bairbre de Brún and the former leader of the IRA. In neither case have bad-mouthers broken ranks and told all. The height of visible disaffection has been an allusion or two in letters to the *Belfast Telegraph* and *Newsletter* reporting civil service unhappiness at de Brún's alleged refusal to refer directly in correspondence to 'Northern Ireland' and preference instead for the style 'here'.

By contrast McGuinness seemed to bask in approval, apart from the unremitting, automatic derision of the DUP and occasional barbs from David Trimble – who famously referred on several occasions to the need for Sinn Féin ministers to be 'house-trained'. It is likely that few Catholics listened to Trimble's 'house-trained' crack without some head-shaking. Whatever else they might think of Sinn Féin's arrival in government, only the most unusual would have expected McGuinness and de Brún to make fools of themselves in office, or that they would behave in a vindictive or sectarian way. The republican public relations muscle is much more highly developed than Trimble's. The behaviour of McGuinness minister has not cost him any fans among Catholics and might have made some converts. Trimble is a different story.

Some surprising sections of Protestant opinion gave McGuinness good marks early. Like Adams impressing new audiences, he benefits today from the bad press of old. A cold-eyed apologist for terror in the past to many Protestants, the McGuinness who visits schools and chairs meetings is a pleasant surprise. Clearly of above average intelligence and a friendly, unpretentious, decent sort, he was off to a good start.

But the sight of him on show doing his job was too much for unionist politicians at first. The images of the average education minister's round took on extra spin. Hunkered down with toddlers in an Irish language nursery or facing a classroom of seven year olds, beaming fondly, he photographed well. Paisleyite pupil walkouts were not a popular opposition tactic; gradually the unionist reaction faded. In the first touchy months his staff made sure he went where a majority of teachers would be pleased to see him, or at least not outraged. The usual shots of teachers smiling beside the minister had more interest than usual. In some schools, principals made speeches telling McGuinness how especially pleased they were to have him.

Invitations came from surprising places, with glimpses of touching generosity. A senior teacher wrote to Belfast papers, anonymously but with some details of his school, to say he would be glad to welcome the minister, though he had been shot and seriously wounded by the IRA while serving in the Ulster Defence Regiment (UDR). He knew what McGuinness had been, but he thought he sounded serious about the job, he was glad a local man now held it instead of a direct rule minister with no knowledge of Northern Ireland, and he harboured no bitterness.

There were new school wings to open, plaques to unveil. Most Catholics over a certain age have memories of such plaques uniformly bearing royal or other titles that to them signified an alien governing group. Only a few years ago republicans were blowing up buildings with plaques commemorating official openings.

Methodist College, Belfast, 'Methody', a bastion of the old unionist establishment, seized the day before many others and invited the dangerous new minister to visit, but without making any prior announcement. There was a partial walkout by senior pupils but less upset from staff and pupils than might have been expected. Later, Methody's principal told a London journalist that to his own surprise he thought McGuinness the best education minister he had met. Stormont officials gossiped that the new minister was plainly 'gob-smacked' by Methody, perhaps most by the courtesy he met but also, openly, by the impressive surroundings. Here was the boy from the Bogside, the ex-IRA boss, now honoured guest in the training-ground of the former ruling class: just across the road from the Queen's University of Belfast, Methody's big sister, all similar weathered red-brick, stained-glass windows, pomp and circumstance – now home to a largely Catholic student-body and a growing quotient of Catholic students. With the arrival of more and more children of the newly assertive Catholic middle class, Methody is itself in the process of change from within, knowingly or not. A good experience for everyone, officials said after the new minister's visit. Given his own involvement in managing transition, McGuinness might indeed have appreciated the day.

The gift for presentation occasionally lets him down, or perhaps the depth of contradiction in the situation make jarring interludes inevitable. When loyalist attacks and threats to Catholic teachers upset schools across North Belfast, McGuinness chaired meetings with teachers' unions and made a strong statement. He would give all teachers the support they needed: schools, he said, must be sacred. A noble sentiment, which must sound strange to the IRA killers over the years who confronted a headmaster as he drank a coffee in the canteen and shot him repeatedly, held staff at gunpoint while they waited for another, booby-trapped a desk drawer with explosives to kill the school principal when he pulled it open, shot at point-blank range the driver of a school bus in front of shocked and terrified pupils. There were many IRA attacks on schools and their staff. Some were members of the UDR, some former members: all were Protestant.

Republicans have always denied the sectarianism that has been part of their violence. McGuinness has been eager to demonstrate that Sinn Féin ministers can be utterly impartial. Easing requirements for enrolment and providing financial assistance to Irish-medium schools has gone hand in hand with support for integrated schools. Paisley's party claims McGuinness has shown sectarian preferences, but the accusation is generally dismissed, nor has the Sinn Féin minister shown dangerous radicalism. Some observers suspect civil service advice may have been followed to the letter. Private funding for school building on the British model, already in train as he took office, began without debate. No room for manoeuvre or the easiest path? The most distinctive move by the new minister has been his declared personal interest in ending academic selection in education at eleven. The Eleven Plus examination is cruel, he says, prefacing all his early remarks about it with the story of how failing it slotted him into second-class schooling, at least in his own mind. But progress in replacing it has been deliberate and slow, by painstaking consultation.

The powerful grammar school lobby, its core the old Protestant establishment favourites, see replacement of selection as a direct threat to them. Perhaps showing McGuinness more warmth than he might have expected has been tactical. One figure well plugged into the network said: 'I've seen him work a room and never seen anything like it.' The early verdicts were favourable, he said, but then this was an open-minded: 'The civil servants say he reads briefs well and can read across, then asks very sharp questions. He's very impressive.' He adds mischievously: 'Wouldn't be the determination and discipline of his past life?'

In terms of making political mileage, McGuinness wiped the floor with the opposition in his first six months, his star power upstaging the rest of the power-sharing executive from the start. No one has ever had difficulty picking out the most newsworthy member, the dullness of the Ulster Unionist and SDLP teams by comparison making McGuinness shine the brighter. With the exception of the SDLP's Brid Rodgers, he showed the only media flair.

His Sinn Féin colleague is alternately invisible or attracts more obvious hostility. Cynical observers of Sinn Féin's women players are not surprised. Giving one of their two jobs to a woman was in line with republican political correctness. Insiders never doubted that the more difficult and under-funded department in which no one could star was more likely to go to the woman. Being required to decide on hospital closures or answer for long waiting lists has swamped Bairbre de Brún as it might have done many others, and the albatross of the Irish language has clinched it. A thoughtful speaker afflicted by a pedantic manner and grating voice, it is not clear whether she chooses to use Irish at every possible opportunity or the party requires her to make the point about cultural equality. She is the only member in the leadership with flawless Irish, certainly the only one capable of answering detailed and unprepared questions in the language fluently.

But the mechanical appearance of chunks of Irish in every speech makes her unpopular even with other nationalists, precisely because it inflames readily inflammable unionists. Some may feel culturally cherished to hear a minister in Stormont routinely speak Irish; others feel de Brún's mechanical usage diminishes the language. McGuinness by contrast, with his token and sometimes stumbling few words, his '*cupla focal*', very much like a Dublin minister paying lip service to the first national language, rubs no one the wrong way – just as well given the other potential strikes against him.

The education figure so initially impressed by McGuinness compares him favourably to his colleague, though at second-hand from the gossip-mill of public occasions. 'She should get a life. You hear stories about meetings with tiny numbers present, maybe no more than six or seven, and she makes a speech in Irish before translating it. No one there except her speaks it. Whereas Martin shakes everyone's hand, says hello in Irish and then says that's all I know.'

McGuinness and Adams may overplay their access to prime ministerial offices and enjoy their new status a bit too blatantly. The balance for their own audience, and for others, is their patent seriousness about their politics. Whatever still lurks in the shadows, McGuinness the minister is on the main stage, under the spotlight.

After the Colombian affair, when nasty suspicion about republicanism resurfaced with a vengeance, one of the few immediate points of reassurance for the optimistic was the education minister's determination to be seen to do his job. When decommissioning finally began, it happened in the same week as the report he had ordered on methods of replacing the Eleven Plus. He travelled to take bows at the White House and to mollify old republicans, now-standard manoeuvres in peace process choreography. Though this was during the early stages of American bombing in Afghanistan, US army chief of staff Colin Powell made time to meet him, an encounter to make unionist teeth spontaneously grind. Powell told an Irish reporter at a televised press conference the next day that no, they had not discussed Colombia. 'We were too busy celebrating decommissioning.'

One official, who had greatly disliked the republican disposition to be contemptuous of those who wanted answers about Colombia, was cheered to the same degree by the start to decommissioning – after a period of losing heart, and faith in their judgement as republicans delayed it. 'Seeing McGuinness taking the applause in the States and then rushing back to deal with the Eleven Plus: isn't that a definition of success?' Knowledgeable as this observer is, he still had doubts about the direction of republican strategy; he had no hesitation in recognising McGuinness as guarantor of its general tendency towards the good. The original hard man is now the bringer of light, to this way of thinking, and working hard at it. McGuinness flew home from Washington, landed in Dublin, drove to Belfast for a press conference to receive the Eleven Plus report in public, then back to Dublin to meet Taoiseach Bertie Ahern. He must have been jet-lagged in Belfast but gleamed with pride as he took questions.

McGuinness has begun making efforts to sound as though he is trying to understand that unionism has other motivations as well as bigotry: hence the Remembrance Day remarks. It may be a sign of growing self-awareness, or another decision by committee that deems it is time to move on. The self-righteous indignation that comes through when he or others are forced to comment on continuing or past IRA violence sounds increasingly incompatible with the conflict resolution they all profess to want. Even the new improved McGuinness still occasionally hits a tone of splendidly injured pomposity, as in his retort to an interviewer who needled him about past IRA violence: 'It ill-behoves anybody to call into question my motivation, or Gerry Adams, in South Africa at this minute meeting Nelson Mandela, a good friend to the peace process. If Nelson Mandela was sitting in this chair, would you even dare to ask him these questions? I think not.'

Republicans grow instantly indignant at litanies of their bloody pasts. Time to move on, they say – though they reserve for themselves the right to rake over the actions of the RUC, British army, loyalists and unionist politicians at the slightest pretext. But there are elements of performance in this also. The Adams–McGuinness leadership is intent on managing its way out of or past the conflict's unpleasant backwash of still unresolved questions: the extent of collusion between security forces and loyalist paramilitaries, or acceptance of a semi-changed RUC as a new police service. Rhetorical outrage may sometimes have to substitute for progress.

One of McGuinness' standard complaints is also a favourite with Adams: the refusal of unionist leaders to shake hands with them in Stormont or on public occasions. Sheer bigotry, McGuinness suggests. Unionists must get over it: conflict management demands more.

It is as though he genuinely cannot imagine how anyone could know his record and feel alienated by the thought of shaking his hand, but leading republicans well know that revulsion is not feigned. Their supporters, however, need reassurance that the conflict is ending with a share of blame distributed away from the IRA, focused squarely on the other sins of the past, in many nationalist eyes the original sins: the neglect and connivance of British governments, unionist discrimination, and repression of 'everything Irish'.

Until recently McGuinness has often used a quote Adams also likes, but there is more relish in McGuinness' claims that there are unionists 'who do not want a Fenian about the place'. He variously attributes the remark to early Unionist prime minister Basil Brooke or David Trimble's Assembly chief whip, the personable Jim Wilson, who is reported to have said it – disapprovingly of some anti-Agreement Ulster Unionists – in an early morning bar-room conversation with a journalist.

McGuinness likes the line so much he has even turned it round: 'The Fenians are about the place and they're not going away.' The retooled quote is obviously meant to be reminiscent of Gerry Adams' off-hand and, some thought, instantly regretted remark about the IRA to a crowd at Belfast City Hall within months of the first ceasefire breaking down: 'They haven't gone away, you know.'

As someone whose mere presence in Stormont sets unionist nerves a-quiver, McGuinness knows that his ministerial office brings many to near-apoplexy, how much of an irritant he is and how little he need say to maximise the irritation. He may insist that behind such irritation bigotry lurks. Like other republicans, much though they deny it, he must know that many people will always think first of those who died at the hands of the IRA when they hear his voice or see his face. Adams deals with that knowledge by becoming crushingly dismissive of those who would recall IRA atrocities, without giving equal weight to loyalist killings and those by 'the British war machine'. The impish McGuinness style is another tactic.

Republicans have come a long way by assessing their own people's mood first and what they can be brought to accept and support. To continue the journey smoothly they know that a reasonable degree of satisfaction in the cheapest seats is essential, and that the vehicle runs best on optimism. If the punters are cheered by an occasional bit of swagger from the driver, a near-the-knuckle remark thrown over the shoulder, that is what they get. At other times, a touch of magnanimous reaching-out makes everyone feel altogether more noble and therefore at ease. IRA leader-become-minister for education may be as neat a symbol as possible of the unlikely itinerary of a peace process.

ELASTIC POSSIBILITIES

None of it started yesterday. As far as northern nationalists are concerned, nothing of substance in the laborious business of making peace has appeared out of nowhere. Although the emergence of a ceasefire was a stunning development in many ways, there are no overnight stars among the main players. Talks which eventually helped spark a peace process began between Sinn Féin and the SDLP in 1988. What has changed over the past 15 to 20 years, at an increased pace since the first IRA ceasefire, is the mood and make-up of the community itself. A dynamic generated by success may be about to precipitate further changes. It is equally possible, and only a little less likely, that the dynamic will falter and fail. For many, a heady sense of possibility is the dominant feature of a new landscape.

From the formation of Northern Ireland until the last 30 years, nationalists faced the same alternatives in tackling the dilemma of finding themselves governed by an alien regime in their own country. They could fight, or suffer with a bad grace. Theoretically, of course, there was another alternative. Northern Catholics could become unionist. Few have chosen to, and in the light of unionist behaviour the suspicion is that most who have so described themselves have been exhibitionists with a touch of masochism. The political behaviour of the Catholic majority was not much healthier. In every generation, the IRA tried to overturn the state and, until the Troubles, invariably retreated fast in bad order. The flag was carried by demoralised constitutionalists bereft of a feasible programme until, a year into the Troubles the SDLP appeared, the first nationalist party in Northern Ireland to develop a serious and positive programme.

Many Catholics before that had mocked the lack of realism of republicans' futility but respected their dedication, while jeering at the pomposity and impotence of the constitutionalists. The memories of the bloody '20s left scars. Faced with an overwhelming, anti-Catholic unionism and with no encouragement from the rest of nationalism, few tried to organise politically. Many emigrated, some south of the border, more to Britain, land of the oppressor, which became more familiar to many than the independent Ireland. Some took refuge in the Irish language, sending school-children to the shrinking Donegal Gaeltacht, not only to learn the language but notionally at least to be inspired by the Ireland that might have been. It was a community huddled protectively around church and culture, with little self-confidence.

Hopes were raised then dashed in the '60s by what turned out to be merely cosmetic 'reform'; increasing disorder and violence followed the unionist backlash against civil rights agitation. But gradually, while the new IRA turned from defence against loyalist attack to taking the offensive on an uprecedented scale, and in the midst of awful communal trauma, nationalism as a whole gradually developed an assertive, buoyant profile. Relationships with Britain, the Republic and the wider world opened up. SDLP leadership boosted the whole community, even those whose allegiance had always primarily been to the 'physical force republicanism' of old and those who began to support the new IRA of the Troubles.

Hume's sheer ability and quality as a political innovator impressed people who had once been tempted to think of their community as second class. Today's republican leadership pay him constant if unavowed tribute by imitating his most powerful technique, his internationalising of the 'Northern Ireland problem', and by using much of the language he developed to chart a way out of fatalism and despair. Hume easily out-shone and out-smarted every unionist political leader of his generation and the spectacle had a powerful effect.

A steady growth in Catholic confidence was matched and fed by a slide in Protestant self-esteem. Both communities have had to question the basis of their political identity. Catholics had a head start, forced by the conflict to weigh up the effects of IRA violence against the SDLP's insistence that violence was wrong and counter-productive. Once a subdued and predominantly poor minority faced by monolithic unionism, they have developed a significant middle class, with a less wealthy section which is highly organised and coherent compared to its Protestant counterpart.

Above all, this community has a shared purpose and sense of identity which bridges the class divide. Catholics make up almost half of the population. The term 'minority' began to sound dated some time ago, as did the quaint fantasy of some misguided politicians that numerous Catholics were voting discreetly for the Ulster Unionists to show preference for the 'wider' British heritage and out of distaste for Irish nationalism. In a less polarised and politically charged time, somewhere over the rainbow, many Catholics might choose to describe themselves as other than 'nationalist', a different proposition from espousing unionism or Britishness. The size of the total vote for the SDLP and Sinn Féin leaves no doubt that the overwhelming majority of Catholics today are anti-unionist, and part of a nationalist political world. They are more deliberate about their Irishness than before the Troubles, more aware that declaring it is a political choice.

But the form of future nationalism is uncertain, as south of the border a separate state evolves at its own pace and as the peace process begins to shape a new political mould. When Sinn Féin squeezed past the SDLP by fewer than 6,000 votes in the general election, many who thought Hume's party unassailable were taken aback, although the leader had been ailing for some time. The first instinct even among the most informed and experienced observers was to regard Sinn Féin's emergence on top as ahead of time and unlikely to be consolidated in short order.

Hume, the almost legendary leader, held imaginations as tightly as Hume, the exhausted man, held on to his post. Denial figured to a high degree: shock has faded slowly. When the local government election count showed a similar result a few days later but left the SDLP still holding more council seats than Sinn Féin, nerves settled. The SDLP would rally, Sinn Féin had been lucky, this was a one-off, some said. There is still an inclination to suppose that this is a purely temporary state of affairs and will be rectified at the next election. In truth, no one knows whether this is indeed the end of an era or the beginning of the end.

It seems reasonable, however, to argue on the basis of experience and probability that a strong party machine such as that of republicanism, having gained the psychological edge, will not be pushed back again by a feeble machine under new and untried leadership. The SDLP is no longer John Hume. Sinn Féin in a power-sharing government and with peace process kudos to its name is no longer merely the IRA's political voice. All has changed: why not the primacy of the SDLP, a tired party without its dominant leader and without an obvious political lodestar, whose tragedy may be that so many of its goals have been achieved?

Until June 2001, some of the most experienced commentators were still predicting that nationalist voters would stick with the SDLP, that in the end the decision for nationalists would come down to a choice between the wise and successful leadership of Hume, and the bloody-handed horrors of the IRA's political wing. Though there was admiration for Adams and McGuinness, the thinking went, the IRA connection would hold back their rise. It was an understandable judgement, if mistaken.

What even the wisest observers failed to foresee was the speed with which events would change perceptions, and the rate at which republicans themselves have developed. This is by any measurement a transitional phase, the outcome of which may see nationalism and unionism both reshaped to take account of new realities. It was not an entirely new phenomenon that voters chose in 2001. Adams and company displayed some of the skills they now bring to the peace process while making war, a phenomenon noticed at the time even by many of those most horrified by the violence. Working on a study of changing Catholic attitudes in the early '90s it became a familiar undertone, one of the most consistent after declarations that 'the war's over' and 'we're not going back'.

One after another, people who were observant about their own community – parents in badly troubled districts, community workers, the sharpest and best-informed journalists – would say that they recognised the talent of many republicans devoted mainly to violence. These were people, they said, capable of immense positiveness if it could be harnessed for peace.

'The IRA as an organisation has to be condemned,' one of the most respected commentators said then, weighing his words so as not to be condemned as a fellow-traveller, a 'sneaking regarder' as Hume's witty deputy Seamus Mallon once termed covert IRA supporters.

'It has taken many lives and wrecked a great many more. It routinely carries out ruthless coldblooded murders: it's a blot on the face of Ireland and the civilised world. But look at some of the people in its ranks. As well as being totally callous, you'll also find that they can be astute, very bright, cunning and resourceful. You can see it in the sheer length of time they've carried on their campaign without being beaten.'

He pointed to the prison record, quoting prison teachers, though that was unnecessary. The discipline, cohesion and general level of intelligence among IRA prisoners, in comparison to loyalists, had become a cliché. For one teacher, the contrast was summed up in the

tea and biscuits with her Provo students on each occasion she took a
class. It never happened in the loyalist wing, where in any case she had
few students. A Protestant from a vaguely unionist background with
very little knowledge of the Troubles, she was unwillingly impressed by
the republicans. Why did the two groups behave so differently, she
asked staff. Republican prisoners were a disciplined unit, she was told,
a collective with a kitty to provide refreshments, conscious of how it
impressed visitors. Most loyalists, by contrast, had little or no interest
in how they appeared as a group.

The Maze had the best education record of any UK prison, most of
its students being republican. 'The lesson I take,' said that circumspect
observer in 1991, 'is that a lot of the Provos are very bright people. If
there were more outlets, more opportunity, many of these people have
it in them to be successful citizens, to be among society's winners: to
make a contribution rather than kill people.'

Sinn Féin is already redefining itself for a new age. As republicans
in Stormont's stately corridors have changed Stormont, so Stormont is
in the process of changing republicans – not necessarily taming them
and luring them into the ways of the most conservative of Dail or
Westminster parties, though they were already well disposed to some
standard parliamentary practices like secretive accounting. As with
every other step they have taken so far, Stormont has worked for them.

Their people warm to the spectacle of Martin the minister, to
young Sinn Féin middle-rankers like Conor Murphy and Dara
O'Hagan sounding articulate and bright on television and radio: in
training, earmarked for progress. The trappings of a unionist Stormont
seem ever more faded and irrelevant as the Adams/McGuinness
leadership grow surer about the steps already taken, and probably more
flexible about what lies ahead. Adams has already said that his people
see the worth of the new institutions, an unusually open endorsement
from such an innately cautious man.

The bounds of possibility turn out to be elastic, like the
terminology the republican grass-roots accepts. They cannot be overly
impressed by the Agreement's north-south bodies, no more than
arrangements for cooperation on health and waterways, as they seem
in the public mind. A shadow of the original nationalist proposals,
thanks largely to David Trimble's last-minute hard bargaining, this is
hardly the once hoped-for dynamic to generate momentum towards

unity. Yet the aspiration is back in place, shimmering above the mundane facts – a united Ireland, an agreed Ireland, a new Ireland – who knows any longer what most republicans see as the holy grail? The only certainty is that they do not believe their journey is over. They are mid-settlement, far from ready to rest in Stormont, as the SDLP have looked only too ready to do.

'Their agenda is not and cannot be a kinder gentler union,' one expert said of the Adams/McGuinness leadership in 1997. He was speaking as republicans nerved themselves for the reinstatement of the IRA's ceasefire, convinced by the new British government of Tony Blair that this time there would be a speedy and definite response, as indeed there was. After years of close study and the development of mutual trust with republicans, this witness saw them still in some doubt.

'It's a very delicate balancing act. They've accepted the consent principle but they believe it doesn't mean there'll be no change. The big question is will the dice be stacked against any attempts to democratically persuade people of an alternative to the union. Are the British determined to hang on to the union, will they change the rules whenever it's under threat, or is it to be a genuinely open ended thing, a level playing field in every sense for the two aspirations?'

One of Hume's least successful themes in later years has been his argument for 'post-nationalism', the suggestion that a new 'Europe of the regions' could best dissolve and neutralise old quarrels. A bit late, the SDLP woke up to the notion that they had prematurely capped aspirations, and Hume's successor, Mark Durkan, introduced the slogan of 'a new nationalism'. Sinn Féin's ambitions remain determinedly undefined but they regularly wheel out unity: not for them to set the boundaries on the march of a nation.

In the minds of voters and potential voters that might do them no harm. Nationalists enjoy speculation about politics, a pastime from which unionists take little but pain. The possibility of a Sinn Féin advance in the Republic is there on the blackboard, the next task. All the evidence suggests that the republican leadership is fairly unsighted about where this next phase will take them. But continuous movement has done them no harm so far and they see the market for maintaining expectations. 'Our wee Northern Ireland' or 'this wee province of ours' are frequently parodied versions among nationalists of what they hear as smug and reactionary unionist patriotism. 'It'll never be that again,' is the instinctive response. Expanding the horizons of 'their' wee Northern Ireland is a popular if still hazy project.

Dispassionate monitors of electoral form and republicans in particular argue that Sinn Féin will have dug in by the time the next election arrives, and that new young nationalist votes will go to them disproportionately, as they did in 2001. An opposite opinion comes from a commentator who, man and boy, has worshipped Hume, and for whom it would feel like treachery to accept Adams and his collective instead. 'I put my faith in the pragmatism of northern Catholics above all. If the SDLP get their act together, if Mark Durkan should come up with a wonderful new product – all right, I don't think he will but he might – Catholics will go for it.' He thought pragmatism would put the SDLP in front again because Catholics would – might – consider Sinn Féin in the round and conclude that because of their baggage Gerry Adams and Martin McGuinness could never deliver the goods like Hume: respect and cooperation from Dublin, initially grudging approval from London that became an unquestioned part of government policy, and acclaim from everywhere else in the world that showed interest.

It is an entirely plausible argument – if Mark Durkan and the SDLP can measure up, and if Sinn Féin falter. Neither course is in plain sight, though for the moment Sinn Féin seem the better judges of customer tastes. The new situation will take time to settle. The eventual intentions of nationalists might not resemble the mood post-election 2001. The realisation that his party has been jockeyed out of place might in time make some feel shame about disloyalty to a hero? In many eyes, Hume's lifetime of service was crowned by the peace process. He was widely recognised as having built the scaffolding for the new institutions, mustered international backing and escorted republicans in from the cold, taking heavy flak all the way.

It is just possible that sentiment and loyalty will swing support behind the SDLP once more, perhaps equally likely regret that in turn will be swept away by reaction to further events. On policing, communal feeling has yet to stabilise. By the end of 2002, a year into recruiting for the new service, Sinn Féin's delaying tactics might look bad if young Catholics enlist in big numbers and implementation of reform is visibly thorough and energetic. If the opposite happens, the SDLP will be badly damaged.

Decommissioning on the other hand has already boosted republican standing. It might have begun in a style that brought no reassurance to unionists but reaction on the streets, in radio phone-ins and newspaper letters pages suggested that nationalists for the most part took it at face value. More than that, they were irritated or disgusted by the unionist response. Many had always been convinced that the demand for IRA disarmament was bogus, designed to be unsatisfiable, or insatiable. The grudging or dismissive reaction reinforced that conviction.

The shadowy nature of the 'event' reported by de Chastelain met many nationalists' sense of what the IRA needed to do and, given its history, what it was capable of doing. Unionists called it a con trick, asked why it had not been filmed and why there were no details. Nationalists never imagined it would happen any other way: in fact, many had begun to think it might never happen.

Many, including both governments if the text of the Good Friday Agreement which they drafted is anything to go by, had imagined the IRA would fade away as politics bedded down, and would have cheerfully forgotten about their armoury. Colombia dented that complacence. The spectacle of Sinn Féin spokespersons blustering and at a loss to explain what three of their people had been doing in Latin America sent a shudder through the rest of nationalism. As the evidence of blatant lies and bad faith piled up, other evidence of the IRA's continued existence began to jar. 'When I hear the news and there's a fella in an alleyway somewhere shot in the legs and arms, I hold my breath before they say where it was and pray it's a loyalist place,' said a Belfast Catholic in her late fifties. 'I don't want it to be the Provos.'

Some began to want decommissioning over and done with. The cycle of republican hints, delays and explanations that the context still did not merit movement on decommissioning irked many. Sinn Féin leaders who preached about security force violence and endlessly demanded inquiries into collusion drew cynicism from outside the republican fold about IRA kneecappings and beatings. A lull in republican attacks for several weeks after 11 September looked like a hurried and tactical response to American government pressure, and did little for the general impression of the state of republican thinking. But the bulk of violence continued to come from loyalists.

'Republicans were really on the spot after Colombia,' said one senior British official. 'They really did look bad there for a while. It was loyalists that got them out of it.' The ambivalence of unionist attitudes to loyalist violence as ever helped justify republicans and shaped nationalist opinion. A year-long, sometimes nightly, campaign of crude pipe-bombings, which usually caused considerable damage though not many injuries, terrorised Catholic families and forced many to move house. The police seemed unable to stop the attacks and made few arrests or systematic searches. Most attacks were directed at Catholics living in mainly Protestant towns or districts. Many other Catholics ignored the pattern but there was a niggling, widespread awareness of it. Unionist politicians meanwhile kept up the demand for IRA decommissioning but tended to ignore or downplay the loyalist violence.

When a loyalist mob began to harass small girls and their parents on the way to Holy Cross, a Catholic primary school in North Belfast, it was impossible to ignore. Holy Cross became a running scandal and drew world publicity. Catholics throughout Northern Ireland were exercised by the sight on television of crying children, angry defensive parents, shouting abusive Protestants who said the parents had intimidated them. Reactions polarised fast. A few Protestant voices straightforwardly told the Glenbryn people to stop, that nothing could justified their actions: many were less forthright.

Perhaps if David Trimble or other supposedly pro-Agreement unionists had risen to the occasion, irritation with Sinn Féin's lies about Colombia and unease at the continuing IRA attacks might have combined to produce a genuinely sharp demand for decommissioning from nationalists. As it was, few wanted decommissioning to meet unionist terms. 'What they want is the IRA to take full responsibility for the Troubles,' was a frequent comment, 'and it isn't true.'

There was a will to see the institutions of the Agreement saved, but not out of any regard for Trimble unionism. In the run-up to the election, David Trimble called on nationalist voters to support his party's candidates against anti-Agreement unionists but told his own voters they should support only unionists. Witnessing Seamus Mallon repeatedly relegated to a back seat by a unionist First Minister left nationalists cold. Unionist behaviour in Stormont and outside it provided no new reservoir of goodwill.

The future line-up of northern nationalism is bound to be coloured by Sinn Féin's fortunes in the south. Success there will feed back into northern organisation. Watching from the south as Sinn Féin took the lead in Northern Ireland ahead of their own predictions, observers began to sound alarmed about the implications for the Republic's politics. A share of the optimism that the SDLP's displacement is purely temporary comes straight from Dublin, perhaps the greater share. Observers close to home are less blithe, more unsighted. 'It strikes me that when they say in Dublin this is just a blip, they're taking their cue from Hume again, as they did for so long,' said one northern analyst, still slightly discomfited by having read the likely performance of SDLP versus Sinn Féin wrongly. 'What's the likelihood of Sinn Féin letting this slip once they've got it?'

At the root of the disquiet that met the SDLP's demotion was a widespread unease, almost a squeamishness. If nationalists have now decided, and will again decide the same way on reflection, to be led by an organisation which has killed so many people, it will be the first time that the majority of that community has opted for the more extreme choice available. Another observer draws up the balance-sheet and finds Sinn Féin likely to stay ahead, without casting any aspersion on the morality of nationalist, Catholic voters. 'If we're going to get out of this in better shape, then, as Hume kept saying, you have to draw a line. And the Provos have drawn it best of all. They look as if they know what they're doing. And what they're doing is trying to make peace. You can't fault that. That's what people voted for.'

Northern Catholics are certainly pragmatic: half their charm as newly effective political thinkers, after decades of self-pity and sentiment. A few years down the line their political choices will be influenced by many familiar factors but might well be dictated by an atmosphere that can only be guessed at now. Reasonable stability and progress in the spirit of the 1998 Agreement would seem like a good deal to many. Freedom from recurring Ulster Unionist crises, a falling away of loyalist violence, further instalments of decommissioning including that of loyalist weapons, the development of a new policing service: all of this would probably produce a considerable will to work the present system.

'A united Ireland's probably on the way all right but a long way off, that would be the judgement for a lot of people,' says an observer who tends to read nationalists accurately. 'Wouldn't they say we've got ministers, let's work this in the meantime, go for the bread and butter issues?' But no one with any experience of the twists and turns in recent years discounts the power of the unpredictable, of random violence, catastrophe or, less dramatically, attrition, to unravel hope and the first fragile underpinnings of stability.

Since the peace process began, republican leaders have occasionally hinted darkly that their lives are more threatened now than when the Troubles were at their height, that as Gerry Adams says, 'this is the stage of a peace process when assassinations tend to come'. It is said flatly, to an extent fatalistically, though with an ear to the effect. The unspoken message is 'I genuinely don't know what effect it would have if someone shot Martin or me.' A different set of circumstances would certainly produce a very different mood.

Nationalists might see a much less bright scenario and take an altogether different tack. 'More Holy Crosses, North Belfast bubbles away there, trouble every summer about marches in the city, Protestants sour as ever – the emergence of Paisleyism as the mainstream of unionism – the inclination might be to say this state's a mess and always will be, accelerator to the floor and head straight for Irish unity.' The observer who paints that picture is also predicting ideal conditions for Sinn Féin, or, at least, for an energetic, ambitious Sinn Féin.

Republicans are not nearly as breezy about their own future as their front-men sometimes imply. A year of mixed fortunes, success followed swiftly by bungling and procrastination, should have disabused anyone prone to overrating their golden touch. Adams and especially McGuinness look reasonably fit, but both are now in their early fifties and Adams is open about yearning for life after Sinn Féin leadership. Those around them have spent almost as long in the public eye. The southern adventure is unreadable and will be arduous.

The next layer of the party may have equal stamina to the Adams/McGuinness leadership, or not. What becomes of an activist, politicised grass-roots in a time of prolonged stability with less political excitement is another question. Working-class communities tend to be less politically active in most societies, the academics note: republicans have to date been largely working class. They have confounded many expectations already. There are signs of determination to break out of the ghettos: a search for candidates who will 'look right' in more middle-class districts, the discreet and unpublicised emergence in republican circles of young lawyers, lecturers, doctors, most but not all from republican family backgrounds.

How the SDLP is to regenerate has preoccupied some observers, but as veterans sometimes remark, this is a party which attracted a substantial vote for many years despite often woeful disorganisation. As SDLP veterans themselves point out, they are not alone: Ulster Unionists have been much more spectacularly shambolic but have remained the largest party. But as the founding generation at last moves on and a new leadership settles in, a few of the older people are most in the dark about future generations. In 1992, a leading figure told me he was sure of the loyalty to the party of those ten years younger than himself. He wondered bleakly how political the children of the new Catholic middle class were likely to be.

One of that generation he trusted said recently that he saw old preconceptions about the middle class beginning to melt. A thriving businessman himself, he felt no antagonism from republicans. 'Sinn Féin's after that vote now too,' he said. 'A couple of their thinkers told me lately that they knew there was a new wealthy breed of Catholic and some were republican. There wasn't a bit of disapproval.' Whatever Colombia was about, the notion of today's Adams-led republicanism exporting a Marxist revolution has not the slightest resonance north of the border: southern republicanism may be different.

This is a community beginning to flex new muscles, looking to a period when the internal wounds of the Troubles begin to heal and the bitter divide over the use of violence gradually closes over. After that, who knows what political alignments might emerge. Given half a chance, this might yet turn out to be an unpolitical community much less exercised by the rigid divisions of centuries. Perhaps the greatest frustration for northern Catholics now is that they see economic growth and political stability within reach, endangered chiefly by Protestant, unionist behaviour. The state of unionism and its ability or inability to change is liable to dominate the next phase of political development.

Some Catholics are still tempted by the idea that the demographic pattern is going their way, that the Protestant majority has effectively gone and that the numbers game will magically transform the mood for everyone. Most know better: a tense 50/50 stand-off may well be the equilibrium Northern Ireland has to live with for decades. There is a wish to be done with the war, to secure the peace and to move on, a widespread stubborn optimism. For the immediate future, the unlikely and unwelcome proposition of exercising patience and forbearance towards unionists will soak up considerable political energy. But for nationalists the future is more a promise than a threat.

3

THE REST OF THE CAST

MAJOR PLAYERS

There would have been no peace process without assistance from outside Northern Ireland. Tony Blair, Bill Clinton, George Mitchell, Albert Reynolds, Bertie Ahern, Mo Mowlam: all were vital at crucial moments leading up to the Good Friday Agreement in April 1998, and Blair has been central throughout. Because so much has derived from relationships between individuals as well as the clout and responsibilities of governments, the personalities of outsiders have sometimes mattered to an inordinate degree: Blair's salesmanship of the Agreement to unionist voters in the run-up to the referendums, his handshakes and let's-go-for-it approach, Clinton's starry circus at a time of general depression, the sheer bounce and fun that Mo Mowlam brought to people accustomed to the formality of English officialdom and many local politicians.

Increasingly, the current phase of the process has resolved itself around the two main groups, unionists and nationalists. Other former players to a large extent have become bystanders: the three governments, British, Irish, and, on another level, that of the US. To the disappointment of many of those involved in the first phase of talks, the bystanders now also include several local players who at one stage hoped to dilute the stark duality of the argument. The Alliance party, the Women's Coalition and the small groups that spoke for the main loyalist paramilitaries have failed to win significant numbers of votes, or, in the case of the loyalists, have all but ceased to exist.

At one point inside the talks that led up to the Agreement, many of those at the table had the sense of three governments urging them on.

Now the outsiders have been pushed into the distance or have adopted a lower profile. Some would resent being called outsiders, or profess to resent it. Others would deny a retreat but no one would deny that it has been exhausting. The initial stage, with its marathon sessions of lengthy debates, harrowed everyone involved. John Hume and Seamus Mallon visibly aged; David Trimble has looked increasingly worn; the energetic former US senator George Mitchell, who arrived with the step of a man 20 years younger, left looking closer to his age.

'Remarkably labour-intensive,' says one historian of the process, 'and ungrateful. It's used people up and then spat them out. One day someone's a star player: a few months on they're gone from our heads like they've never been.' He might have added that Northern Ireland judges outsiders in advance wholly on how they are expected to line up in the contest of interests. To date, only the Americans have come out with across-the-board approval from the pro-Agreement parties. For anti-Agreement unionists, all intervention conceived as assistance to the process was bad by definition.

Outsiders have run into dirty tricks: resistance to 'interference in internal UK matters' dies hard in some quarters. But American involvement has by now become part of the furniture, not to mention the long-time presence of Canadians and Finns as members of the under-employed decommissioning body.

The relegation of briefly familiar faces to the land of the forgotten is a measure of how many twists and turns there have been. As Blair's first Northern Ireland Secretary and the first woman in the post, for example, Mo Mowlam jarred a male political society to its roots. Yet her 28 months of office seem almost as remote as the distinctly different political atmosphere before the paramilitary ceasefires. Such has been the pace of startling developments that even the most striking personalities are already fading from popular memory.

America

Bill Clinton gave distinctive and lasting shape to the American contribution, an unprecedented demonstration of sustained presidential involvement outside the United States. Although Clinton as president was famous for his skill in projecting interest without real or indeed any commitment, the possibility of peace in Northern Ireland seemed to genuinely engage him. He clearly judged, and rightly, that being associated with a settlement of the conflict there could do him nothing but good.

Clinton managed at once to celebrate and encourage the fledgling peace, acknowledged and tried to quieten genuine fears. 'A class act,' commentators agreed. As a British government press handler commented wistfully while listening to his keynote speech on his first visit in November 1995: 'The Taigs were always going to be easy. But he never put a foot wrong with the Prods, which takes some doing for an American president.' Or for anyone, he might have added.

In a place where the most familiar outsiders were a string of Northern Ireland Secretaries given to patronising or wheedling in stilted, upper-class English accents, the occasionally syrupy Clinton style suited people starved of warmth. John Major's government had treated the IRA 'cessation of military operations' with suspicion and a measure of distaste. Nationalist hopes deflated as unionists probed and queried the genuineness of the IRA move; Tony Blair's optimism was still far off over the horizon. Clinton arrived into a disappointed and strained society, only three months before the cessation ended with the bombing of Canary Wharf in London's newest business district.

Diplomacy behind the scenes had been struggling to recover a sense of momentum. White House aide Nancy Soderberg later recalled how 'furiously we worked all Fall to ensure there was some substantive progress'. The day before Clinton arrived, a new twin-track approach to the stumbling block of decommissioning was announced: preparatory talks for negotiation in parallel with efforts to resolve the decommissioning argument, chaired by the man who until then had been billed as Clinton's 'economic envoy', former Senator George Mitchell. 'And it was the most euphoric trip in all my five years in the White House,' said Soderberg. 'I was on the phone to Mr Adams till two or three o'clock the night before to make sure it was all well-balanced – the trip started on the Shankill and we had maybe a couple of thousand people watching and then we went to the Falls Road and we had more and by the middle of the day we had hundreds following the car just as if the president was a rockstar.'

The highly choreographed and scripted visit had a corn count much higher than local taste would normally tolerate but a depressed atmosphere soaked up the syrup. Apart from grouchy anti-Agreement unionism and a few voices listing the immoralities of American foreign policy, the reception was sunny in spite of the cold. Announcements of a 'twin-track' did not truly register on the streets. People had been too bruised and wary to show much jubilation in 1994. At a moment when foreboding was in the air and the IRA had secretly begun the countdown to Canary Wharf, the welcome for the Clintons at Belfast City Hall in November 1995 became a belated celebration of the ceasefires.

Clinton, a cheer-leader who could at least pretend believably to be above the local quarrel, may be remembered for providing the excuse for a party and a temporary surge of hope. In the autumn chill, he and Hillary beamed from a platform at well-wrapped crowds and smiled as though with real affection while the Lord Mayor of Belfast, an earnest fundamentalist who eventually drew a scattering of boos, struggled through a lengthy and over-religious speech. In a place with no universally acceptable much less beloved store of memories, American visitors were pretext enough for nostalgia that could offend no one: a band playing Glenn Miller arrangements plus a politically correct duet from Van Morrison, originally East Belfast Protestant, and Brian Kennedy, born on the Falls. Soderberg was elated, but probably accurate when she said: 'As devastating as the ending of the ceasefire was several months later, I just knew it was never going to be back the same way. You can't have a trip like that and see that support for peace and not know it was going in the right direction.'

Clinton's lengthy televised session listening with his trademark intensity to East Belfast teenagers from both communities, walking on the Shankill and Falls, standing at the Guildhall in Derry with John Hume by his side, amounted to as clear a demonstration as there could be of how totally Northern Ireland lacks a shared, civic culture. Elaborate advance planning merely succeeded in setting up enough appearances by the visitors to acknowledge separate communities. The only true common denominator in the public occasions was Clinton and his wife. No local touchstone gave them an accurate read 'across the divide'.

Hillary hooked up with the Women's Coalition and other feminists, and went home to work on a women's network. At the Guildhall one analyst, original sympathies largely with nationalists, was shocked to realise that the organisers had omitted to invite the Church of Ireland Bishop of Derry, Dr Jim Mehaffey, a warm supporter of Hume and the fledgling process. The bishop spoke publicly about his disappointment.

The analyst said later: 'I think I preferred nationalists more when they were the underdogs – don't see much sensitivity in this.'

White House and State Department staffers who did the preliminary work for visits had also established contacts and insights for Mitchell as economic envoy. The American connection became multi-faceted, managing Protestant unionist fears by showing interest and sympathy and helping the Adams/McGuinness leadership to handle Irish-American suspicions. Clinton's interest and the Irish-American lobby that hooked him in the first place produced a 'floating seminar', as one early enthusiast described it. The eventual arrival of an energetic American contingent to assist negotiations added visible, tangible optimism. Mitchell and his staffers would not have been a thinkable addition to any previous political initiative. Trips back and forth across the Atlantic of leaders and potential leaders in many permutations pushed out horizons and tested individuals on their capacity to see beyond their own group, class and position. It was the period of the peace process that raised most hopes and most excitement among those involved, and it seems very long ago.

The psychological boost Clinton provided began with decisions on visas for republicans to enter America, when he was convinced that it was essential to achieve the 1994 ceasefire by the Irish government, John Hume and the Irish-American lobby who first hooked him into the process. Gerry Adams was boosted inside his own organisation by a visa for the septuagenarian Belfast IRA figure Joe Cahill, so Cahill could persuade stubborn Irish-American republicans of the merits of a peace process.

A decision on a visa for Adams himself had the additional merit, in republican and Irish eyes generally, of being taken against British government advice. To someone familiar with the preoccupations of official British lobbying, that still seems an amazing shift: 'Hadn't that been the most useful thing for Britain down the years, to create this etiquette that America stayed out of it – during rows about human rights issues, for example.' It broke with an iron diplomatic law, that in deference to the special relationship with Britain, Washington would forswear even the slightest comment that might be thought favourable to Irish republicanism or the aim of unifying Ireland.

The visa came through in February 1994, with the IRA still engaged in violence, though at a comparatively low level. Adams arrived in New York to a celebrity welcome, appeared on prime-time television and was mobbed at social receptions. John Major was so furious he refused to accept telephone calls from Clinton for several days.

When Tony Blair became Prime Minister three years later, forming an instant and apparently genuinely close partnership with Clinton to usher in another IRA cessation, the Clinton genius for glad-handing bridged the next stage. A conference season began, a sort of floating pre-negotiation. Politicians, paramilitaries, some police officers and a growing and shadowy tribe of 'community workers' flew into Washington to debate the ending of conflict. St Patrick's Day in the White House became an overseas study trip. Unionists met nationalists far from home: American razzmatazz diluted tension and hostility. Republicans released from wartime restrictions took to the new world with a will, the emerging loyalist paramilitary spokesmen not far behind. Unionists were slower to lower their guard.

At the time, some queried the glitz and socialising so obviously orchestrated to help gunmen and killers make a comfortable transition into politics. Back home critics mocked the White House 'jaunts', but few outside their own supporters were impressed. Against accusations that the US pre-negotiations were extravagant, even distasteful, many seemed to feel that the end result – people who had been deadly enemies were now beginning to talk seriously – was justification enough.

In the process, at least one major barrier collapsed, if only mentally. Unionists complained for decades that nationalists had an unfair advantage in US propaganda terms because Irish-America supported them emotionally and financially. Encouraged by the Clinton White House's carefully impartial language, they discovered that they too could lobby in Washington. His status and patient networking still gave Hume the edge, and the media in Washington and New York had clearly taken to Adams. Yet unionists could see that they were welcome and would be listened to on Capitol Hill, and in editorial offices, with respect and a visible even-handedness. The Clinton years established America on a unionist map which once extended no farther from Belfast than London.

During the negotiations running up to Good Friday, Clinton phone calls famously encouraged both Adams and Trimble, helping steady nerves in the last fraught hours before agreement. By this stage, though the Clinton charisma undoubtedly still mattered, the involvement of former Senator George Mitchell had created an altogether more densely textured involvement. As the president's economic envoy, then joint architect of the compromise on decommissioning and chair of negotiations, Mitchell introduced a novel element into Northern Ireland wheeling and dealing. Complete with high-calibre staff and the president's blessing, he became the principal deal-maker.

Clinton provided occasional star turns and an open house, Mitchell complemented that with years of hard graft. Though initially unionists refused to credit it, he arrived, as a knowledgeable official said, 'innocent of Irish-American sentiment', having taken the job 'as a service to the president rather than a burning zeal to right the ancient wrongs'. Four years on and in the midst of the interminable effort to produce agreement on decommissioning, a task he shouldered again after the feat of chairing the negotiations that produced the Agreement, Martin McGuinness heard the strain in Mitchell: 'On one memorable occasion he said to Gerry Adams and myself, "You guys have a life and this is it. I have a life and this is not it."'

The comment was apparently made with a smile, perhaps in the hope of encouraging more self-reliance and sense of responsibility among local parties. Mitchell's contribution struck many insiders as committed and selfless to a remarkable degree, the gleam of white American teeth and resolute calm creating an optimism few Irish or British players felt, a sense of possibility that buoyed up spirits. One observer at the talks sessions thought Mitchell was 'well on the way to canonisation', having watched his even temper survive grim Paisley jests about his alleged closeness to the Kennedys, and interminable monologues from the UK Unionist Robert McCartney, the Paisley–McCartney duo mainly interested in breaking Trimble's nerve. A few complained from time to time that less patience might mean more speed.

'It's an extremely courtly and permissive chairmanship at the moment,' an insider said early on, though with the immediate rider that this was clearly in the hope of civilising otherwise uncivil participants. Many at the table were already tiring before Paisley and McCartney left and Sinn Féin arrived.

When negotiations began in earnest, insiders watched with some fascination as the predominantly youthful American staffers dipped in and out among the parties, lobbying, gathering and sifting. Mitchell's chief of staff Martha Pope, who had worked with him in Washington, brought a new dimension to the male world of senior officials in Belfast, London and Dublin, by being female, serious-minded, very good-looking, and a Capitol Hill veteran not disposed to tolerate condescension from second-raters at Stormont. A diplomatic and sensitive woman, her presence alone caused a degree of culture-shock. For Ian Paisley, of course, her surname provided material for jeering outside the talks. 'Miss Pope' was the subject of many cracks in the Martyrs Memorial. Some officials noted that in the talks complex, he avoided shaking her hand. One of the Americans figured: 'You can see him thinking "eccchh, the devil in a skirt".'

To observers inside and outside the talks, the Americans stood out among more strait-laced British and Irish officials. Their most distinctive contribution was a willingness to take those they met at face value, with none of Northern Ireland's judgemental, highly coloured selectivity. It was a quality that alarmed or offended several British officials, schooled to think of themselves as on a front-line by harsh experience – the death, for example, of Judith Cook and serious injury to Brian Cubbon, both civil servants, caught in an IRA landmine in July 1976 while travelling with the British Ambassador to Ireland, Sir Christopher Ewart-Biggs, the chief target, who was also killed.

The sight of the Washington crew chatting easily with some republican described by British intelligence services as a major IRA operator, or with Billy Hutchinson, a former UVF lifer, 'is not entirely comfortable to contemplate', as one once confessed a trifle thinly. Like several others, he had been inclined, not surprisingly, to think of paramilitaries as beyond the Stormont pale. The Americans had their own reservations. Biographies of the major players handed to them by the Northern Ireland Office (NIO) on arrival lacked interesting details, they thought. The Trimble file, for example, omitted the initial period of the Ulster Unionist leader's career, when he belonged to the erratic William Craig's hardliner Vanguard Unionist pressure group.

What Mitchell and his staff brought to the other players was a novel perspective. Nationalists and republicans who assumed American sympathies naturally lay with them found they faced constant pressure to move beyond traditional positions. American 'can-do', a quality initially praised on the nationalist side as likely to move the process on, became for them as well as for unionists a 'why can't you?' Early in the talks one republican concluded a shade grumpily that 'Mitchell's people' were an unfamiliar breed, entirely uninterested in Irish-American sentiment.

The discomfort and distaste that eddied around the Americans clearly did more than ruffle feathers. Intervention by a foreign state might have become an integral part of the process but was not universally loved; some still clearly hoped to derail the process before it began to run smoothly, preferably by attacking the most offensive element. Six months into the talks, jokes about 'Miss Pope' went sour when the DUP showed a leaked document, supposedly of a internal security briefing, to newspapers in Belfast and London. It suggested that she was having an affair with Sinn Féin negotiator and former bomber Gerry Kelly. They had never met, inside or outside the talks. The papers hastily apologised, withdrew the story and paid Martha Pope sizeable damages.

The leak, and the way it was handled by the NIO, did lasting damage. Few observers had any doubt that it was meant primarily to strike at the impartiality of Senator Mitchell as talks chairman. Some thought the anti-woman element was gratuitous, though probably revealing about the type of individual or individuals involved. Others thought targeting Martha Pope had been a bonus for the leakers. It was the nastiest incident of the entire negotiation, a serious attempt, in the opinion of many insiders, to strike at the whole business of American involvement and indeed the entire peace process.

The leak came from a very sensitive document through someone with high clearance. Only people of considerable importance to the official system would have had sight of it. 'It took major malice towards the process to leak that thing,' said one observer. Yet when the story broke, neither the NIO information service nor the Belfast minister Sir Patrick Mayhew expressed anger, much less outrage, on behalf of an official from another jurisdiction tasked to assist a vital political operation. Senator Mitchell and people on Capitol Hill were said to be furious on behalf of a valued colleague. Inside the talks, many on several sides decided that an element in a threatened establishment had behaved in an unpleasant and sinister fashion.

Mo Mowlam, though still getting her bearings as the Opposition's Northern Ireland Secretary in waiting, found a way to show solidarity with Martha Pope. In typically flamboyant style she came up to her in the central, journalist-haunted Europa Hotel and invited her for a drink in the crowded bar with the new Chief Constable of the Royal Ulster Constabulary (RUC) Ronnie Flanagan, and an international group of visiting police chiefs. It was as public an endorsement from an impeccably establishment group as could be found. It may also have made Mowlam enemies in high places, even before she arrived to be the Labour government's first steward of the peace process.

From Mitchell himself, the untouchable front-man, nothing emerged in public in the wake of the Pope leak except determination to finish the job and get home to his new wife, as he began to say with slightly more regularity as time went on, even more often when their first child was born. His subsequent extra spell of involvement won admiration verging on awe, that someone in his early sixties should give such a slice of his life to try to help a difficult and often apparently ungrateful society.

The American dimension is durable. Clinton's successor George W. Bush appointed an incisive 'point-man' on Northern Ireland, Richard Haass, who within months had convinced unionists that this would be a presidency disposed to listen more sympathetically to them than to nationalists. He adopted the line originally proposed by Tony Blair's third Northern Secretary, John Reid, that with nationalism viewing implementation of the Agreement as unadulterated advance, unionists needed convincing that Northern Ireland 'would not be a cold place' for them. But Haass also delivered the message that the two communities must build a shared future or have none at all, blamed loyalists for the bulk of residual violence, and stuck to the Clinton line that republicans were committed to politics.

Well-informed monitors of American involvement reported that he had been terse with Sinn Féin leaders in the wake of the Colombian affair, perhaps had even used four-letter words when he met them in Belfast in the wake of the 11 September attacks and again in a meeting in Washington. They were left in no doubt, clearly, that the arrest of three of their people among Latin American guerrillas had better be an isolated case. They were not told that Bush considered them to be terrorists, nor anything remotely similar. The Haass speech on the plight of Protestants congratulated the Adams leadership on the 'ground-breaking achievement' of the start to decommissioning, recalling that republicans had traditionally viewed their weapons as 'valid instruments' of their historical opposition to British rule. Before the Clinton embrace of the peace process, no such statement would ever have been made by an official American spokesman.

With Clinton's departure, American policy on Northern Ireland may have lost an unrepeatable momentum and personal interest, but Washington looks signed up to a hefty degree of commitment to an inclusive process. Now that settled British policy is essentially to support republicans through a transition phase from war to peace, American presidents are set to stay on board. Increasingly, it looks likely that they will take their cue from Downing Street, which in Tony Blair's time has a very different steer on Irish affairs from that of previous governments.

A South African dimension has been a mixture of involvement by individuals in Northern Ireland, and efforts to provide example. The most varied groups trooped off at the invitation of the Mandela government to explore the handling of another conflict, including several with both Sinn Féin and DUP membership. Though many unionists saw and still see the ANC primarily as friends to republicanism, the Mandela personal magic worked. Stories came back of slightly sheepish unionist politicians queuing to shake the great man's hand.

One of several South Africans who became involved, a lawyer who had worked with the ANC, Brian Currin, went home for good late in 2001, admitting defeat. He had tried and failed to mediate between the Orangemen at Drumcree, County Armagh, and the Catholic residents in nearby Garvaghy Road, Portadown. In his farewell statement he seemed to suggest that mediation had been undercut by a private deal between Trimble and Tony Blair to review the powers to restrict marches.

Like the Canadian General John de Chastelain, waiting for years while paramilitaries played games about decommissioning, Currin needed official political efforts beamed directly on the issue he tried to resolve. Some would argue that de Chastelain has only seen action when republicans cut deals with government. Tony Holland, the English lawyer who heads the regulatory Parades Commission, has made a sizeable impact, some would say decisive. A Trimble–Blair trade-off could reverse the Commission's effect. The roles of some outsiders have been invisible and ignored, as well as thankless.

The South

'What the hell has happened to the south? Does even the dumbest DUPer think them ones down there still represent a real threat?' The questioner went on to wonder whether nationalists still thought the south a real friend. She thought not by and large, probably an accurate assessment of much nationalist opinion. As a Belfast Protestant who had once feared the Republic, her main point was that for her at least it had transmuted into an unthreatening neighbour. Still exotic to a degree in its difference to the north, it now lacked the overlay of what she had always taken to be a forbidding, hostile Catholicism and unmoderated irredentism. As a professional observer of unionist attitudes, she concluded that for many, whatever unionist politicians choose to say, today's Republic is very different to the alien Celtic enemy of the past.

'Haughey has gone; Articles Two and Three of the constitution, remember them and the threat they posed to unionism? Slipped away in the night. Now you've got unionist politicians and businessmen and God knows what turning up to earnest seminars on cross-border cooperation. Not much sense of menace there.'

For another observer, southern attitudes had also changed: 'The love affair the chattering classes had with David Trimble, Ken Maginnis, the McGimpsey brothers, that's long sundered. Okay, it was never much more than a scary fling with Trimble. And Trimble has no support base in Dublin.' The view seems widely shared. In the early '90s when John Hume took such punishment for his talks with Gerry Adams from an assortment of anti-republicans and pro-unionists, there seemed to be growing sympathy for Trimble, and a belief in a new Trimble unionism. A matching new element seemed to be emerging in southern politics, but it was insubstantial and short-lived. To judge from the tone of discussion (what little there is now) on developments in Northern Ireland, the argument that unionism had been maligned unravelled, thanks to successive Drumcree clashes, the violence surrounding them, and the general trend of unionist behaviour. 'Even the *Sunday Indo* [*Sunday Independent*] is more anti-republican now than pro-unionist,' said one analyst, naming the paper which ran the anti-Hume campaign.

By this account, borne out in conversation with assorted academics and cross-border travellers to the rash of seminars in recent years, an emergent new north–south relationship is much less heated and much more pragmatic. 'I can't sense any form of residual fondness for unionism, but there's massive interest in Belfast from the money men. There's your invasion scenario: Dublin buys up Belfast,' an enterprising and unpolitical Dubliner said cheerfully.

The view among nationalists of the likely direction of southern involvement is cloudy, perhaps a surprise given that the political structures put in place by the Agreement supposedly provided a concrete relationship. But the cross-border bodies make few waves and create no sense of impetus or dynamism. Bertie Ahern, having been thrown into the same pitching vehicle as Tony Blair at various points during the roller-coaster ride of recent years, is not seen by nationalists as a champion or an enduring friend. Appreciation of his 'good political compass', as one said, leads to suspicion that he hopes the intense period of involvement with the peace process has passed, and that he has more of an eye now for Sinn Féin's southern ambitions than a care for the thorough implementation of the Agreement.

Ahern's predecessor as Fianna Fail leader and Taoiseach, Albert Reynolds, probably retains more affection in northern nationalist minds, for the chances he took to advance and sustain an IRA ceasefire. Again, like Mo Mowlam and indeed George Mitchell, Reynolds has been carried into the past by the speed of events. He was vital for a time, the commitment of his government and his personal qualities as wholly pragmatic negotiator central to the establishment of a peace process. The fact that even the most paranoid unionists could not type him as other than amiable and unthreatening was a major bonus. Ahern inherited the leadership of Fianna Fail from Reynolds, plus a process that he could see guaranteed popularity. His watchword on Northern Ireland, says one spectator, might well be 'steady as she goes. I doubt Bertie lies awake at night thinking about the north but he'd mean them well, the lot of them,

Reynolds and Ahern

although he gets a bit worn by all the carry-on.' Others point to the steel behind the amiable front, the reputation for deviousness.

The 'carry-on' from Ahern's perspective presumably includes persuading Gerry Adams of the need for progress on decommissioning to keep the machine running smoothly, as well as playing host and non-ideological neighbour to Trimble. Ahern has put long hours into the process, notably in the week of the Agreement when he flew back and forth to Dublin to bury his mother between final sessions of negotiation. His chief contribution has been to develop a friendly and uncritical relationship with Tony Blair. Implicitly, this leaves the heavy thinking to be done by the British prime minister, though to a blueprint originally drafted by Dublin's Department of Foreign Affairs. By contrast, the combative intelligence of Foreign Minister Brian Cowen made some headway against Northern Ireland Secretary Peter Mandelson, at a time when nationalists and republicans felt the Agreement was about to be steadily unpicked in the name of helping Trimble against anti-Agreement unionists.

The durable Dublin contribution to developments north of the border, indeed to the establishment of a peace which, however imperfect, has benefited the entire island, has come from the permanent element of government, the Republic's diplomatic service. They needed Hume, as he needed them. The strategy that used Irish-American influence to 'transcend' the narrow ground of Northern Ireland depended on a series of bright young Irish diplomats in Washington and New York to underpin Hume's ceaseless travels and networking.

Curiously, it is in part due to the success of their state's good servants that Bertie Ahern and his government have become less important in Northern Ireland. Throughout the early stages of what came to be known as the peace process and earlier, a series of talented and occasionally inspired officials – Dermot Nally, Noel Dorr, Michael Lillis, Sean Donlon, Martin Mansergh and Sean O hUiginn – produced advice, policy and strategy to preserve constitutional nationalism in Northern Ireland, then to neutralise and convert armed republicanism into a constructive political force. From an early stage, they liaised with Hume to develop international opinion, as a check against the recurring British tendency towards doing as little as possible on Northern Ireland.

Tony Blair has successfully worked a plan originally developed by officials in Dublin, not London, on the back of the gamble by an intuitive northern nationalist that his republican counterpart genuinely wanted to bring his organisation in from the cold. This is an odd scenario, and appearances suggest it has met with considerable resentment inside both Irish and British bureaucracies. In the run-up to the Agreement, the most formidable of the Dublin officials, Sean O hUiginn, was redeployed away from the talks as a sop to the loathing of him that had built up among unionists and some of his British fellow mandarins.

O hUiginn won the supreme compliment of attracting venom as the power behind nationalist negotiation, therefore dangerous. The best brain nationalism has had, a unionist commentator called him in private, 'better than Hume'. Among unionists, British officials and ministers, O hUiginn's well-stocked mind and swift tongue won another accolade: the nickname Prince of Darkness. His surname added to his offence. Really he was John Higgins, scoffed monoglot unionists, as though it was pretentious or fraudulent for an Irish-speaker to have an Irish name.

Being cast as the embodiment of nationalist wiles eventually neutralised an outstanding figure. Critics could argue that the fixation unionists had with him made his involvement a hindrance to agreement, that he had lost the impersonal, impartial façade essential in senior civil servants. A sizeable number of insiders thought that precisely wrong. O hUiginn's supreme accomplishment, they argued, had been drafting skill which helped produce an agreement capable of winning wide allegiance and delivering fairness. Their conclusion was that he drew the map for others before leaving.

A number of negotiators displayed shrewdness, even magnanimity on occasion and some vision. But it was an ordeal, often protracted beyond the point where tired minds could function, hampered by having to talk in 'the original sick building' in the words of one participant. The parties brought their own individual agendas, which in many cases were then jigsawed together without much care for how they fitted or the overall effect. The bulk of the systematic emphasis on human rights, theoretically important to nationalists and republicans but not something their delegations had worked on in usable detail, others thought were from the start a red rag to unionists. Much of the detailed work came from Irish officials countered by proposals from unionist negotiators, with contributions from the more thoughtful smaller parties like the Women's Coalition.

It has been difficult to spot Dublin's line in later developments. Where once their Department of Foreign Affairs maintained control over policy, guiding the Taoiseach's office very much as experts to amateurs, in recent years many hands have been involved with a consequent loss of coherence and force. Dublin has also 'lost Hume', as one analyst openly dismayed by the switch says, 'and got the Provos in exchange'. With internal southern politics due to put pressure on government–Sinn Féin relations, close and usually amicable cooperation with the main northern nationalist party may become a memory.

For the political class in the Republic and in particular for Fianna Fail, interest in Northern Ireland's politics has been strained by direct self-interest. Rivalry with hungry republican activists in inner-city Dublin and several rural areas concentrates Fianna Fail's attention on its own backyard. Having frequently interpreted republican intentions with amazing charity, for example on intent to decommission, and having coaxed David Trimble to share government with Sinn Féin ahead of any measure of disarmament, in January 2002 Bertie Ahern announced that he would not consider a coalition with Sinn Féin while they retained a connection with the IRA.

There was no contradiction in Ahern's assertion, a Dublin parliamentary correspondent explained fluently, identifying with the government of his state in a fashion no northern journalist can manage as yet. It had to be understood, he said, that the Stormont government was merely a devolved administration, without control over security forces including an army: so it was fine for Sinn Féin to be in the Stormont executive. It would be utterly different to have them in the government of a sovereign state, in control of that state's army, while they remained linked to a secret army of their own. Unionists responded with words like 'shameless' and 'hypocrites'.

Southern politics would clearly prefer the evolution of republicanism to stop at the border. Sinn Féin's displacement of the SDLP as leaders of northern nationalism, even if it should prove to be temporary, is deeply uncomfortable for the Republic's politicians. Not long before the establishment of the Stormont executive, a prominent political and legal figure in Dublin foresaw something like the results of the 2001 election with distaste, telling northern journalists off the record: 'I don't think you realise how much people here dislike the Provos. No unionist could loathe them more. The sight of them hanging around our parliament with not a shred of shame for all that murder and mayhem and our governments smarming over them . . . The prospect of them getting into the Dail in numbers makes people feel sick.'

Although the passion evidently came from his own soul, it did not take wide-ranging research to discover that the general sentiment was widely shared among Dublin's politico-media chatterers. A majority of the political class had eventually accepted that Hume's efforts helped end the IRA's violence. It was easy to accept that power-sharing in Belfast must include Sinn Féin and Ian Paisley as well as Ulster Unionists and the SDLP, but the republican march into politics should have stopped in Belfast.

There is another side to the story. Bertie Ahern's ideology-free amiability and personal lack of anti-republicanism kept tensions below the surface for some time. As unionists pushed for a start to decommissioning, Ahern went into meetings with Sinn Féin to coax, rather than hector. 'For a politician, the guy has remarkably little ego,' said a commentator familiar with London, Dublin and Belfast. 'He was never going to throw tantrums at the Shinners, like Peter Mandelson or Trimble.' It was a temptation that the least egocentric Taoiseach might have entertained, however controlled his approach. The 'Shinners' have treated the prime minister of a sovereign state with scant respect, and others resent it on his behalf.

An icy *Irish Times* editorial lectured Sinn Féin and the other political parties on the way ahead. It pointed acutely enough to the hypocrisy of expecting more from northern unionists than any southern party was willing to give them in the Dail, in the view of the *Times* quite rightly. 'If Sinn Féin wants a share of power in this state, it has work to do. It has to choose finally, irrevocably and completely between the armed struggle – in any guise – and politics.' Shortly afterwards, a poll found Gerry Adams second most popular party leader to Ahern. Metropolitan Dublin's grasp of what 'the country' thinks can be skewed by its own convictions.

A dispassionate Dublin monitor spotted a quantity of partitionist double-think. 'The electorate in the south has one kind of mindset when they're looking at guys they would see as getting off the tiger's back, coming out from under a very difficult history and travelling in the right way, even if there's some baggage they don't like. I think they apply another filter when the guys have acceded to, in quotes, normal politics, and then they see they're still carrying an awful lot of the baggage, like punishment beatings.' This came into sharp focus, as he put it with restraint, when Sinn Féin looked like becoming politically ascendant close to home.

Southern observers are divided between those who fear a Sinn Féin surge and those convinced nothing of the sort is likely, thanks to what they take to be irreducible distaste among voters for what republicans have done in the past, and the unpleasantness of the habits they have not bothered to break. The latter may be proved correct. Some in the north, however, are still insisting on much the same grounds that the 2001 results do not mean permanent eclipse for the SDLP. Northern nationalists will not forget Sinn Féin's past, they say, and so on. But in advance of the June election, observers of this mind also believed that the SDLP's lead was secure.

As Dublin's political position adjusts to developments close to home, Northern nationalism looks southwards with some amusement, tinged with bitterness in the case of the SDLP. What they see is a governing party, accustomed to dominance either by forming administrations on its own for decades or lording it over less significant coalition partners, now guarding its flank, by whatever means it thinks necessary, from attack by a comparatively tiny player. Southern politicians may think northerners intransigent: northerners think them to be utterly unprincipled – an opinion for once shared across the traditional unionist–nationalist divide. Whatever sniffiness Fianna Fail, Fine Gael and Labour now display, experience of Dail power-plays suggests that the respect Sinn Féin commands in future will be decided not by their bloody past and uncivilised habits but by their performance in elections.

In the meantime republicans cultivate Tony Blair, not Bertie Ahern. 'I think he's a good guy,' a leading republican said of Blair some time ago. 'I think he genuinely wants to do the right thing, whatever about some people in his political machine.' It was a spontaneous comment, with not the slightest sign of awareness that warmth about a British prime minister still comes oddly from Irish republicanism. For all Bertie's efforts, there was no such complimentary remark about An Taoiseach: no longer vital to republican purposes.

Britain

Republicans who have dealt amicably with Tony Blair for several years still denounce British policy but senior Sinn Féin figures no longer say 'the Brits' as they once did, spitting out the word.

It is one of the more intriguing aspects of the past few years. They may try his patience, but Tony Blair's gamble on the good intent of the Sinn Féin leadership probably ensures his continuing interest in the peace process, at least at times of crisis. His involvement is unlikely ever again to resemble that of 1998's negotiations or the rescue efforts of 1999 and 2000. In defence of his own investment and reputation it seems unlikely that as prime minister he will ever be able to push Northern Ireland to the back of his mind, unless the miracle happens and peace beds down without further ado. In the meantime, a relationship continues to develop with republicans.

A Blair–Trimble relationship looked central for a time. Trimble 'likes his prime ministers', an official said once. Mo Mowlam was quickly bypassed in favour of meetings with 'Tony', from which Trimble claimed she was swiftly excluded on his recommendation. Peter Mandelson enjoyed the most consistent unionist approval of anyone in the Belfast post, thanks largely to the perception, which he assiduously fostered, that he was 'Tony's' alter ego. The resolutely modest and low-key John Reid, deliberately unlike his two controversial predecessors, had a relatively lengthy honeymoon period. Then he began to take the flak for his boss as it steadily became clearer that republicans and Blair formed the new axis. From the republican point of view, dealing directly with Blair made more sense than detouring through Dublin, Blair's thinking has not been as clear, or as consistent.

British micro-management of the peace process has been hit and miss. Blair's initial close personal involvement could never have been sustained; he had spent more time on it than on any other issue, he said at the end of his first term. Much as the new prime minister's lustre eventually dimmed on his home patch, personal appearances have inevitably had diminishing returns. The initial swing through Northern Ireland to declare himself for the peace process and reassure unionists, the barnstorming that brought out enough of the silent to secure a narrow unionist majority in the referendum on the Agreement – these were early Blair, the bright-faced Tony with more hair and less strain in the eyes.

Appealing over the heads of local politicians came naturally to a man with a landslide victory and huge parliamentary majority at his back. He might have sounded a shade less empathetic than Clinton but he came across as well intentioned, even handed and, like the Americans and his first Northern Ireland Secretary, purveyor of the most welcome of messages to a battered population: confidence that all would be well. In those first visits Blair trucked round audiences of wary unionists steadying nerves without disheartening nationalists, even when he tacked on the personal pledges about decommissioning that became a liability further down the line. Sharp instincts and a good ear helped. Blair might have metropolitan sheen but at that point in his career was trouper enough to find precisely the right tones for Belfast listeners. The era of Sir Patrick Mayhew, last in the line of Conservative emissaries from Westminster, cursed with the plummiest of voices and loftiest airs, disappeared into the mist.

If Blair ever truly warmed to Northern Ireland and its political representatives, the integrity of the quarrel and constant reminders of British responsibility in time brought a chill and a weariness. The new Labour prime minister was decidedly less chirpy on later trips to batter decommissioning back and forth, between stony republicans and a

Reid, Blair, Mandelson and Mowlam

Trimble who agreed one minute and withdrew support the next. The long ordeal of hope alternately raised and dashed took its toll on Blair, as it did of most people.

Passionate advocacy remained, the drive to communicate with what sounded like religious conviction the possibility of a peace which could deliver sane and healthy political development. 'John Major took a middle line between nationalists and unionists, traditional British detachment: the difference with Blair is that he seems to say there's a question of justice here too,' says one usually astute observer. This is a secretive process: the motivation of key players is more than usually hard to assess. 'Maybe he simply said right, whatever works with the republicans to get peace, that overrules everything else. But I think there's something deeper than that.'

Northern Ireland was the stage for the first appearances of the would-be Messianic Blair, launching a project of potentially epic proportions. The first two of his Belfast ministers were by far the most controversial personalities to fill the post, and caused waves accordingly. They may have made more work for their boss than they saved him. Mo Mowlam, first Labour appointment to the Belfast job, crashed headlong and wilfully into Northern Ireland's social conservatism and probably reduced her own effectiveness as a result. Many from both ends of the spectrum and both sides of the divide enjoyed the spectacle, even more felt real affection for her. For women in particular, memories will linger of the first female to hold political power, and the reaction she evoked in some of her own officials: shock, verging on revulsion. Others, including officials, thought her the best thing in the process to that point.

'She heightened the atmosphere,' said one. 'We needed someone to say everything's changed, you have to look at the whole thing afresh, and Mo did it just by being herself.' It proved to be a high-risk enterprise. Largely by being herself she made serious enemies in an establishment still partly pickled in the style of Conservative administrations: stuffy, proper, intrinsically patronising to a society which some NIO mandarins seemed to think they transcended by virtue of working out of Stormont, close, as they imagined, to the real power of Whitehall. Yet over the years the general tenor of NIO advice to incoming ministers coincided to a remarkable degree with that of middle unionism.

It was a simple formula, if unworkable: that a centre ground could be built to accommodate moderate nationalists and moderate unionists, if only moderate nationalists would drop their insistence on a central Irish dimension. The fundamental precept of the peace process – inclusivity, the drawing in of the extremes – was a flat contradiction of everything many in the NIO had worked for. No wonder there were shivers at the peace process.

Accustomed to dispensing wisdom on the local scene to variously naïve arrivals, and filtering the input from others, some NIO people were alienated instantly when Mowlam answered the phone herself and talked directly to journalists. They disliked her insistence on being 'Mo' in public and private: they would have preferred at all times, or at least in public, that she act as Dr Marjorie Mowlam. They cracked when it came to the four-letter words and the kicked-off shoes. Her rude-girl behaviour subverted Stormont's pomposity and mucked up the chintzy sitting-rooms of Hillsborough, the formal residence that for some still conferred on latter-day British administration a desirable echo of the Viceregal. They had heard the tales of Mo changing her tights while giving interviews. It did not happen in Belfast. But the mere possibility underlined how times had changed.

To some unionist-leaning official minds, Mowlam was subversion incarnate, a dismissive flip with the back of the hand to the idea of an enduring British connection, like the wave she gave as she finally handed over to Peter Mandelson. That wave, some close to her said later, actually masked an emotional moment. Mowlam had not wanted to leave, and chose to clown as usual.

Her stint was always going to be fraught with danger, not least because she was a risk-taker. Hackles went up and stayed up when it became clear that the new Secretary would maintain links made in her shadow spokesperson days with community workers, many of them women, occasionally consulting them before asking her officials for guidance. In retrospect, Mowlam must herself sometimes think that she made her own life hard. The exhibitionism that played so well in metropolitan Labour, the fizz of rugby club manners in an attractive woman: neither was suited to the small, introvert and stressed world of Belfast's newly transitional political scene. There was enough trauma to the system, in the shape of republican gunmen en route to political power. Mo was a one-woman culture shock.

Others thought the value and sharp political direction of her public role more than compensated for bureaucratic noses out of joint. While negotiations dragged on and public spirits drooped, the boisterous, nonconformist Mowlam shook up impressions of British ministers and their relationship with people in Northern Ireland. Her staff had to adjust to lightning changes of plan, sudden safaris to places not until then on any official list: a down-town women's centre; the Brook Clinic, where she dispensed sympathy to staff disheartened by a year-long fundamentalist picket. It was not all feminist special interest: Mowlam's first visit was a punctilious call to formally open a trauma centre for victims of the Troubles. Civil servants complained about her pace and split down the middle on the techniques: indiscriminate bear-hugs for civic worthies, old people on walkabouts, leading politicians; jokes in place of boring speeches. Like the politicians and the wider Northern Ireland, some loved it, others were less won.

'Hello, my darlings,' she carolled to the press pack. 'Like bloody Benny Hill on speed,' one listener groaned. Mowlam once held up the printed copy of a speech, already distributed, to demonstrate how she would deliver it: 'You needn't try following this because I'm going to read it upside down and in no particular order.' A Paisley swipe at her complained that 'the Secretary of State gabbled and rambled'.

Behind the fooling there was serious intent. Mowlam convinced a large number of people that the arrival of the Blair government marked a qualitative move towards neutrality on the union. It was a stance that must have been directed by Blair, which fitted the policy of tying republicanism firmly into constitutional politics, drawing a line under the old ways of treating them as pariahs. Mowlam used first names often when she spoke of republican leaders, very much as she did with everyone else: shock, horror. She performed public duties as though she were in Britain: never mentioned Britishness, the importance of the link. More, she openly played it down – outrage.

Nationalists predictably warmed to her informality, even more to the glaringly obvious lack of identification with unionists, and the patent determination to talk up the chances of the peace process. Unionist politicians by comparison noted with pain that the Northern Ireland Secretary of Her Majesty's Government refused when asked to say she valued a British identity. When she arrived talking about the need for reform of the 93 per cent Protestant RUC, they complained. As Shadow Northern Ireland Secretary she had shown comfort and support to the

Catholic residents of Garvaghy Road who opposed Orange marches. Next she was introducing plans for a commission to restrict and standardise marching.

It also fell to Mowlam to introduce the Agreement's scheme for early release of more than 400 paramilitary prisoners. There seemed to be widespread acceptance among Catholics that it was an unavoidable part of any settlement, though many found it distasteful. Protestant opinion across a wide spectrum was affronted and angered, with only the paramilitary-linked fringe parties defending the plan. 'We're big on justice and none too keen on forgiveness,' a Protestant involved in evangelical but ecumenical groups said ruefully at the time. 'There's a lot of insistence on the letter of the law when it suits us.' Anti-Agreement unionists attacked the scheme unceasingly, blaming Mowlam as though she were personally responsible and singling out the release of specific republicans for condemnation.

'Fucking useless that woman, I think she's hostile to the Prods,' said a man who not long before thought Mowlam a breath of fresh air. 'She walks all over the things that touch them, like the security forces,' he complained. Unionist attitudes towards her had changed dramatically since she was first appointed party spokesperson in place of the strongly pro-nationalist and SDLP-supporting Kevin McNamara. Then it was the SDLP who were wary, potentially hostile, unsure how Blair as prime minister would handle republicans, decommissioning and the peace process. Unionists meanwhile, still convinced IRA refusal to decommission would scupper the process, saw the replacement of McNamara as proof that Tony Blair had finally ditched the pro-nationalist strand of Labour thinking. Dislike of the contrary agenda that Mowlam brought with her blended into distaste for her rude habits. 'Just plain vulgarity,' complained a senior unionist. 'You wouldn't have her at your dinner-table,' another declared.

Even her cheery openness about treatment for a brain tumour rebounded, though not with the public. When she whipped off her wig, complaining that it scratched and was too hot, but also apparently to discomfit the stuffier unionists in difficult meetings, it confirmed for them her 'vulgarity' and lack of conventional, old-fashioned femininity. The mixture of unnerving spontaneity, bravado and what was sometimes unguarded talk, scattered with sensitive security detail, also made less hostile men uncomfortable. Long after unionist distaste and derision set hard, however, people in general continued to warm to Mo.

As, with painful slowness, negotiations got under way, Mowlam simultaneously disappointed some nationalists and became a scapegoat for the growing unionist discontent with Blair. The vexed question of Orange marches crystallised attitudes in both directions. A typical lightning tour from Catholics on the Ormeau Road in Belfast to Orangemen in Portadown, on the day of local government elections, got no marks from unionists for even-handedness. Instead they focused on her hug for an Ormeau spokesman who had been an IRA prisoner, Gerard Rice: the charge was 'hugging terrorists'. Her attempts to maintain a relationship with protesting Catholic residents on the Garvaghy Road, begun while Shadow Secretary, outraged unionists and raised Catholic expectations that were dashed when the Orange march was allowed to pass. Several leaks of documents, clearly malicious, unsurprisingly suggested a degree of bureaucratic disaffection from 'the process' inside Stormont.

She won much lasting affection and admiration for the real achievement of slogging through night after night during the negotiations inside Stormont's Castle Buildings, doing the donkey work of carrying message and drafts back and forward with suitable encouragement or chiding. But by that stage Mowlam had been comprehensively belittled and marginalised, an outcome the few women insiders, and some of the men, thought unfair but predictable. 'It would make you boil,' said one woman. 'There's Blair in his room like a king, cool and comfortable, never budges. And Mo slogging from one to the other.'

Several of her admirers in the talks thought republicans had also done their bit to damage Mowlam. What was the point of her iconoclastic behaviour if not to reassure them of a new British approach? 'But they give her nothing. They're treating her in there as if she was a perfidious Brit. It makes her look like she didn't know what she was doing, and she's very sharp.' In the fraught months of haggling over the setting up of an Executive, supposedly pro-Agreement unionism dithered and splintered and arm-wrestling over decommissioning sidelined the SDLP. It sometimes seemed that only Mowlam's effervescence sustained the idea of the Agreement, of power-sharing and political progress, in the public mind. The fact that Mo liked Northern Ireland mattered. Many liked her in return and continued to like her, perhaps all the more as she became a unionist target.

Trimble began to deal exclusively with Blair and called for her dismissal, claiming that she was inefficient and badly briefed. He let it be known that he favoured Peter Mandelson for the job. Hints followed that Blair had the same idea. Under strain, Mowlam began to look reckless and petulant, for example becoming locked into a silly row with the Ulster Unionist MP Ken Maginnis, where both obviously lost their tempers too easily. The real harm was done when Downing Street failed to counter the Trimble claims. Instead snippets of unattributable briefings, never pinned down as coming from official spokesmen, hinted that Tony was losing faith in Mo.

As 'helping David' became the watchword of a policy daunted by confused unionism, Mowlam's performance was more and more shadowed by suspicion that she had been abandoned by her own team. It was in the end another score for a side which rarely felt lucky. Unionists who ironically were a party to the Agreement had now managed to get rid of two enthusiasts for it: Mowlam and the Irish diplomat O hUiginn.

Peter Mandelson's impact was a lot more narrowly concentrated than Mo's: the public was not an audience he wanted to impress. Mowlam had handled things very badly he suggested to unionists, nationalists, republicans and journalists. Exiled from London, having lost his first Cabinet post, he settled for a version of his usual intrigue that entangled politicians, but left the wider public cold. In particular he put the Patten proposals for reform of policing back into play as bargaining material between unionists and nationalists. Mandelson may have genuinely thought, as he claimed off the record, that he was 'creating room for negotiation', which would eventually allow both Trimble and his partner in the Executive's chief office, the SDLP's Seamus Mallon, to claim credit for a new compromise. Mandelson appeared to think he would right the balance in favour of the central parties against the extremes and that Blair would be delighted.

Instead unionists ended up further embittered when the next man in the post reinstated much of the original proposals. While Mandelson tinkered, nationalists became more split on the worth of the reforms and republicans' long-fingered acceptance of a police service. At the cost of losing trust among nationalists of all shades and possibly delaying the start of decommissioning, Mandelson had won some unionist approval, but no lasting affection for Blair. Uncharmed Belfast observers suspected they knew his true motivation: desire to put a personal stamp on a settlement, the outline of which had been agreed under Mowlam, the person in post on 10 April 1998.

Some insiders suspected a visceral dislike of republicans also played a part; others thought Mandelson's estimate of his own negotiating ability and desire to shine was sufficient explanation. 'The story's just give, give, give,' he said off the record but often in front of several people in London soon after taking the job: 'Adams and co. get everything they want.' Or as he put it to a series of London journalists, none of them familiar with the details: 'Republicans have over-negotiated. It's time they were cut down to size.' The next man in the job struggled to restore nationalist trust in the central issue of police reform, while attempting to manage unionists who had gone back to campaigning on policing as well as decommissioning.

John Reid opted for a more traditional low-key performance than either of his controversial predecessors, playing the plain man whose Scottishness and familiarity with sectarian hatreds in Glasgow helped him understand both communities. Firm but fair, Reid declared himself, a modest but efficient manager of a process well under way, with the main issues substantially tackled: devolution, decommissioning, demilitarisation, policing. Protestant alienation from the Agreement might be a problem but was not beyond solution. He felt relaxed enough to begin to address what he deemed the root of division: sectarianism.

His honeymoon as even-handed quiet man ended when Blair finally weighed the effort needed to please or support Trimble against winning movement on decommissioning from Sinn Féin, and plumped for Sinn Féin. Blair's man in Belfast took the brunt of Trimble displeasure. The initial darts included allegations that the NIO was 'full of republicans', an accusation that was said to make Reid smile wryly at how little Trimble seemed to know. As unionist politicians turned against him, the Glasgow Catholic and Celtic supporter, as he habitually and jokily referred to himself, seemed less amused at having to field needling remarks from leading DUP figures about his Catholicism.

A Stormont insider remarked on an odd feature: 'Wee barbs when delegations of them come in, innuendo about Celtic supporters. The kind of thing that, as Reid might say, would get you a dig in the heid in a Glasgow pub. But it doesn't happen when the Doc's there: amazingly, he's the brake on the others. Reid's happier when Paisley's there, and they get on fine.' Implicit in the story was the Northern Ireland Secretary's effort to avoid even thinking of 'a dig in the heid'. Bringing Paisley's party more fully into the Agreement they now work, camouflaged by continuing to criticise, was a central task for Blair's man in Belfast. Telling them their sectarian gibes were unacceptable would scarcely help the diplomatic effort. But at a time when Reid was urging sympathy for the hurt feelings of Protestants, the DUP performance must have struck him as falling short of the tolerance and pluralism he called for from public representatives.

Close observers think that for Reid, as for Tony Blair, the element in the situation that needs most work is unionism. It may be the old Communist in Reid, the veteran of Old Labour become shameless partisan of the New, that helps him adapt without any sign of effort to a process which includes representatives of the IRA. 'So that's three shameless Labour people we got in a row,' a Belfast commentator jokes. While he shows no warmth towards the republican leaders, it is clear that Reid, the ideologue turned pragmatist and moderniser, recognises their skills.

His enthusiasm is history and political science. Among the Cabinet papers released in 2002 from 1971 were a few nuggets for any historian, the most striking of them reflections by British civil servants and politicians on the calibre and personalities of the Unionist government they found in Belfast. They were unflattering verdicts. The man who two years later emerged as the first unionist power-sharer, Brian Faulkner, was over-interested in repressing Catholic agitation and under-interested in removing grievances. 'Perhaps too sure that we need him,' said a memo home from Belfast. Some of his ministers were 'not house-trained', clearly a reference to the hardliners in the Cabinet. That nugget might give Trimble pause, its language echoing his own about his Sinn Féin ministerial colleagues who 'need house-trained'. Ministers wanted to do as little as possible on equality and discrimination because they would be hard to sell to their supporters, another judgement said.

Shortly before Trimble launched an open attack on him in the Commons, Reid announced that Trimble had done more than any other unionist to 'reach out to Catholics'. He might even believe it. In any case, the view is that hectoring unionists to root out their own sectarianism will not work: hectoring republicans failed, after all. The British disposition will be to continue praising Trimble as a brave pioneer of compromise, to encourage him and others, if increasingly through gritted teeth, while hoping loyalist violence will fade away rather than rekindling the violence of republicans.

MINOR PLAYERS

One previously favoured avenue seems unlikely to be explored. Despite official flirtation down the years with the idea of encouraging non-sectarian politics, government attention is now monopolised by the two large blocs. The small cross-community groups, Alliance and the Women's Coalition, have probably had their day in the sun. NIO partiality for decades towards Alliance did not help the party; similar approval of 'the women', as the other players call them, brought no benefit either. With a comprehensive effort towards a settlement between unionism and nationalism in play, those who try to avoid or downplay the traditional divide might have known they would be sidelined.

Alliance was shaken by a 3.6 per cent total vote in the June 2001 Westminster election, half their tally in the previous election, and 5.1 per cent on the same day's poll for local government, also a drop. Some veteran figures suggested it was time for voluntary dissolution before there was nothing left, as one put it, to hand on. 'But there's strong opposition to that idea,' says a clear-eyed former Alliance activist and supporter. 'The group that most would see as their likely heirs are the Women's Coalition, and some people in there hate the women.'

A new and determined Alliance leader may have arrived too late to halt the slide into oblivion. David Ford played his moment of glory in November 2001 for all it was worth, agreeing that three Alliance members would redesignate as unionists to save David Trimble. As pay-off, he won a promise to review the arrangements set up to ward off majoritarianism, which demand majority support from each community on particular votes, in which the votes of the cross-community groups are not counted – blatantly unfair, as Ford says. The big blocs are reluctant to begin unpicking arrangements: the review proposed no change. Alliance still hopes to regenerate but has had a cruel few years.

The Women's Coalition was formed with NIO encouragement in the run-up to the Agreement as an unprecedented women's party, with a deliberate policy of representing both main communities equally. They attracted much attention but have since failed to increase votes. Its two members in the Stormont Assembly make an impact. Its leader Monica McWilliams is perhaps the female politician with the highest profile in

Northern Ireland; she is at least in contention for the title with the SDLP's Brid Rodgers. But the early promise has dimmed, a disappointment many women's groups feared was always likely, despite the concentration of talent and enthusiasm behind the coalition's banner. Women's groups in Northern Ireland have always struggled to bypass traditional divisions.

Even before negotiations began, 'the women' created a considerable stir in the abortive Northern Ireland Forum, set up as a form of elected discussion group as John Major delayed acceptance of republican bona

McWilliams and Ford

fides, boycotted by the SDLP and Sinn Féin. McWilliams and colleague Pearl Sagar, a working-class Protestant, were the nearest thing to nationalists the Forum contained. The Coalition's rule was to be represented by women from both main groups, and they argued strongly from the outset for all-inclusive negotiation. DUP and other anti-negotiation Forum members decided this made them pro-republican: the fact that McWilliams was a Catholic made her a lackey of Sinn Féin and the IRA, and Sagar was attacked as a traitor. They faced constant heckling. 'I've seen Pearl overcome with nausea before going in there and both of them near tears when they come out,' one of their researchers commented in the early days. Once, when McWilliams began to speak on agriculture, the bulk of the DUP present made mooing noises throughout her speech. The spectacle and their treatment in general caused ripples of shock and some discussion in the world outside on the depths of misogyny in Northern Ireland politics.

The Coalition's greatest hour was in the talks that led to the Agreement. Volunteer drafters and researchers gave them a seriousness disproportionate to their size and their presence made an impact, the sight of women negotiating for themselves being enough to attract attention in the male-dominated talks. Attitudes towards them said something about the need to redress the gender balance in Northern Ireland's lop-sided public representation. Some unionists treated them with blatant contempt, others ignored them. SDLP leaders tended to be patronising or dismissive. Sinn Féin behaved with more political correctness on the surface and were occasionally happy to use them as intermediaries, but, despite talking directly to them on serious issues, froze them out, as they did everyone else, when it came to discussion on crunch decisions. Some insiders thought they did well as mediators, but nostalgia lies heavily on a very young party.

Even more than Monica McWilliams, the two Progressive Unionists in the Assembly, sometimes uncomfortable front-men for the still active paramilitary UVF, made a disproportionate splash. David Ervine and Billy Hutchinson are both ex-prisoners with very different approaches: Ervine fluent and daring, sometimes more fluent than sensible; Hutchinson direct and emotional. They both served long sentences: Ervine for possession of explosive, Hutchinson more than 13 years of a life sentence for his part in the murder of two young Catholic men shot dead from a car as they walked to work. They handled their past in a distinctively different way to that of republicans asked about IRA convictions. Neither bristled; Hutchinson has always said he thinks expressions of regret serve no purpose, but he hopes his political involvement will make some reparation for what he did as a paramilitary.

The effect disposed surprising people to like them both. They were candid and easy with journalists from the start, which distinguished them immediately from most leading unionists, and Ervine in particular had a nice turn of phrase, often deliberately witty, occasionally funny by accident. With sectarian tensions spilling into street riots in North

Belfast, he once announced with great seriousness to the delight of listeners at a social function: 'The intimacy of fear leads to populism.' One listener turned away in giggles to note it down. Another was fascinated by the reaction of the nearby Sinn Féin Assembly member for North Belfast, the usually poker-faced Gerry Kelly. 'Kelly looked stunned. You could almost see him thinking, hold on, is that in the Agreement?'

Republicans, like nationalists in general, have had a soft spot for the loyalist fringe parties. Both Ervine and Hutchinson admit that Catholics were treated badly by unionists, with a frankness and generosity unmatched by any mainstream unionist politician. Ervine identifies this as the chief cause of unionism's poor image in Britain. Like the Women's Coalition, the Progressive Unionist Party (PUP) has failed to win votes and Ervine and Hutchinson's flair may not find a political home elsewhere. The fringe parties emerged suddenly and as quickly faded, their roots in shallow soil. When the most prominent figures in the paramilitary group openly admitted they had turned against the Agreement after steadily stepping up their violence, they undermined spokesmen with apparent commitment to political development, Gary McMichael and David Adams. The UDA's front, the Ulster Democratic Party (UDP), collapsed, overnight.

A long-running feud erased remaining credibility, with the spectacle of hundreds of Protestant families evicted from their homes on the Shankill or fleeing ahead of gunmen, changing streets to resettle where the group they supported held sway. The feud was kindled by the openly anti-Agreement local UDA leader, Johnny Adair, dubbed 'Mad Dog' by the tabloids to his evident delight, but the UVF response was equally violent. Between them the two groups brought fresh misery to people in the blighted Shankill, and Hutchinson's apparent role as linkman to the paramilitaries dragged him back to the streets. The invisible barrier of fear now cuts UDA supporters off from UVF territory, much as the brick and metal peacelines of nearby North Belfast run between Catholics and Protestants.

For all that the loyalist fringe groups lacked roots and substance, the loyalist ceasefire announced in October 1994 had a vital political role. Against expectations, it turned out at least initially to be substantial and disciplined. Without it, if loyalists had kept on killing Catholics at the rate they kept up in the first years of the '90s, republicans would not have been able to hold their first ceasefire as long as they did. There was another, equally powerful benefit. At a stroke, mainstream unionists who abhorred the process were deprived of the ultimate threat against it, an all-out loyalist attack.

When in 1997 David Trimble at last agreed to talk to Sinn Féin, and walked into negotiations accompanied by Ervine, Hutchinson, the UDA front-man John White and other paramilitary figures, he was mocked and criticised. But the effect was significant. For the leader of a party which had made so much of the bloodstained hands of republicans, it certainly did not look pretty. Loyalist paramilitaries are responsible for 1,000 of the Trouble's deaths. But as the voices of the angriest section of grass-roots, supposedly the most extreme end of the unionist spectrum, the fringe parties gave Trimble cover against the Paisley anathema of 'sell-out'. Without the loyalist paramilitary spokesmen at his shoulder, the Ulster Unionist leader could not have mustered the courage to begin negotiations with republicans and nationalists for a fresh start.

At the table, he reverted to the practice of keeping them at a distance, though several turned out to have at least as much ability and greater appetite for negotiation than most of the Ulster Unionist team. Primarily, their usefulness was their ability to be more open with republicans. Except McMichael, all the main spokespeople for the two fringe parties had been jailed for paramilitary offences, several for murder or attempted murder. The PUP duo, in particular, openly suggested from the start that only those who had tried to kill Catholics, or who had actually served time for killing, could, with impunity from unionist criticism, denounce sectarian violence as a failed and immoral policy. They were remarkably radical and forthright spokesmen, for a still violent organisation. The wonder was that they emerged at all, and that they felt able to be so open and truthful.

A cocoon of wishfulness surrounded them. They were gentled along by government, praised, funded and, in some minds, wildly over-promoted. Nationalists and republicans secretly wondered how genuine their mandate was, but openly praised them and avoided asking too many questions. If only David Ervine were leader of Ulster Unionism, said many inside the pre-Agreement talks. Mainstream unionist reaction ranged from angry characterisation of them as godless socialists and duplicit gangsters – Ian Paisley – to Ulster Unionist distaste twinned with need. The effect was to boost the temporary standing of fringe parties further.

'There is more to politics than decking out some UDA men in shirts and ties and giving them briefcases,' a rueful commentator wrote years later. Many thought the same thing initially but were willing to swallow doubts in the mood of the time. McMichael and Adams had ability, like Ervine and Hutchinson: it was just that neither party came from a culture which respected paramilitaries, for good reason.

Crime and gangsterism in loyalist areas blighted the fringe parties' prospects. 'Look at the communities they come from,' says one historian of the conflict. 'Loyalist paramilitaries have no record of organised political thought and none of the mythology of republicanism. It's hard to see how they can build vote-getting organisations.' He added: 'Yet they're the only voices in unionism who sound halfway serious about building a new political identity.'

Through the seemingly interminable months of talks, with Doomsday cries constantly agitating the grass-roots, Ervine and Hutchinson, McMichael and Adams were the voice of calm and reason in front of cameras and mikes. They talked down the scaremongers and, more remarkably, they explained that compromise was a strength not a weakness. On the night before the Agreement was signed, when Paisley stomped up to Stormont in the dark with a few dozen supporters to bewail the imminence of treachery, noisy and tough-looking loyalist paramilitary supporters surrounded them, shouting abuse about Paisley's past. Holding a flustered press conference in a portakabin, known UVF men only feet away from him hurling contempt with every word, Paisley looked thrown and slightly scared, for once barracked rather than barracking. Ervine intervened to calm the atmosphere, sounding commanding while the DUP leader blustered.

A few years later, little remained of the early promise. By the time the UDA told its political front to fold up, Ervine's refrain of how maltreating Catholics had almost cost the Union had disappeared from the communal memory. It never amounted to much more than talk, analysts reckon now. The limitations of the brave new voice were clear once the novelty faded. 'The PUP left nothing,' a political correspondent says sadly. 'It was only words in a torrent of other stuff. So much else was happening no one remembers what they said.' Loyalist spokespeople, he pointed out, were given to describing fluently the modesty of their backgrounds, routinely winding up with the observation that working-class Protestants had no advantages over working-class Catholics.

'I just heard one of Ervine's mates on the radio today saying the same thing again, that the lives of working-class Protestants were the same as

McMichael and Adams

those of Catholics because they had the same houses. But it wasn't the same,' said the journalist, himself working-class Protestant in origin. 'What we had that the Catholics hadn't was the chance of jobs in the shipyard or Mackies or Sirocco. Protestants still don't recognise that, and the PUP didn't tell them.'

Ervine and Hutchinson have always talked about the under-emphasis on education among working-class Protestants, the belief that you could leave school early and be sure of a shipyard job, and how it penalised many now that the old jobs have gone. Even for the most daring, protected by their violent past, some things were unsayable. It was never made crystal clear by the most radical of the loyalists that Protestants had enjoyed privileges denied to Catholics, and the basis on which these privileges were granted. There were limits to their licence.

In the view of most monitors of the unionist mood, when John Reid talked of the evils of sectarianism and suggested both communities were equally to blame, he would hit no nerves and spark no new unionist thinking. 'There are an awful lot of Protestants out there saying "that's very true", and not giving it another thought,' said one. 'It hasn't stuck, it's not in print. There are young ones coming up who don't know that Ervine said that stuff.' The PUP's impact was fleeting, is the general judgement, and what remained as the fringe parties faded was the feuding on the Shankill and elsewhere, and steadily more obvious corruption, largely among the UDA.

For many watchers there was always too great a contradiction, between personable, resolutely non-sectarian front-men like Ervine and Hutchinson, and the less successful McMichael and Adams, and the continuing loyalist violence directed at random Catholic targets or corrosively turned in on their own community. The comparison with republicans is one the fringe loyalists often made themselves, in the course of admitting how much they gained by imitation. It is harder to admit why they are so different and to tackle those differences in public. The contradictions became clearest when Billy Hutchinson was sucked into first the Shankill feud, then the Holy Cross confrontations. Hutchinson turned up initially at the school as some kind of mediator between police and the loyalist mob, an awkward and unsustainable role; Ervine stayed off-stage, unwilling to comment. As Holy Cross became an arena for the degradation and poverty of loyalist tactics, the harshest of lights shone on the PUP's spokesman, trapped in the contradiction between the fine words of loyalist politics and reality on the streets.

Republicans occasionally complain, though with little heat, that more is expected of them than loyalists. The lack of heat is acknowledgement that they know they are thought of as an altogether more serious group. The loyalist parties were probably damned by the legacy of gangsterism and corruption, played out in increasingly anarchic battles for territorial control. The best hope is that a few individuals who have travelled a long way from their origins will try again.

4

A PROFILE OF UNIONISM – THE RETREAT

IAN PAISLEY: INSIDE THE TENT

In June 2001, a crowd of noisy DUP supporters attacked David Trimble and his wife in the car park outside the election count. Daphne Trimble's terrified face, and the Trimbles' dependence on an outnumbered police guard to get them from their car to the count and back made the tea-time news and front-page photos next day. Elections in the Irish Republic, England, Scotland and Wales tend not to inflame such passions. Men and women jostled the couple, elbowing each other to get at them, faces red with fury, pointing accusing fingers, kicking wildly and trying to land punches. The candidate struggled to stay upright and hold on to his dignity. Some of the crowd were almost incoherent, frothing as they shouted, 'Traitor! Trimble the traitor! You've sold Ulster!'

The DUP had a good election. The mob was also theirs, followers of the Reverend Ian Paisley. To judge from radio phone-ins and the letters pages of local papers, the spectacle of unreconstructed and rampaging Paisleyism renewed a distaste among some Protestants that has always capped his party's vote. This time, however, it looked as though political calculation in the secrecy of the polling booth came close to seeing off that residual fastidious reserve. The DUP looked on course to knock Ulster Unionism out of their lead position next time around. In his 75th year and after almost half a century on the political scene, Ian Paisley at last appeared to be within grasping distance of power. It has been a slow and tortuous rise.

Paisley is a lifelong troublemaker, his considerable talents dedicated to wrecking. He has seen off several leaders of more polite unionism.

Ian Paisley

He has harried many others into impotence. The main Protestant churches are mortified that his is often the international face of Northern Ireland Protestantism, but their criticism has always been muted by dread that he will steal their congregations. For several decades business leaders have been blaming him for blackening Northern Ireland's image. British ministers regard him with open distaste and mention of his name is the cue for worldwide derision – Paisley is synonymous with antiquated bigotry. There is a long history of promises to set up citizens' armies which will use any means necessary to take the war to Ulster's enemies and defend Protestants. Paisley and several of his closest associates have helped form groups which have then faded into obscurity, but in several instances some previously involved in those groups were charged with possession of arms and explosives. Paisley himself twice served prison sentences for disorderly behaviour.

The most recent and most balanced history of the last 30 years, *Making Sense of the Troubles*, summed up the British government estimate of him: 'James Callaghan accused him of "using the language of war cast in a biblical mould". Reginald Maudling wrote: "He was one of the most difficult characters anyone could hope to deal with. I always found his influence dangerous." William Whitelaw marvelled at his "unrivalled skill at undermining the plans of others. He can effectively destroy and obstruct, but he has never seemed able to act constructively." Roy Mason remembers him as "an oafish bully, a wild rabble-rouser, to many a poisonous bigot because of his No Popery rantings". James Prior thought him "basically a man who thrives on the violent scene. His aim is to stir the emotions of the Protestant people. His bigotry easily boils over into bombast."'

Yet more than 40 years after his first public disturbance, the bulk of unionists, a constituency which reveres law and order, look tempted to make him their political leader. Given his history and what he still stands for, it scandalises many that even so late in life he should have won such support. It does not surprise anyone who analyses unionist thinking. As a respected local commentator puts it, only slightly tongue-in-cheek: 'There are three types of traditional unionist voter. One is your middle unionism/establishment, which is embarrassed by the big troublemaker. Too sectarian, vulgar. Another lot is very pro-

Paisley. The rest don't like him but they turn to him in a crisis, like the ferocious Alsatian in the backyard.'

According to Paisley, unionism, indeed Ulster, is perpetually in crisis. He likes to deliver solemn warnings, offering what can look like strong and definite leadership in the emergency. It has never been declared at an end; Ulster can never stand easy. Because many Protestants do indeed believe that their chronic state is dire, Ian Paisley fills an uneasy and presumably unexamined need for, among others, those Alsatian-lovers who do not vote for the DUP but allow themselves to support him personally. They put an 'X' beside his name in each European election – he has consistently won 30 per cent of the vote in Euro elections. This means that more than half of Protestant voters consistently support him, although on reflection they might surely realise that he has never been able to end the emergency or win them security.

The conclusion has to be that some Protestants fool themselves. They refuse, or have refused until recently, to vote DUP in local government, Westminster and Stormont Assembly elections, presumably because they think the DUP is anti-accommodation and thus bolsters sectarian division and perhaps a climate that validates violence. Putting Ian Paisley on top of the Euro poll, however, can scarcely be construed as anything but a reminder to the world that Northern Ireland is unionist and Protestant. Moreover, it keeps a nationalist out of the top slot. Ian Paisley has no doubts: 'Vote Paisley Number One To Save Ulster' remains his favourite slogan. The Euro vote is his crowning and lasting validation. It is like a linguistic tic, cropping up on every major outing. He cites it on every occasion his party's policy is questioned. 'I speak for the majority,' he says, and sometimes, 'I speak for Northern Ireland,' or more simply, 'I have the biggest vote in Ulster.'

Many middle-class unionists spurn politics to stay clear of Ian Paisley, arch-extremist. Others support him because they think an extremist is what Ulster Unionism needs. The twist, though some may still not recognise it, is that the immovable Ian Paisley moved some time ago.

Paisley's fly-swatting routine during the count to a presenter on camera, eyes bulging with malicious glee, was a vintage example of his favourite technique, eating-the-media-for-breakfast. 'Pestiferous scribbling rodents,' he once christened print journalists, condemning them routinely as drunken atheistic liars. 'Let me smell your breath,' he famously bellowed at an inoffensive new arrival from Dublin. During the 2001 election campaign, a male colleague was told to 'shut his mouth' because he intervened when a reporter from the Irish language station, TG4, was told she could expect no cooperation, since she conducted her business in a foreign language. Ranting on camera and the car park mob scene are both typical Paisleyite behaviour, designed to intimidate, while playing to the faithful watching television in their homes.

These and other techniques have done double-duty. While the DUP shifts shamelessly to stay in the game of the peace process and share power with Sinn Féin, Paisley has continued to pose as the last man to compromise. Yet the surest sign that the process has already come too far to be reversed has been the spectacle of the DUP and its leader, camouflaged by tough rhetoric, inside the Agreement's structures and working alongside the legion of Irish republicanism. They still maintain a careful veneer of hostility. 'Do you sit with the Sinn Féin in the Assembly?' a potential voter asked DUP contender Gregory Campbell near the Co. Derry town of Coleraine. 'Yes, but we confront them every time,' Campbell assured her. 'We don't sit and have coffee or talk with them.' The leader's biblical injunction to his Free Presbyterian congregations down the ages to 'come ye out and be ye separate' is still invoked but the pretence involved is at times farcical.

When Trimble and a delegation attended a White House function on St Patrick's Day for what had become the annual jamboree to boost the 'Irish peace process', at which Sinn Féin president Gerry Adams was present, Ian Paisley thundered: 'The freeborn sons of Ulster will rise again and wash out from Ulster's public life the black and treacherous spot of betrayal. They will rid themselves democratically of all those who in Ulster's darkest hour went over to the enemy and were found being entertained in the tents of the conspirators.' Three years and a change of president later, in 2001, Paisley himself was in the Bush White House. As another guest noted, the DUP leader waited to meet the President of the United States in the same small room as the Sinn Féin leader.

Paisley met President George W. Bush, not the pro-Irish 'adulterer'

Clinton, Peter Robinson by his side, to tell the most powerful man in the world that unionists were very unhappy to see Irish republicans in the 'government of Ulster' while hanging on to their terrorist weaponry. Then he sped home before the St Patrick's Day festivities could suck him into green beer and shamrockery. It was a sanitised excursion, though in remarkable company. Who knows what his people truly thought?

A relatively dispassionate observer remarks on the 'amazing difference in perceptions of Paisley. Some think he never lies, others that he rarely tells the truth, or at least the whole truth.' As the former civil servant turned commentator Maurice Hayes observed, after having worked with the DUP leader in an earlier Stormont Assembly: 'I have often thought there are about six Paisleys. Two of them are very nice people, two quite awful, and the other two could go either way.' They say the lawyers scissored out another four.

There is no argument that even into his eighth decade Paisley still towers over both his party and the church he founded, though the size and force of his personality makes dispassionate assessment of his significance difficult. Often the same person will offer conflicting views of him, in the process unconsciously using more than one of Paisley's nicknames or titles, as though admitting he cannot be categorised or contained in one persona.

'Ian Paisley's genuinely a big man, a big personality,' says one unionist, long disaffected from his politics but still reluctantly impressed. 'The others in the party are unlike him, small creatures. The Doc's capable of going from brutal and vicious to being your friend. And the evidence is when you're his friend all else goes out the window. Ian's actually capable of being extremely warm, human and kindly. Genuinely very funny at times.' The last is recognised by many whose main reaction to Paisley is horror. After a pause he adds: 'When he turns on you he is as nasty as they come – but he is at least human. Some of the people round him by contrast are just eternally nasty.' Even in a summing-up that covered all the bases, the larger-than-life quality outweighed the rest.

The DUP's internal workings are almost as hidden to the outsider as those of republicanism. Did Paisley agree with his underlings that the party must not be left outside the Agreement tent, or did the ambitious, much younger would-be dealers around him manoeuvre the big man into place, like small tugs manoeuvring an ungainly liner? MPs Peter Robinson, Nigel Dodds and Gregory Campbell, the party's brains trust, while keeping up the chant of 'Trimble the traitor who let terrorists into government', were clearly determined to be in that government. They persuaded their leader to their way of thinking, or, still unpersuaded, he allowed them to prevail. Most evidence suggests the latter. Either way, as one insider says, 'They needed the big man's clout. The little squirts couldn't do it without him.'

Another adds: 'Can you imagine the younger Ian Paisley going for this? It wouldn't have happened ten years ago. He'd have been outside the tent calling down fire and brimstone.' The speaker is a moderate who knows David Trimble's weaknesses but supports him, who regrets that unionist leaders have left it so late to deal, losing clout in the process. In 1974 other unionist leaders made common cause with Paisley, and with loyalist paramilitaries at the height of their killing campaign, to bring down the first power-sharing Stormont government. Unionism flexed a communal muscle and society buckled. In 2002 Paisley looks within reach of becoming acknowledged leader of Unionism at last, but unionist clout is not what it was, and nor is Paisley.

The record shows that he will never argue for compromise, in fact will scourge any unionist who does. He has a weakness for a *fait accompli*, which he then accepts with bad grace or with breathtaking disingenuousness. Going into government, with the enemy he wanted to 'smash' only a short time before, has called for displays of old-style doomsday scarifying as well as shameless pretence. Campaigning for the June 2001 election, aged 75 but with the vigour of a man 30 years younger, after more than a decade of rumours that his powers were failing, Paisley told voters that to save Ulster from the evil of the Good Friday Agreement they must support him. Yet from the start two DUP ministers have been been members of an Executive with two Sinn Féin ministers. The fig-leaf is their insistence that they are not sharing power, since they refuse to attend collective meetings. 'We will never sit down with Sinn Féin or the IRA,' Paisley and his ministers-to-be solemnly intoned, before he nominated them and they began work.

Irreverent Stormont officials wondered initially if ministers Robinson and Dodds might shout their contributions from another room, or consent to teleconferencing. David Trimble and the pro-

Agreement parties played it calmly for the greater good, and the DUP ministers were kept informed by civil servants. Few other than the faithful were fooled. As one seasoned unionist commentator puts it: 'Look what the DUP did as opposed to what they say they did. Paisley sustained the Agreement. He could have brought the whole thing down and forced the Ulster Unionists out at any time by telling Peter and Nigel to walk. But no chance.' By the end of the Assembly's first year of existence, it was clear that the DUP would be the last to stage a unilateral walkout.

The old techniques of intimidation emerged again in the new version of the cause. David Trimble's car park ordeal on the night of the election gave a platform to a freshly enlisted Paisleyite, local businessman David Simpson. Cameras caught him cheerfully watching as the mob gathered, as he waited for the recount he demanded. Simpson's real significance was that his noisy confidence made Trimble aides suppose for a few hours that he was about to win the Ulster Unionist leader's seat, which would have been the upset of the election. In the end he cut Trimble's majority enough to leave the fear of next time dangling in the air, the most damagingly concrete manifestation possible of Paisley's debilitating effect on the standard-bearer for moderate unionism. The leader must have been proud of Simpson and his airy defence of the crowd scenes: 'natural rage at Trimble', Simpson said. The DUP tend always to exculpate their own and blame the media for exaggeration and hostility, loudly, and preferably on air.

Shouting at interviewers is a Paisley speciality and his lieutenants imitate him with varying degrees of success. The hectoring, nasty lashing-back by Paisley, Robinson and Dodds, the noise-level and aggression involved in any exchange other than with the softest, least probing question, all work. They have certainly cowed interviewers. The outcome is a level of tolerance for the intolerable. Newcomers, by contrast, still reel at the nature of Paisleyite invective.

Soon after Trimble had been reinstalled as First Minister, courtesy of Alliance and Women's Coalition votes 'redesignated' as Unionists in a crude procedural fix, a visiting British official expressed shock at what he termed a 'grossly anti-Catholic' Paisleyite figure of speech. 'I heard him at his party conference the other day talking about the Transubstantiation of Pope Trimble,' he said. 'That's not the kind of language you'd hear anywhere else in the United Kingdom today. And I must say, it doesn't offend me personally because I'm not a Catholic, but it surely must offend many Catholics here.'

The locals listening smiled at his innocence. The Transubstantiation of Jesus into bread and wine might be Catholic doctrine but is hardly first-rate demagogic material. In Paisley terms, the crack was rarefied, more suited to his pulpit in the Martyrs Memorial than the DUP conference. Undoubtedly such language offends Catholics, but they are more galled by his utterly unselfconscious and coarse abusiveness, gibes like 'are we to become priests' women and nuns' men?'

The outsiders are right in one respect. It is a fact that Paisley and his followers, both political and religious, have no qualms about publicly insulting Catholicism, that they breach no unionist/Protestant communal taboo and pay no penalty. If anything, the reverse is true. Once a fresh eye and ear points it out, the startling aspect is that such behaviour is not only cost-free in terms of popularity or electoral support, but brings rewards. Bullying interviewers is not an aberration but the norm for Paisley's party. Boorishness, real or assumed, and an aptitude for stunts is an asset to the DUP member on the make. Display of offensiveness about Catholicism, Catholic clerics and a whole range of others is regarded as a useful attribute, at the very least a tool of the trade.

'You could say they're highly politicised as a bunch of people but insufficiently socialised,' says one local journalist, wearied by loud, abrasive press conferences. There was no surprise when Stormont's internal security team found a DUP member primarily responsible, though they did not identify him or his associates, for 'the Brawl in the Hall' in autumn 2001 which followed 'redesignation' and the reinstallation of Trimble as First Minister. The fracas spoiled Trimble's post-vote press conference and onlookers detected the main culprits instantly. 'Wasn't Paisley in the middle of this kind of carry-on before the Troubles even started?' as some nationalist elders muttered. Like Trimble's party, they watched in cynical disbelief as the DUP leader strode to the mikes to claim that his people had been roughed up by 'republicans and nationalists of the pan-nationalist front, furious at our defence of true unionism'.

In his church Paisley lashes out at a range of targets, from 'ecumenical weaklings' to political betrayers, quislings, traitors. In political guise he lacerates other unionists, British governments and ministers for their perfidious intent towards unionism, their alliance with the Irish Republic, and American and other outsiders for interference and conspiracy with the 'enemies of Ulster'. The enemies are legion: Catholic church, republicans, nationalists, a weak and pagan Britain, the European Union, the World Council of Churches, journalists who have been critical of Paisley's lifetime in politics and therefore do the enemy's work. Denunciation is the stuff of his politics, his lifework the detection of betrayal of Ulster into disaster.

The least suggestion that he ignores or underplays loyalist violence has always brought instant depiction of the questioner as 'an IRA man' (or woman) or 'a republican'. Other unionists also favour the tactic in public or on air, knowing that with an utterly polarised audience it immediately downgrades the journalist for at least half the listeners. 'Liar' is an epithet that tends to trip more easily off DUP tongues, especially that of their leader, who invests it with all his status as leader of a fundamentalist church.

There is an element of cod in some of Paisley's performances. Bad intent sits easily beside a wicked sense of humour, and a wide and perhaps dominant streak of shamelessness. In the new Stormont, bombast has covered a multitude. He continued to berate David Trimble for agreeing to share power with Sinn Féin without IRA decommissioning, and for agreeing the structures in the first place. But as well as DUP ministers functioning alongside Martin McGuinness and Bairbre de Brún, the leader himself has chaired the Assembly's agriculture committee with several Sinn Féin members, and by all accounts takes their questions for the most part with civility and even occasionally with humour. Shortly before the election campaign began, he appeared on television as committee chairman, side by side with the minister for agriculture, the SDLP's Brid Rodgers, to talk about the current foot-and-mouth outbreak. Like other unionists Paisley usually refers to her as a 'foreigner' or 'Brigid Rodgers'. By her side on television he was impeccably courteous, though neither ever looked directly at the other. Just as remarkably, the third interviewee was the Republic's minister for agriculture, from a Dublin studio. Paisley made not the slightest comment, though he has walked out of studios on air rather than have such contact in the past, and for decades has fulminated about the Republic's evil designs on Protestant Ulster.

The turnaround is blatant enough to render many onlookers almost speechless. David Trimble's party have pointed out the scale of contradiction involved in vain, and often feebly. As though he had not already forfeited the high ground of intransigence, as though only Trimble had moved, the DUP leader brandishes the benefits of his traditional position, lofty superiority over the compromiser. Paisley-watchers, all too familiar with his history of destroying any and all unionist leaders as soon as they broached compromise, have looked on in amazement. Those who know the history of the early Troubles are not surprised. There is a consensus about Paisley. Back in the '70s an insider said sharply, 'He loves Stormont. He loves being the big fish in the small stagnant pond.' The view still holds.

This is a man who loves an audience, another muses, to preach to in his churches entirely as he chooses, or in parliamentary institutions where he is guaranteed a hearing. 'So as well as Stormont he goes to Westminster and to Europe. In fact he has been in Europe for over 20 years, even though before that he used to denounce it as a Catholic work of the Antichrist.'

Ian Paisley has been a constant in the lives of everyone in Northern Ireland for more than three decades, a phenomenon so huge that he defies succinct analysis. Instantly recognisable for decades at home and far afield, he is a big star in a small place and much of the positive reaction to him is fan-worship. Many hate him, but perhaps as many adore him. Others detest Paisley and yet are fascinated by him. In his mid-70s he is more celebrity than anything else, swaddled in incessant attention, lord of all he surveys. 'Leader for life of his own church, head of a party, MP, MEP', as one much less starry politician said. 'He's led an unreal life, as shut off from normal life as any Hollywood star or a member of the royal family.' What was probably exhibitionism from youth has been encouraged by the constant presence of a retinue, and by years of being the recipient of both mass adulation and abuse.

An increasingly bizarre and garish wardrobe in latter years had precedents in the Russian-style fur hat of '70s marches, the swaggering greatcoats with velvet lapels and collars, one fine walking-stick after another. These days, Ian Paisley Senior affects a movie gangster-style pinstripe, hefty, wide black and white lapels below slightly shrunken jowls and draped over-sloping shoulders, and technicolour ties. His son, smaller in every respect, wears what looks like a scaled-down version of the pinstripe. To the irreverent, the effect suggests *Guys and Dolls*, or a mini dynasty which considers itself a model for the followers, perhaps even, among a sedate and largely puritanical people, a setter of trends.

In 2000, soft-focus coverage of the 50th anniversary of Paisley's Free Presbyterian church and of the man himself at 75 appeared in quantity in the two unionist newspapers, the *Belfast Telegraph* and the *Newsletter*. For the past 30 years both papers have had occasion to chide him for rabble-rousing speeches and demonstrations, the *Telegraph* much more consistently and for the longer period. Now it was as though they were writing about someone else. The almost fawning tone of columns and features on his personal kindness, his humour, his warm family life, photographs of him kissing his wife, cuddling a baby granddaughter, interviews with his wife attesting to his devotion as a husband, all contributed to a portrait of a major figure for whom society should feel respect.

But the perception of Paisley as dangerous and destabilising is widespread. He may indeed be a loving father/husband/warm friend. Most local media operators are well aware that this has no bearing on his role in recent history. The trouble is that he is also feared, even among a number who profess to scorn him and who would angrily deny that he intimidates them. The effect is almost as pernicious as his effect on the rest of unionist politics, and on the other, bigger Protestant churches.

Where David Trimble represents a people torn down the middle, himself ambivalent about the agreement he concluded, Paisley is the perfect representative of the naysayer, corralled into compromise but determined not to show approval no matter how implicated. It is hard to detect even a glimmer of late-flowering civic spirit in his Stormont participation. What mellowing is there in an undiminished willingness to insult Catholics, with whom he now shares Stormont committees several days a week, by continued use of epithets like 'Papist' and 'Romanist'?

'Here he is at the end of his life,' says a political analyst, 'having split unionism and split it again, having made it just too bloody difficult and painful and distasteful for most of that time for anyone else to lead Protestants forward.' From this perspective, David Trimble's progress had been too crab-like to build momentum, and the DUP's growing electoral strength was on track to displace Ulster Unionism. But the analysis put the old wrecker himself firmly inside the tent, no matter what belligerent triumphalism his possible emergence at the head of unionism might bring. 'There may be a rich irony in his screwing up unionists' ability to deal, then sneakily dealing himself as he approaches the end. And you could certainly argue that he's screwing his own supporters most – but this time for a change it's for their own good.'

Even with another half-century's perspective, historians may decide that Ian Paisley carries a daunting responsibility, as huge as his own charisma. A fundamentalist preacher of time-honoured style haranguing those in authority in the name of an unforgiving Old Testament God, he emerged from the fringe where unionist politics intersected with fundamentalist Protestantism. His first big moment came in the edgy '60s when Catholics began to demand reforms. The unionist establishment tried for a time to dismiss him as a buffoon. Church leaders teetered between dark forebodings about fascism and muffled complaints about his targets. Like many other Protestants, Paisley equated reform with capitulation to ecumenism, to Rome, and therefore to the wolf at the door, Irish republicanism. His was the voice and the talent that said it best and with the most inflammatory effect. There was no wolf at the door, nothing but nightmares, or the memory of nightmares. At his most potent Ian Paisley turned the scrawniest, oldest nightmares into ravening monsters.

Terence O'Neill, the first scalp Paisley claimed, made angry speeches calling him a fascist. But Cabinet papers released in recent years show O'Neill's Cabinet spending hours working out how to appease him and limit his appeal. Paisley's corrosive scorn scorching their grass-roots unnerved many who would have backed O'Neill, and urged Cabinet hardliners into competitive intransigence. When O'Neill's own party turned from him, it was Paisley who took his parliamentary seat.

The Troubles roared in and the unionist monolith collapsed. Paisley preached in his pulpit and made speeches declaring that the Catholic church and the IRA were indivisible, their purpose to destroy Unionist Ulster and Protestantism. From the outset many could see what Paisley did to crowds, the mistrust and anger he fomented in the hearts of individuals. Taking him on became a more and more unpleasant prospect and many avoided it. The sheer scale of Paisley's genius for destructiveness was denied by some, wished away, as in more recent decades he has occasionally and prematurely been consigned to oblivion. Fellow reformed Christians have made little effort to refute systematically his decades of vocal and inflammatory anti-Catholicism. As a recent Paisley biography (*Persecuting Zeal*) written by Presbyterian cleric Dennis Cooke puts it, with perhaps an excess of circumspection: 'Protestants have generally refrained from challenging the accuracy of his statements.'

Yet awareness of what ignoring or tolerating him had loosed was there very early. John Hewitt's 'Demagogue', anthologised now, said what many whispered: 'a Samson self-ordained, his strength destroys our canting state'. As the Troubles erupted in 1969, Hewitt wrote an indictment of a lazy-minded, complicit class, the poem 'The coasters':

> But you said, admit, you said in the club,
> 'You know, there's something in what he says . . .'
> Now the fever is high and raging;
> Who would have guessed it, coasting along?

It was never painless to speak out against Paisley. From his earliest days as a gospel-hall preacher, those inside fundamentalism who challenged him found it a wearing experience. Enemies were pursued, vilified, hounded. Political critics suffered from his growing army of followers. Paisley listed them from his pulpit or had them written up in his Protestant *Telegraph*. Anonymous phone calls and bomb scares expressed the wrath of the big man's supporters. To many observers, the silence of middle unionism has an explicable if not entirely sympathetic explanation.

Watching Paisley outface David Trimble since 1998, a reminder of a younger Trimble comes to those who were around to witness his Vanguard Unionist days. The combatants have never seemed well matched. Trimble is least effective when trying to compete with Paisley on his own ground of denunciation, as in his red-faced fury at the Patten proposals for police reform. But it is a measure of how far Trimble has come that Paisley pulled out of a face-to-face debate on television with him before the referendum on the Agreement. Those who remember the big man twitting the then nerdish, weedy Trimble in Stormont in the early '80s can see the difference now. Trimble may be a fitful champion of moderation, but he is a more substantial political animal now than then. Paisley's showman qualities stand up well, but his politics are less considered and consistent than ever. To those who do not worship him, the sense of overriding duplicity is striking.

Yet he is often reported as though his utterances were unexceptionable. The man who berates journalists for giving republicans an easy ride throughout the Troubles is given his place as a major party leader, his words infused with newsreader gravitas and parsed with care. Paisley's sheer longevity is a major media benefit. His career of negativity began well before many present-day reporters were born. As controversy built, for example, over Catholic objections to loyalist marches past their homes and the consequent rerouting or banning of marches, a running theme of the past ten years, Paisley repeatedly denounced what he called the 'Sinn Féin/IRA' tactic of using the device of a counter-demonstration to force a reroute. He made his name with the self-same tactic, starting in 1959 and using it ruthlessly throughout the '60s into the early years of the Troubles, adding vastly to the problems and pressures faced by the RUC.

But his effect on the media means the contradictions are rarely if ever put to him in public. BBC handling of Paisley versus republicans down the years is an interesting contrast. Republicans are constantly pressed to explain or condemn violence, though never strongly enough to satisfy unionist critics, then more recently put under constant pressure to explain why the IRA do not decommission, while a single critical question to Paisley tends to be the limit in any exchange.

The threat of simultaneous protest, usually met by Unionist governments with official capitulation, served him well for many years. The official Cameron report into the scene-setting disturbances of Armagh in 1968 and at Burntollet Bridge in 1969 said he must bear 'heavy responsibility for the disorder'. The record shows that Paisleyite counter-demonstrations to civil rights marches sparked many clashes boiled over into the riots that eventually launched 30 years of violence. His savage indignation at the gall of Catholic counter-demonstrators, and what he depicts as the fakery of their objections to Orange marches, is almost comical to anyone who has watched Paisley work himself and his audiences into a lather of rage, up to and including the past few years.

Age has not softened his anti-Catholic rhetoric. Derided by the world outside, revered by followers in the church and party he founded, Paisley is regarded by many, Catholics and others, as personally responsible to a large degree for stoking Protestant fear and hatred by a still fevered anti-Catholicism. Preaching in the year 2000 he was still throwing out words like 'Romanists' and 'Papists', taunts parroted in speeches at Stormont by Ian Junior in feeble imitation of daddy's speciality.

In the '60s, Paisley railed against would-be reformer Terence O'Neill: 'The Prime Minister in his stupidity can preach about "bridge-building". Where are we going to build the bridges to? Are we going to build them back to darkness, back to Romanism, back to the tyranny and superstition of the Dark Ages? I can take no part in such bridge-building. No true Protestant would ever suggest such a course.'

In the new millennium he was still using the text Catholics first objected to in the '60s, which many think of as his signature tune: 'Come ye out from among them and be ye separate.' In a divided and bitter Northern Ireland, as one now retired nationalist politician remarks, 'that's a seriously malevolent text'. The comment has a personal edge. This is someone who was advised for years to vary his movements and stay out of supermarkets and cinemas to avoid assassination by loyalist paramilitaries. 'It praises segregation as good in the sight of God,' he says of Paisley's text. 'It damns those who would live together peaceably. But then Paisley's always thrown petrol on the fire. He's never knowingly tried to make peace. He's a man of God who feeds bitterness in men's hearts – isn't that an awful thing to say about someone?'

A unionist commentator insisted that any book on the attitudes of Northern Ireland Catholics ought to include a section on anti-Catholicism. Reporting and analysing a couple of Paisley sermons would take care of it, he reckoned. 'It's not that far-out an idea. You present Paisley, you're presenting a lot of people. They would tut-tut, but they hold views not far off. They regard the Church of Rome as inherently evil as foretold in scriptures, the Bishop of Rome the Man of Sin etc.' He stopped, pink in the face at a quotation that recalled the earlier part of his life. 'Don't you smile,' he said. 'When Ian Paisley says he's "loyal to the crown being Protestant", he speaks for many. The ones who don't think that way, they're the minority.'

The circle of Paisley supporters has certainly always reached well beyond the fundamentalists who come to his churches to hear 'medieval theology', as one stunned London visitor called it. At his best, Paisley's sermons provide great theatre. A Belfast journalist who has shelves full of Paisley files agrees. 'It's probably the real Paisley in the pulpit, the bedrock. Sends an enjoyable chill down their spines. Hell is real to many of these people: it's a united Ireland.' But like most long-time observers who have charted Paisley's impact on politics, for him talent and showmanship were not the most significant qualities. 'Listen to him in the Martyrs Memorial and what does he tell them? What's the effect? He breaks down their self-confidence. The message is always the same: disaster is nigh, Doomsday's coming. But I'll save you.'

Paisley's favourite texts intrigue this observer. 'There's "come ye out" and there's "If you compromise God will curse you: if you stand God will bless you." Even in the purely religious stuff, what's he preaching? Ulster in deadly danger, lots of secrets, lots of difficult and detailed references. He says: "I was looking at that last word in the original the other day." Original what, Hebrew, Greek? Few of the flock have any idea what he's talking about.' Like many who have watched Paisley's progress for a long time, he gives a sharp estimate of the gap between preacher and congregation: 'Paisley's obviously very clever and cunning, but his congregation is noticeably thick.'

It is a view widely shared among those who study the development of all the local parties. 'You can't miss the fact that while people like Robinson and Dodds are clever people, the mass of Paisley's regular support out there are nearly always very obviously less intelligent. I'd say the least intelligent of any party's supporters,' one commentator says.

Paisley may respect the simple faith of his congregation, though having listened to him scarify and mystify them for decades, several writers on his intertwined religion and politics have their doubts. But then who does he respect, who does he listen to? Long ago Paisley and then up-and-coming barrister and politician Desmond Boal came together to found the DUP. Boal drifted out of politics into a full-time and illustrious career at the Bar, famed for his quick wit, defending among others many accused of IRA murders. The two men are said to be friends still. It is not clear where else Paisley might find intellectual stimulation, much less an honest appraisal of his strategy and tactics. The relationship with his much younger political colleague looks more unequal than anything else.

He goes nowhere alone. He is surrounded on a daily basis by sycophants and dependants. When he laughs, those around him laugh. When he raises his still powerful voice, the circle obligingly flinches. Like many over-exposed people, he gives the impression of putting little value on privacy and an inner life. A man of remarkable gifts, high intelligence and considerable mental versatility, but perhaps a performer with no still centre, self-awareness sometimes lets him down. When, in his role as self-proclaimed man of God, he occasionally from his pulpit half-jokingly quotes from his own conversations with the Lord, the Lord sounds remarkably like Ian Paisley. It is hard to imagine the Big Man, the Doc, Big Ian – nicknames constantly used by his retinue either out of real respect or in the knowledge that he likes them – minus microphone, pulpit or audience, sitting by himself, thinking. The audience is the important thing.

And yet a booklover discovered by accident recently that Paisley had bought hundreds of books at a second-hand sale. He has written scores of books and pamphlets himself, mostly theological exegesis with a sprinkling of political tracts. He must read, and he writes; clearly he thinks. Yet apart from perhaps at most six smart associates in the party, he is surrounded by strikingly mediocre minds or slavish admirers. One veteran observer wonders, 'Does he sometimes think, why is it that only dopes like me?'

An Irish-American pro-republican commentator, Niall O'Dowd, gives a glimpse of him for a moment alone and in unfamiliar surroundings. O'Dowd plainly dislikes Paisley but the account rings true. Describing the 2001 arrival of the DUP leader for the first time at the White House St Patrick's Day reception for politicians from Ireland, north and south, and remarking that this represented a considerable and surprising advance, he throws in an earlier Paisley sighting. 'One memory stands out. He spoke at a foreign affairs luncheon in New York and afterwards several of us went to dinner with him. Through sheer coincidence a leading Irish-American and myself arrived at the restaurant at the same time as Paisley, well ahead of the rest of the party. He became very uncomfortable, though we tried to put him at ease. He shifted his eyes continually to the door of the private room, desperately hoping that some of his retinue would arrive . . . unwilling or unable to engage in dialogue with those who disagreed with him.'

Although Paisley is above all a performer, his performances highly stylised, his behaviour sometimes brings the contradictions in his own position into focus more sharply than he would like them to be seen. One of those moments came in a brief press conference in July 1999 in Stormont's Great Hall, when the first attempt to set up a power-sharing executive collapsed in farce as unionists refused to nominate ministers. Paisley went straight to the top of the queue of parties before the group of waiting journalists, which included Scandinavians, Germans and Japanese as well as the more usual Americans, British and Irish. He launched in with much of the old attack but also the now more frequent flickers in concentration, when the word that emerged sounded second-best. Flanking him were his son, Ian Junior, and his long-time deputy, Peter Robinson, cold eyes characteristically flicking between his leader and the press pack.

Robinson intervened twice as Paisley held the floor, each time to supply a date or fact, and Paisley Junior offered an unnecessary aside. The contrast between star and sidekicks was as always instructive. Ian Junior, in his mid-30s, still strikes many as immature, childishly rude when he tries to imitate his father's vitriol. By contrast an official on the other side of the negotiating table once said of the able Robinson, who has seemed middle-aged since his twenties, that 'he sits there like a cobra'. That snake-like quality has made several public appearances as the DUP struggles to adjust to the post-ceasefire situation.

But on this occasion the ageing leader produced a few vintage remarks, replete with his own inimitable, almost camp delivery. The best crack was at the expense of David Trimble, who had boycotted the Stormont proceedings with a misguided press appearance near his party headquarters, in a slightly seedy street beside the city's bus terminus. 'While Mr Trimble and his friends pouted about the bus station,' scoffed Paisley, 'we were here.' British and Irish journalists smiled a little. The message by contrast that most struck the foreign media was Paisley's blatant contempt for the tiny loyalist fringe parties, the spokesmen for gunmen whose ceasefires bolstered that of the IRA, and thus the prospects for the entire peace process that Paisley had opposed from the start. An American reporter asked: 'Are you concerned that the vacuum will be filled by loyalist violence?' Paisley swung to face him, nostrils flaring in scorn. 'You have nothing to fear. Aren't they all dedicated to peace? They've given their word.' The mighty actor's voice poured contempt into 'fear' and swooped up in mockery on 'their word', the culmination of half a century's practice in demagoguery. The pack broke up, brows furrowed. A number wondered if their understanding of English had failed them. Some innocents asked Belfast journalists to explain why a political leader, a churchman, should sound derisive about paramilitaries stopping violence.

But the only judgement that matters to Paisley is that of his own people. The disapproval of foreigners, outsiders, whom he frequently writes off as 'the dupes of Rome' or 'fellow-travellers of terrorism', is immaterial, indeed reinforcement of his own rectitude. He swept off, stage-guffawing to his underlings. But the outsiders were onto something, a point that the local media often ducked because the reaction when they pushed it was so hostile and abrasive.

Paisley's people, like many unionists, were confused and wrong-footed by the IRA ceasefire, memorably described soon afterwards by the low-key Jim Molyneaux, then leader of the Ulster Unionist party, as 'destabilising'. Molyneaux said it was 'not an occasion for celebration, quite the opposite. It has started destabilising the whole population in Northern Ireland.'

The loyalist ceasefires that followed were equally disconcerting to some unionists, on the basis that they aggrandised an IRA action many still preferred to characterise as bogus. Paisley excoriated the loyalist fringe parties as republican stooges, because they now urged pragmatism and negotiations to include themselves and Sinn Féin, the IRA's political voice, as well as nationalist and unionist politicians. Inside the talks that preceded real negotiation, an astute official noted the frustrated tone of the DUP and singled out the most significant consequence of the loyalist fringe party presence at the table. 'It means that Paisley and Co. can't use the bloodcurdling threats of loyalist violence that they otherwise might.'

As it became clearer that to be a credible majority voice inside unionism Trimble needed loyalist fringe party backing in negotiations, and then as the referendum on the Agreement approached, the DUP antagonism towards pro-Agreement paramilitaries became steadily harsher. Paisley scoffed at the proposal for early release from prison of paramilitaries whose groups had called ceasefires. The government was calling these people 'good terrorists', he said, expressing concern and outrage at potential discrimination against other loyalist prisoners. By contrast, for paramilitaries who opposed the process and refused to call a ceasefire, there was something like solicitude, with visits to their prisoners in the Maze and statements by party spokesmen voicing their complaints.

Paisley's clerical lieutenant, the Reverend Willie McCrea, famously shared a platform with the splinter Loyalist Volunteer Force leader Billy Wright, when Wright was threatened by the parent group, the UVF, for his opposition to their ceasefire. Wright liked to boast of his reputation for being involved in the murders of more than a score of Catholics. McCrea's public appearance with him brought angry criticism and demands that Paisley disown him. The reply was instantaneous and characteristic. How dare the critics impute support for paramilitarism to Paisley or his party? McCrea's support, Paisley bellowed on radio, was for freedom of speech, and a man victimised by Godless gunmen.

When faced at a press conference with questions about a rally the night before the Loyalist Volunteer Force (LVF) killing of a young Catholic, at which DUP speakers addressed a crowd containing a considerable number of people wearing LVF T-shirts, Paisley and Robinson rounded on the questioner, accusing him of 'asking stupid questions' and 'dirty tricks'. One experienced political correspondent wrote that as the questioner persisted the two leaders became 'extremely agitated'. Paisley at one point said, 'What about people who go to IRA rallies who wear pioneer badges? Does that mean that the Roman Catholic Church is associated with the violence of the IRA?' Given that Paisley himself had been claiming for years that the church actually masterminded the IRA, it was an odd remark, a sign that he was slightly off-balance.

Paisley's reaction to accusations of ambivalence towards strands of loyalist paramilitarism has always been robust and pugnacious. He angrily denies it, sometimes threatens legal action and complains at length about victimisation. Major media outlets have settled out of court with him rather than contest his denials. The tally of uncontested settlements, some substantial, must surely have stoked Paisley and the DUP's fondness for bullying reporters. It may also feed his own opinion of his life's work. The perception that he can say whatever he likes and contradict whole areas of his career with impunity has certainly fed nationalist frustration. They hear the familiar big voice demanding IRA decommissioning, plus a string of further moves to prove that republicans have given up violence and are in truth committed to democracy. But to many minds Ian Paisley is never pushed to confront his own role in the continuum of bitterness, in helping produce the hatred which helped produce the Troubles which produced all those murders – a litany like a children's rhyme of a singular career.

An unguarded glimpse of him in the mid-'80s helped convince one observer, with considerable appreciation of Paisley's ability and personal magnetism, that vanity is the key to him. A loyal Free Presbyterian on the fringes of the Paisley family circle told him artlessly how he called to the Paisley home at Christmas with a present for 'the Doc', and was delighted to be invited to have a chat by the fire. The fan asked respectfully how Paisley saw the future. He was impressed by the response: 'Brother, I'll keep you out of a united Ireland for as long as I live. After that, well . . .' And the Doc raised his arms heavenwards, his habitual evocation of the divine guarantor and his own egotistical projection that he and he alone could 'save Ulster'.

Paisley's behaviour in the mid-'80s tested the attitudes towards him of a whole section of unionists. It was a period when the DUP leader ricocheted between calling crowds onto the streets, attempting to raise quasi-paramilitary groups, mustering men in darkness to wave gun licences on a hillside and marching at the head of ranks of men with Peter Robinson, both of them wearing red paratrooper-type berets. He allowed Robinson to take part in drafting a blueprint for talks, then shelved the result. The disillusioned former associate says he concluded bitterly after this circuit that 'the big bastard only cares about himself. As long as Ian Paisley can keep on shouting "No Surrender", that's all that matters. As long as no one can see his name on any deal. Meanwhile the Protestants get weaker and weaker. They can deal after he's gone. He doesn't care. He'll be dead and buried.'

It is a view lent credibility by other accounts from within unionism and from British politicians. A series of Northern Ireland Secretaries have left swingeing descriptions in memoirs and interviews of meetings with Paisley, in which he ranted at them or urged colleagues on to deliver near-hysterical diatribes. One of the most bizarre was an early encounter with the Labour minister Merlyn Rees in 1975, described by both sides later as ending with Rees rushing into an inner office and locking the door when the Reverend Willie McCrea chanted passages from the Bible at him and Paisley accused him of telling lies, a frequent charge against British ministers.

The Belfast minister from 1979 to 1981, Humphrey Atkins, had a strikingly different experience with Paisley. Opinion in London and Dublin at the time flirted with the outlandish and unfounded notion that Paisley might now make a deal with nationalism because his first European Parliament win in 1979 magnified his leverage in unionism. But then for all the ministerial scorn of him recollected in memoirs, several British, and indeed some in Irish, governments had also toyed early in the Troubles with the notion of a moderate Paisley. Recently released cabinet papers show that fanciful souls in London in 1971–72 thought Paisley might just be the leader to win Protestants for power-sharing.

Atkins told journalists that Paisley had made intriguingly moderate noises in talks. 'I said to him, Ian, you'll have to show a bit more leg.' He had no Paisley response to report, but one of the journalists present maintained that for years he was haunted 'by a vision of a thigh of biblical proportions'. The fantasy of a power-sharing Prime Minister Paisley dissolved overnight in May 1981, when the teasing talker reverted to noisy demonstrator, picketing the installation of a new Church of Ireland Archbishop in Armagh because Taoiseach Charles Haughey was a guest.

Yet another Northern Ireland Secretary described a Paisley contemplating compromise, though covertly. This time he was accompanied by the then Ulster Unionist leader Jim Molyneaux, the two of them persuaded into discussion about a devolved administration with nationalists, though this had been described as firmly off the agenda. A Westminster correspondent recalls that the minister dined out for years on his depiction of a suddenly complicit Paisley: 'But you do realise, Secretary of State, that you will have to impose this, and we will have to tell our people that you have imposed this?'

Paisley rejects all such accounts as British black propaganda, scurrilous lies. Yet now the compromise is in place, and the disguise has been crafted. Stunts serve a purpose. Rural members of the party, many of them members of Paisley's church, are regularly bussed up to Stormont for tours of the grand parliamentary building, to be couriered around by some of the keener young Assembly members. Stormont insiders note that the parties who organise most tours around the building are the DUP and Sinn Féin, which is comment enough on the strangeness of the new institutions. The DUP top the league by a considerable margin. Passers-by note suitably dark sidelong glances from Paisleyite visitors at the Stormont Sinn Féin contingent, but considerable lingering in the monumental Great Hall, still dominated by the black statue of Craigavon, father of the Unionist Northern Ireland.

Paisley may be able to tell his followers anything, but the White House trip had to be matched by hostility to a nationalist/republican icon. So Easter 2001 was marked at Stormont by a row between the DUP and Sinn Féin over a display in the entrance hall of two bunches of white lilies, symbol for republicans of the 1916 Rising. It was the first emblem of any kind of nationalism to make it through the gates of Stormont. The approach road to the parliament building is dominated by the towering image of Lord Edward Carson erected by a grateful unionist people, the base of the statue decorated with metal bas-relief scenes of the time: Ulster Hall rallies, mammoth demonstrations, great crowds of martial men, though not, irreverent moderns note, a single visible illegally imported German rifle. Paisley struck an identical pose for a photographer beside the Carson statue some years ago, raised in the pick-up cab of a crane to equal height with the man his father followed, and whom he hails as inspiration.

In the year 2000, Sinn Féin complained it was time Stormont served as backdrop to something other than unionist iconography, and the complicated voting systems set up by the Agreement won house room for their lilies. The battle of the flowers was fought to a standstill by Jim Wells, a particularly excitable DUP Assembly representative with a 20-year history of rowdy protest and a latter-day sideline as chief party courier of the Stormont tours. He lost, but only after the recall of the Assembly from holiday for an acrimonious emergency debate.

While Stormont staff looked for suitably impressive vases and prepared to mount a guard on Sinn Féin's lilies, Wells spluttered furiously to a TV reporter about betrayal and his leader hove into camera-shot alongside. Paisley said nothing. But as one bystander remarked, 'Even when he's silent, Paisley's more eloquent than the likes of Jim Wells. With the two of them there you couldn't take your eyes off him – that curve of shoulder lowered like a bison, the big head doing that thing he does, half-nod, half-toss, where you don't know if he's registering approval, disapproval or readiness to charge.'

Though once he was clearly seen as a wrecker outside the social and political establishment, a big ungainly preacher on the edge of organised religion, Paisley long ago became a significant and central player in the politics of his people. Someone snatched from the local scene by aliens in 1960 then restored by flying saucer in the year 2001 might find this the most stunning transformation of all. Perhaps they would be cheered to see that the wrecker is now inside the structures he has fought so long and so hard to pre-empt. They would be unlikely to moderate judgement on the man.

The massive personality has had a massive effect, and nearly always for the worse. Republicans admit that the IRA never seriously considered killing Paisley, though they killed much less significant figures ostensibly because of their anti-Catholic or anti-nationalist stances. There was never any doubt that Paisley was an IRA recruiting sergeant. His existence, his hate-mongering, or so they privately thought, graphically illustrated to the world the justice of the republican cause. That belief was shared across the nationalist spectrum.

Many Protestants, unionists, unsurprisingly have the greatest difficulty in seeing past Martin McGuinness the IRA commander to McGuinness the minister. For Catholics, nationalists, there is equally strong distaste for the spectacle of Ian Paisley as leader-in-waiting of unionism. To some unionists, this is itself distasteful. Paisley might have an unpleasant record of bigotry and troublemaking, they say, but unlike McGuinness he has never led an organisation which has caused 2,000 deaths. The nationalist response is that Paisley is a Christian clergyman, a man of God who has primed minds for violence but never taken responsibility for it. He has, in many minds, both nationalist and unionist, done an awful thing, endlessly.

In mid-1996, when hopes of progress were at their lowest, against the backdrop of a broken IRA ceasefire and unionist cries of 'told you so', one government official with wide experience of Northern Ireland sat back to consider Paisley's significance. Paisley had a genuine constituency, he said, that had to be recognised first. 'He's the tremendous awful warning, in capital letters, from O'Neill onwards to people who try to change; in other words the insistence that there are no degrees in this situation, that it's either/or, that the moment you take your foot off the windpipe you're dead yourself. That's certainly had an inhibiting effect on unionism.' A full two years before Trimble nerved himself in the face of Paisley's scorn to accept the Agreement, at what the speaker supposed was the last phase of Paisley's career there was a chill summation: 'His legacy is almost entirely negative; he has done huge damage to his own community's capacity to adapt healthily.'

The final indictment might be the harm he has done to those around him. Disparity in physical size between leader-for-life and retinue has lessened over the years, as the massive head sagged and the big shoulders began to slope, but it is as if the followers have also shrunk. There was a period when Peter Robinson was flattered by some officials, built up as leader-in-waiting. As the years ground on and Paisley remained dominant, Robinson seemed increasingly dulled.

In his final years, political victory is at last in sight for a man who has always seemed best suited to opposition. It is hard to imagine him exercising power and responsibility, probably an unlikely outcome even should the votes come his way. It is much easier to visualise him outside First Minister Peter Robinson's door roaring denunciation. A cartoon, from the period when London (and Dublin) briefly flirted with the notion of a power-sharing Paisley, showed the DUP leader at an office doorway, clearly angry. The civil servant facing him is saying: 'But Mr Paisley, *you* are the Prime Minister.'

Yet the slogan of 'No Surrender' is now a sham. In 1974 Ian Paisley helped bring Northern Ireland to its knees, because of power-sharing with John Hume and a limited Irish dimension. In 2001 Paisley's own party shares power with Martin McGuinness and in practice accepts Dublin governments in partnership with London. The legacy is dark, but this is progress. Only republicans have come farther along the road to compromise, dissembling and fudging on a heroic scale to cover their tracks. The DUP have been sitting in local government for more than a decade now with Sinn Féin councillors. They began by hissing, spitting, spraying air-fresheners, playing cassettes of loyalist songs, turning their chairs to sit with their backs to the republicans. But they now share council chambers relatively amicably and get on with council business.

Lies are only to be expected; ranting in retreat should perhaps be acceptable, if not admirable. Much of the time neither Sinn Féin nor Ulster Unionism in government is a pretty sight. But grumpy, ill-mannered, sometimes offensive behaviour is a small price to pay for escape from an entirely unlovely period. Life after Paisley, force of nature and monument to bigotry, has been delayed too long. The consolation is that he may himself have begun the transition to a new era, leading his impressionable flock with a kind of contempt, to an end they could never have imagined.

PETER ROBINSON: MAN AND BOY

The problem for DUP deputy leader Peter Robinson is the length of time he has spent in Ian Paisley's shadow. He has the look of a man whose soul has shrivelled. On too many occasions when decision was called for, or initiative, he failed to make the move. Ambition and ability are still there, but something looks out of his eyes: anger at himself? The big man still stubbornly towers over him.

Number Two in a party which until recently was chiefly noted for its nuisance value, Peter Robinson must have spent hours musing on how playing second fiddle to Ian Paisley illuminates the frustrations of all deputy leaders. The bigness of Paisley, in talents as in physical stature, has always diminished those beside him, even the most able by far of his associates. It is a position that would have wizened a greater soul. Robinson's principal problem is one he can do nothing to solve. He spent decades being 'Young Peter' to 'Big Ian'. The years diminished the bigger man but never dulled his charisma or craze for prominence, scarcely grazed his vitality. 'Young Peter' is now over 50, older than Tony Blair, more than ten years older than the SDLP's new leader, within a year or two of David Trimble. 'Not so much *Waiting For Godot* as waiting for God,' unkind observers joke.

There was one moment when it looked as though Robinson had decided to go for it on his own. It happened in 1986, in the aftermath

Peter Robinson

of the Anglo-Irish Agreement, when unionists summoned up their forces and discovered that mammoth marches and Days of Action which degenerated into thuggery would not move the British government, except to stronger policing. Ian Paisley forged an odd alliance with the Ulster Unionist leader of the day, Jim Molyneaux, a quirky figure who believed unionism's best hope was refusal to negotiate and silence. Molyneaux announced that he would make no statements for an indefinite period, because the media preferred sensationalism.

Robinson's personal history in 1986 was highly erratic, swinging from highly charged rhetoric to direct action of a particularly crude, somewhat embarrassing and unheroic kind, and then towards enigmatic accommodation. As the year began, he made angry speeches about the threat to Ulster from the Republic, warning of unspecified economic sanctions against the southern state and the likelihood of loyalist paramilitary attack: 'The Republic is only an isolated, unapproved road away.' In August 1986, he drove or was driven across the border in the middle of the night and watched scores of cudgel-carrying men in hoods and balaclavas break windows in the tiny Monaghan village of Clontibret. They had scrawled 'Ulster Says No' on a number of walls, including that of Clontibret's Protestant primary school, before an unarmed Garda arrived on the scene and hastily summoned reinforcements. Robinson was the only man arrested. On remand in one of the Republic's jails, he refused to eat, apparently fearing poison. Iris Robinson arrived with a basket of 'good nourishing Ulster fare'. The history of the Troubles (*Making Sense of the Troubles*) says the protesters claimed the incursion was intended 'to demonstrate inadequate border security', adding waspishly: 'The security was, however, sufficient to effect the MP's arrest, a second humiliation coming when he pleaded guilty in a southern court and paid an IR£15,000 fine for unlawful assembly.'

Robinson's defence was that he had merely been 'observing', but he changed his plea to guilty. His standing with the paramilitary world dissolved overnight when he paid the fine rather than serve a jail sentence in the Republic, which would also have cost him his Westminster seat. 'Peter the Punt' appeared on walls next day in the tougher parts of his loyalist East Belfast constituency.

The party leader promptly organised a collection to pay the fine, advertised with a fetching photo of Iris and Peter, heads together, smiling winsomely. Shortly afterwards, Robinson complained about the amount the protest had cost him. He addressed a crowd outside the Secretariat set up to service the Anglo-Irish Agreement at Maryfield, outside Holywood, County Down, jointly staffed by London and Dublin civil servants, watched while young men tried to break down the gate and ineffectually advised them to stop. Then he turned his back while a police car burned and became exceedingly tetchy with journalists who asked if this was not conniving at violence.

Finally, in 1987, Peter Robinson sat down to write proposals for an alternative to the Anglo-Irish Agreement with two members of the bigger unionist party, the dying Harold McCusker and the young and able Frank Millar, whose frustration with the poverty of unionist strategy was to drive him out of politics inside the year. The three-man Task Force canvassed a cross-section of Protestant life, and concluded that unionists should sit down with nationalists and hammer out a deal. Talks should cover all relationships, including that of Northern Ireland and the Republic. The report was titled 'An End to Drift'; a second part has never been published. It is thought to have contained a savage analysis of the causes of 'drift', which directly criticised the two unionist leaders. Not surprisingly, Paisley and Molyneaux received the Task Force document with few words and consigned it to outer darkness.

Millar, who stood out from most other unionist politicians then and since, by so unequivocally condemning the loyalist violence during protests that he became a target for the Ulster Defence Association (UDA), went to London to become a journalist. As one close associate at the time said, 'Robinson waited until Millar was practically on the plane and then resigned as deputy DUP leader. It was pathetic. Too little, too late.' Robinson never publicly explained the resignation, made no explicit criticism of the leadership. Veiled accounts of unhappiness appeared in the press, but as though this was a private matter, rather than an expression of fundamental disagreement about strategy and tactics. Inside three months he was back, again with no explanation. His post had been kept open for him. There was just a hint in the air of paternal solicitude, even faint amusement. Had Peter been having a little tantrum, stamping his tiny foot? A loving father understood.

The price may have been what was left of Robinson's self-respect. A one-time admirer wondered shortly afterwards if want of conviction had been as damaging as lack of nerve. 'You actually had to believe in your heart that a deal was required: it was always clear when the Task Force reported that the shit would hit the fan, and that this was going to be a very nasty ride. You had to believe that an accommodation was necessary and desirable and right. I don't know if that conviction was ever there in Peter.'

Whatever Robinson's innermost thoughts then, political associates suggest he has an unsure side, at odds with the deliberately off-putting front. 'He goes off into himself sometimes,' one confided around the Task Force period. 'He can withdraw for weeks at a stretch. You'd think he never doubts himself, wouldn't you? But I don't think that's true. There's a blackness in him, when it's like he loses faith in himself.' It was said with a degree of sympathy. But the most common image of Peter Robinson is glaringly unsympathetic and appears entirely a construct, in keeping with the party's overall image.

For years he practised the icy smile, the curt put-down, the politically incorrect reactionary remark. Like much else, dislikeability seems prized in the DUP, aped from the leader's example. Far from wanting to appear likeable and unthreatening, many routinely sneer and mock, with occasional resort by the lesser ranks to jostling journalists or political opponents, secure in the knowledge of approval from on high. Paisley's sheer bulk and booming voice shook people for decades, aided by the powerful suggestion that he had no brakes, and that no protest he made would be constrained by manners or convention.

Robinson, by contrast, for some time appeared to cultivate an image of thin-lipped ruthlessness. Photochromatic glasses darkened dramatically, 'first reflecting light', says an unappreciative broadcaster, 'and then the degree of sinisterness he wanted to project'. While he was playing Mr Moderate in 1986, a visiting London journalist from the more intellectual end of the market was shocked in an interview when Robinson said something that sounded remarkably racist to her, apparently assuming she would think none the worse of him. The language he has chosen is another study, habitually harsh, sometimes grotesque, often of nauseating ugliness. In February 1995, Robinson said of the Framework document meant to guide the negotiations that eventually produced the Good Friday Agreement that 'this monstrous and hideous Irish mutation will be found to be still-born'. Paisley said: 'The document is already stinking. It is like the body of Lazarus after four days in his bed and it is stinking.'

In more recent years there has been slightly less menace, more dispassion. Long-time watchers detect boredom and detachment more often now in the flat speech rhythms, the ostentatious slouch while others are speaking. Some years back, he took to modish light-framed spectacles. His hair became spiky and moussed. Reporters sent to chart the progress of Iris Robinson towards her own Westminster seat, with human-interest 'Swish Family Robinson' headlines in mind, were shown Peter's sizeable tie collection while Iris chattered about her husband's awe-inspiring intellect and how she chose the new hairstyle and glasses to make him look younger. Despite the effort, the dandified effect is undercut by a deadness in the made-over gaze, the remains of the old menace; Robinson is more sour now than sinister.

For someone with immense ambition and a sense of his own talent, the career he fashioned has hardly had the peaks he might have imagined. Most of his energy seems to have gone into building an empire in Castlereagh Council, the Belfast suburban borough in which he's been a councillor for the past 30 years, about which he repeatedly boasts: lowest rates in Northern Ireland, an ice-rink which brings in healthy revenue, unsurpassed leisure facilities in the egocentrically named Robinson Centre. He and Iris dominate council debates with much self-indulgent mutual reference, generating considerable irritation. She agrees with Alderman Robinson, he lauds Councillor Robinson, both speak at inordinate length. All that is missing, as non-DUP members of the council have been known to muse, is a statue or two around the borough of Iris looking rapt while Peter orates.

The Castlereagh stage would scarcely satisfy most would-be major players, but clearly it gives Robinson something he does not find at Westminster. An MP since 1979, he has never warmed to the House of Commons. 'I would reckon he's no more comfortable on one of his day-trips to London now than when he was first elected,' says a lobby correspondent who studies unionists with considerable curiosity. 'Scurries off as fast as he can. Doesn't like London. He likes home, his ice-bowl where he's king, his little empire.'

In his early fifties Robinson's ability and ambition is still unmistakeable, probably undiminished. But like many over-fifties, his glory days must seem in the past, and for an unchanged, unchangeable reason: the immovable mammoth who dominates him. When the DUP finally sat down in the 1996 negotiations, from which Sinn Féin were excluded, one government functionary who had always disliked him recognised how Robinson still shone among mediocrities. 'Like him or not, he's by far the most intelligent unionist at the table.' More impressive, he reckoned, than Trimble, the self-styled 'trained lawyer' proud of his ability to dissect documents. Although contemporary government interest in boosting the stock of the Ulster Unionist leader showed in this official's unwillingness to specify how Trimble was outshone by Robinson, there was no hesitation in ranking the university lecturer behind the DUP man who left school at 16. 'Best forensic mind on the unionist side – a bit of a star, as always.' A little later in proceedings, it was the constraint of Paisley on Robinson that stood out: 'He's trying to hang in there. But he has to manage the Ayatollah.' Later again he added: 'Poor Peter, he has his work cut out for him hosing down the elephant.'

Managing Paisley, which Robinson has signalled he's been doing for years, was at its crudest in the mid-'80s. Several journalists in Belfast at the time recall how 'Peter' – first-name terms were cultivated – would catch their eye at press conferences and raise a surreptitiously supercilious eyebrow while 'the Doc' was in full flow. He went further during a particularly fraught press conference inside Downing Street, after a meeting between Margaret Thatcher, Paisley and Jim Molyneaux. The group dynamic was vividly recorded by journalist Ed Moloney in the Dublin *Sunday Tribune*, in an account pieced together from several sources within hours, with Moloney's trademark thoroughness and eye for detail.

The leaders had gone to Downing Street to tell the Prime Minister they would not return to talks, or have any dealings with her ministers while the newly signed Anglo-Irish Agreement remained. They were to demand suspension of the Agreement before any new negotiations. But they emerged flustered and hot-looking, to tell reporters they would be talking to Northern Ireland Secretary Douglas Hurd when they returned to Belfast. There was a sudden sharp cough when Paisley made the announcement, Moloney noted. 'No, no,' Robinson hissed from the back of the room, white with temper, then briefed generously to the effect that 'the two old men' had been handbagged by the Iron Lady.

Around the same time, the first tales of Paisley's declining powers began to circulate. Some came from the bigger unionist party. Robinson left a considerable number of journalists with the impression that it was impossible to get a decision out of Paisley, either for radical street action or sustained political negotiation. Paisley was slowing up, it was said, and against expectations, becoming deferential to the mediocre Molyneaux and his delusions of influence in Westminster. The unionist position was disintegrating. Rapid negotiation was essential before the rot worsened, but Paisley and Molyneaux had nothing to offer.

Robinson had never been more accessible, even occasionally displaying what looked like a sense of humour. Journalists found themselves gossiping with him, some uncomfortable in the unaccustomed complicity but aware that Robinson was enjoying talking politics outside the narrow confines of the DUP. Some thought the tone was that of a slightly irreverent clever child, poking affectionate fun at his ageing parent, others that it was meant to belittle and was distasteful.

Robinson, some said, particularly enjoyed dismissing the pretence that there might be a Paisley dynasty. Ian Junior and his twin Kyle were 22 at the time, Ian showing signs of an unsophisticated interest in politics, like climbing on a pillar in Belfast's City Hall to attract journalists' attention. 'Junior', it was whispered off-stage, was very immature. The implication was occasionally spelled out. The failing leader could not bring himself to negotiate. No one else in leadership had the requisite ability and authority, but the able deputy would seize the moment. The local British government handlers played their part in building up what became almost the shadow of a regency. At a time when unionism in general was supposed to be spurning every NIO advance, Robinson and his close friend of the time, Sammy Wilson, then the party's press officer, were visibly embarrassed to be spotted by a journalist in a secluded Chinese restaurant with their partners, supping on the friendliest terms with a senior NIO official and his wife.

Paisley's deputy featured in articles which foresaw a realignment of unionism with him as leader, able and refreshingly willing to deal with nationalists. Lunches with Robinson were scheduled for important visitors, academics, opinion-formers. It came to nought.

'It never was the right time, was it?' says a former associate. 'Peter was never prepared to face the big man down.' One legacy of the period is a reputedly icy relationship with Ian Junior and his sister Rhonda. Robinson clearly feels no need to disguise his low estimate of the most political Paisley children. A striking spat a few years back had Rhonda chiding him none too subtly for supporting the idea of a NIO in Brussels because her father did not approve, and Robinson lashing back, 'If the girl knew anything, she would know that I am perfectly in tune with party policy.' The 'girl' was 32 at the time. She has since withdrawn from politics, while Ian Junior appears to detour round Robinson on his own career path of lightweight sectarian abuse and under-whelming agit-prop, like the raucous long-running picket of a Catholic congregation in his father's home town of Ballymena, for which he occasionally acted as spokesman.

The leader for life's two sons, his first names divided vaingloriously between them, together cannot match their father's sheer energy even now, much less the talents and appeal of his heyday. Kyle, like his father a Free Presbyterian minister, tends a modest English congregation. Ian Junior has his Assembly seat for North Antrim, and numerous appearances as a party spokesman. Paisley is a famously fond parent, but the contrast between the ability of his sons and that of Robinson could not be starker.

There was a time when Paisley would have made his own lightning analysis of documents but the formidable brain is not what it was. He knows Robinson has the appetite for negotiation as well as forensic skills. It was Robinson who made the party the election machine of today, albeit on the back of the Doc's unparalleled vote-drawing ability. He also now has his own dynasty, Iris in Castlereagh and Westminster, bright and personable son Jonathan – more likeable than either parent – on the payroll as assistant. Robinson and Paisley clans co-exist. The tie is only mutual at the top, where Paisley knows what he owes his deputy and the deputy recognises how he is outshone, presumably more dourly with every passing year.

Back when the NIO was trying to build Robinson into a believable unionist leader, John Hume and Gerry Adams were beginning the contacts that eventually produced the peace process. Ulster Unionists belatedly realised that the 75-year-old Jim Molyneaux, denying reality every step of the way, had delivered them into yet another nationalist-inspired arrangement. In 1995 they replaced him with hardliner David Trimble, aged 51. It must have been a harsh moment for Robinson, only four years younger. So much now for the always fanciful notion of coming out on top in a post-Molyneaux, post-Paisley unionist realignment, able and ready to deal. For all its limitations, Trimble's leadership destroyed the realignment fantasy. Within the year, while Robinson went on managing Paisley, it was Trimble who found himself enmeshed in preliminary negotiations. Trimble, however unwillingly, began grappling with reality; Peter was stuck with the Doc.

He still looked determined to be at the table and was effective in taking apart early nationalist proposals. But it was never clear what the DUP alternative to agreement was to be, which meant that Robinson once again came to be seen purely in destructive mode. Divisions among Ulster Unionists refocused around the Trimble personality. Relations between the DUP deputy leader and the media cooled again, and Peter Robinson withdrew from the position he seemed to have been preparing on the wider stage.

In recent years the suggestion that the big man is somewhat diminished has taken on a mechanical quality. When rumours began that some in the DUP wanted to take part in the Assembly, the party leader was said to be putting up strong opposition. When the party unveiled their half-in, half-out policy, it was clear that participation had won, but not at all clear that Paisley had been brought to it unwillingly. 'There will be a lot of temptation for Paisley to hang around the tent,' said one scholarly observer, pointing to the DUP leader's constant preference for opposition, but equal unwillingness to be left out of developments or deprived of opportunities for grandstanding. Another detected diplomacy among his closest aides: 'Robinson will be trying to keep some escape route open.'

He has certainly enjoyed his ministerial role. 'Never seen him happier,' said one old associate, 'this is the thing he's enjoyed most in his political life, even more than building his earthly monument in Castlereagh Council.' What was also clear early on was that the party had settled into Stormont, Paisley visibly blooming as he trundled along corridors and into committee rooms to chair Sinn Féiners, uncomplainingly, among others. By contrast, it was almost painful to watch the under-stretched Robinson, during his time out of office, as part of the party's tactic of rotating ministers. When Trimble was on his feet, Robinson affected to be too bored to listen. It seemed like a long time since the moment in the pre-Agreement talks when the two of them looked briefly like potential allies, born to conduct a pedantic but effective joint attack on nationalist proposals.

But in or out of office Robinson continued to play his part in the charade of DUP opposition to the presence of Sinn Féin. When health minister Bairbre de Brún goes through her routine of speaking Irish intermittently through every speech, DUP backbenchers begin to chatter to each other, break into wild peals of laughter, yawn, grunt and gibber. Robinson is too important for monkey-noise duty. He sits in front and make notes in the margins of important-looking papers, awarding the backbench performance snide smiles from time to time over his shoulder. He must wonder occasionally who the farce is intended to fool.

As the DUP went into the June 2001 election geared to cut the Ulster Unionist lead, Robinson statements made plain that while continuing to pillory Trimble, he wanted to keep his own party in play. 'Unless we have a structure that can enjoy the support of unionists and nationalists alike, it is not going to last,' he told one reporter on the record. In the *Irish Times* he said of north/south cooperation: 'If it's a matter of having good cooperation for practical purposes then I'm your man. But if it's a matter of advancing the nationalist agenda I'm against you.' David Trimble has always made a similar point, though with more laboured condescension to the south.

Something that might be identifiable as melancholy in a warmer person shows through occasionally now, most often when he is listening to Paisley. Like most people in late middle-age, Robinson must have begun to realise that the choice ducked may not come round again, or worse, that the offer might recur and he might make a bad decision for a second time. People who have followed his path through stunts like Clontibret, the moderation of the Task Force, and the indeterminate periods between and later, are convinced that he knows the last chance is not far off. 'Here he is at another testing point,' says an insider who watched the 1986 débâcle. 'And he's not finished yet. Hope springs eternal and all that. But it must be getting to the point where he wonders if he's blown it, where he thinks he's had the optimum opportunity. If that is what he's thinking, he might waver and blow it again.'

He faces another version of the mid-'80s problem. Without a realignment in unionism there is no ready-made vehicle for a new departure. Paisley has always out-polled his party. How will it fare without his electoral pull? Few observers believe the empire will survive him intact. A gradual splintering is the most likely outcome, no one sticking by the big man's much smaller son, the fundamentalists hiving off with the fiery Reverend Willie McCrea while an incalculable number follow Robinson. The prospect can have brought Robinson little cheer. 'He doesn't like his party. He likes it less than David Trimble likes his, which is saying something,' one insider reckons. 'He probably calculates his best bet is that Trimble goes and is replaced by Jeffrey Donaldson. Then Donaldson, the inferior tactician, would defer to his superior brain and political skills. But his prospects of dwarfing Donaldson are less now than they were even a few years ago.'

Some wonder if Robinson might have despaired of emerging as his own man at the head of a considerable grouping. Even dead, Paisley will wield influence. Anti-DUP feeling is strong among the anarchic Ulster Unionists, the roots deep and well nourished by decades of rivalry and mutual abuse, a fascinated dread of Paisley, the seepage of votes to him, the authoritarian contempt he and Robinson have always lavished on the bigger party's 'weakness' and willingness to compromise.

After the June 2001 election, a scholarly onlooker summed up the situation as hopelessly tangled. 'The culture of the Ulster Unionists is so different from the DUP. I find it difficult to see any realignment. While the Ayatollah's still there any move in that direction would be over his dead body. Can Robinson make an overt break with him and risk anathema? I doubt it. He needs to be the chief pall-bearer. Coming out on his own before that would be seen as treachery against the great man.'

Not many major parties split and survive, political scientists point out. It is too difficult to separate assets, buildings, activists, voters. The route towards a Robinsonite union with a pro-deal section of Ulster Unionism is hard to envisage. If Robinson should somehow emerge at the top he would still face the dilemma that stumped David Trimble:

how to craft an accommodation with nationalism more palatable to unionists than the existing agreement.

But a major component of the dilemma would be absent. Political life in Northern Ireland without Ian Paisley is hard to imagine. For the man most chilled by his huge dark shadow, balked of succession by a bigger man's refusal to give way, the prospect may have been fatally delayed. Peter Robinson may find only fragments of unionism to lead.

DAVID TRIMBLE: DIVIDED INTERNALLY

'He's not a politician at all, or if he is, he's most unusual.' Delivered with a sigh, it is a common view of David Trimble. Assessments of the man come readily from those who deal with him, though almost always hedged with mystification and anxiety. This is the politician who has become central to the peace process. Unless David Trimble – or a new leader of Ulster Unionism – develops authority inside his own party and in the community he represents, the future is likely to be as rocky as the recent past. Late in 2001, and not for the first time, it became clear that the Blair government did not know what to do with Trimble. How to help the Ulster Unionist leader secure his own position as First Minister of the Stormont Assembly? How to rally support among Protestants for the Agreement he had signed and the devolved government he headed?

It was clear that the glaring disparity between nationalist and unionist coherence and confidence threatened political progress. The malaise ran from top to bottom of the Protestant, unionist community, Northern Ireland Secretary John Reid diagnosed in a thoughtful speech. Unionists and nationalists must persuade each other of the merits of their respective political identities. Nationalists were confident about their place in Northern Ireland now, but unionists were insecure and despondent; unionists must take heart and make common cause with nationalists to defeat sectarianism. The last seemed to be a coded reference to the threat from Trimble's strongest enemy, DUP leader, the Reverend Ian Paisley.

Off the record, officials were more frank. Their most pressing problem was Trimble: 'He's not great, is he? But he's what we've got. We're trying to make the best of a bad job.' The difficulty for those who wanted to help was that Trimble complained of any statement made without his prior knowledge, but 'had a go' at every suggestion offered.

David Trimble

Even consultation and apparent agreement did not guarantee satisfaction. Quibbles about Reid's speech arrived next day. 'There's always a comma in the wrong place,' said one civil servant. A blast from Trimble in his local newspaper, the *Portadown Times*, accused Reid of having a 'narrow agenda', but Trimble let it be known that this was a 'misrepresentation'. One ageing apparatchik said wearily: 'What he says today he's capable of turning on its head tomorrow. Who's the real David Trimble?'

In Northern Ireland's political circles, there is little respect and not much liking for Trimble. New arrivals sometimes express surprise at this. Late in 2001 a visiting diplomat remarked, in puzzled tones, that he had 'the least loyalty among his own people of any successful politician I've ever seen'. It takes an outsider to point out that internationally Trimble is seen as successful, and more than that, as brave, skilful and enterprising. Occasionally, in London, where he has a tireless set of advocates, and for a time in Dublin, the Ulster Unionist leader has been portrayed as near-statesman, a visionary prepared to make a historic new start with ancient enemies, trying to forge a new democracy, courageously taking on the bigots in his own tribe. The picture is hardly recognisable at home.

Yet this is indeed a man who has led a divided party into a novel form of government, against sharp internal criticism and in the face of denunciation from a fearsome, premier-league demagogue. These are considerable achievements. The pity is that close examination of their author steadily diminishes any sense of conviction in him or of proper pride in what has been achieved. A baffling and barbed personality complicates the picture. Trimble has some international status because he is linked with the process of attempting to make peace in Northern Ireland. Closer to home, his ambivalence about that process shines out. On his own turf he can scarcely bring himself to use the name of the political enterprise which gives him lustre abroad and significance at home. 'Peace process' is a term he resolutely avoids.

Clearly, his friends in bigger cities flatter Trimble. As clearly, he finds their assurance and metropolitan panache a tonic to what is perhaps fundamentally an anxious soul, over-conscious of provincial origins: born in dull little Bangor, living outside even duller Lisburn. For someone who finds Belfast broadcasters and newspaper editors less than attentive to his frequent complaints, it must be a delightful contrast to bask, even occasionally, in the editorial offices of the nation's capital. He is probably a natural Tory, and there are signs that he loves his brushes with the aristocracy. The most elevated of the Westminster allies in Trimble's eyes has been the senior Tory Lord Cranbourne, member of the family that provided Elizabeth I with a first minister. Acquaintances say Trimble has become an expert on the intricacies and etiquette of titles.

In his thirties he used to boast that he had never been out of the British Isles. Now by all accounts, a plane journey out of Belfast is enough to turn him into a more relaxed, some say charming and almost cosmopolitan, being: a sociable Trimble can be found in foreign parts. The radical deal-maker of London legend remains elusive. On the local stage he erratically promotes himself as an innovator in a brave and radical cause, elsewhere he sometimes seizes on the persona provided for him. Inside Northern Ireland, Trimble is seen more as puzzle and problem than as model statesman. Yet at home too there are efforts to talk him up, to sustain an image and hope that the reality might in time resemble it more. David Trimble is presumably aware that he inhabits different worlds, in different guises. Occasionally, his worlds collide.

A Belfast-based journalist describes an uneasy encounter at a function abroad: as they exchanged words in a hotel lobby, Trimble became increasingly embarrassed as strangers came up to congratulate him on his 'bravery' in agreeing to share power with republicans, his fearless stand against bigoted hardliners. 'You could feel him wishing they'd stop. He cut the compliments short. He didn't want me to hear them.' But what he would have said to the wellwishers if alone left, the journalist baffled. What Trimble thinks of his own achievements is a puzzle.

His morale and motivation in the years immediately after the Agreement concerned everyone keen to see steady progress rather than a series of fits and starts. Both pro- and anti-Agreement lobbies were almost continuously obsessed with his chances of staying in place as Ulster Unionist leader. Both camps have watched him with raised eyebrows. The truth may be that the flickering personality which has baffled and frustrated prime ministers, presidents and politicians, in his own and other parties, is that of a man whose concept of himself as a political leader is fitful and more than a little eccentric. David Trimble might be a riddle not worth solving, a minor political talent inflated to a significance well beyond his capability or claim to seriousness. The problem, as weary mandarins and the ministers they service on both sides of the border admit, is their lack of choice, the 'best of a bad lot' syndrome. In some exasperated minds, Trimble, with his quirks of speech and behaviour, personifies the political shortcomings of unionism.

Even in the midst of his many crises, he dashes off newspaper articles for Belfast, London and Dublin, worrying endlessly at the details of his engagement in negotiations, reinterpreting and revising as he goes. Republicans also play this game. The difference is in Trimble's obsession with detail to the point that no coherent picture ever emerges. One tired observer says: 'There's no vision that anyone could sign up to, only the endless making and scoring – well, he thinks he's scoring – small and insignificant points. What will the legend on Trimble's tombstone say, I wonder?'

In February and March 2000 Trimble wrote several times to refute what he took to be an attempt by nationalists to blame a unionist police officer for murdering a Belfast Catholic family, the McMahons – in 1922. Another of his own interminable trials by his party's policy-making Council loomed. But the charge against a long-dead policeman had to be refuted, like the picture of Catholics in Belfast in 1922 under widespread attack. The Ulster Unionist leader delved back in time and wrestled facts into submission to produce a version of 1922 that showed unionists in a better light. 'What sort of message was that to send nationalists today?' another observer wondered. 'He'd just been made First Minister in a power-sharing administration, he's meant to be offering a new unionism, and he's off fighting the case for a man judged extreme in his own time.'

The McMahon murders happened a few weeks before the Royal Ulster Constabulary was formed, and the suspect police officer, like others, moved into the new force. It never won nationalist allegiance. When Trimble turned historian/detective, nationalists and unionists were locked in disagreement over plans to transform the RUC into a new police service, unionists bitterly objecting. Even as he lost the battle to preserve the RUC, Trimble seemed to think that he still had a mission to clear its name retrospectively. But the revision was all assertion. His articles on the McMahons displayed little research and a lax approach to fact, and were easily dismissed by Eamon Phoenix, the academic Belfast historian he unwisely challenged. In an effort to clinch his case, Trimble quoted a priest writing in the '20s in Belfast, mistakenly, as Phoenix pointed out, in fact so badly that it was tempting to believe he had not read the original text.

No modern unionist politician has invested more effort in personal accounts of his own contribution. Trimble's predecessor, Jim Molyneaux, was a man whose idea of leading the Ulster Unionist party was to do and say as little as possible. Trimble had negotiation and change thrust upon him. His central theme is that the 1998 Agreement merely rationalised measures already in train. What must be understood, clearly, was that no historic reversal happened. That would amount to an admission of previous unionist inadequacy, or worse.

Inevitably, Trimble was condemned by other unionists from the moment he entered negotiations. For most unionist politicians, as for many in the community they represent, it is an article of faith that nationalist demands for reform must be opposed because they represent a variation on the old joke: when did you stop beating your wife? Some in Trimble's own party say he dare not contemplate what was agreed in 1998, so he denies, distorts or minimises. It is simply becoming modesty, say Trimble advocates. This is a man, they argue, with no inflated notions about his own importance.

Yet in ways he behaves as though possessed of iron vanity, not unusual in a politician. Watching his career develop has convinced at least one perceptive witness that Trimble is not a politician of any recognisable kind. Nor is it easy to find a thread of personal development from the young lecturer who in his own words looked among unionists in the turbulent early '70s for coherent political thought, rather than be content to 'shout at the television'. The leader he chose to follow, Bill Craig, had little coherent political thought to offer, instead he was developing a reputation as wildly erratic. There followed years at the most abrasive end of unionist protests, against the principle of allowing Dublin consultative rights on how Northern Ireland was governed, and the idea of accommodating northern nationalist demands.

Though he had surprised many by leading a delegation into talks first with the moderate nationalists of the SDLP, then with republicans, and surprised them again by staying at the table through fudge after fudge on the decommissioning of IRA weapons, many were still amazed when on 10 April 1998 Trimble accepted the Good Friday Agreement. Not that he or other unionists call it that – for them it is 'the Belfast Agreement', as though ducking the memory of the dreadful day.

Two years later Martin McGuinness recalled a piece of Trimble behaviour when the Agreement text had been settled, in the final plenary session to seal the deal, an example of the republican eye for propagandist detail, but it fits a Trimble pattern many have traced: 'At the table he had a pencil in his hand. We all had these intercom systems in front of us and when we had to speak we had to press a button and a red light would come on. David was uneasy, and rather than push the button with his finger he hit it with the pencil. From that stage on I knew that we had problems. He said yes, but it was a very conditional yes, and I could sense that we were going to have great difficulty up the road . . .'

The unionist observer who thinks Trimble an odd class of politician finds it easy to explain why he disbelieves in Trimble the statesman. 'No moment of conversion you can spot,' he says. 'There he was in the Ulster Clubs etc, chaining himself to Land Rovers. Then he starts the Ulster Society to build some peculiar form of Protestant identity and sets the non-existent Ulster Scots language upon the world.' The Ulster Clubs was a short-lived umbrella for protest against the Anglo-Irish Agreement, bringing politicians and some senior paramilitary figures together in what were already slightly dated forms of agit-prop, usually peaceful. Trimble helped form the Ulster Society as an overt attempt to strengthen a sense of Ulster Scots identity. It is one of his achievements the London fans choose not to mention, as they try to fit him for an international stage.

The observer who disbelieves in Trimble the statesman has a punchline: 'Then he prances through Portadown with Paisley as a triumphant Orangeman. At which point in all of that did he decide Unionists had built a cold house for Catholics in Northern Ireland?'

In a sardonic sketch of Trimble's past, this is a tongue-in-cheek reference to the most quoted sentence in Trimble's acceptance of the Nobel Peace Prize he won for concluding the agreement. The speaker knows well that the phrase first swam into Trimble's head while the Nobel speech was being concocted, or was presented to him by someone with a feel for public relations and a less heated view of history. According to those around him, the most likely source is the curious assortment of extra-party well-wishers, a mix of academics and journalists, whose project it has been to confound and wrong-foot nationalists by substituting a vision of a tolerant, widely read, modernising and liberal Trimble for the older picture of an ill-tempered lightweight from the right-wing fringe.

Soon after he won his Westminster seat in 1990, an odd but congenial job lot of patrons adopted him, the group expanding when he became Ulster Unionist leader five years later. Perhaps the most intriguing was the odd figure of Sean O'Callaghan, former IRA prisoner turned anti-republican campaigner: in 2002 Trimble employed him as a Westminster research assistant as an angry response when Sinn Féin's MP's gained access to House of Commons offices. The nucleus of the London fan club was the gaggle of right-wing leader-writers and journalists who for various reasons championed unionism and saw in Trimble what they had despaired of finding, a figurehead of passable intelligence. A dislike or suspicion of the Good Friday Agreement, which most of them share, has strained their attachment to First Minister Trimble: they fall back on claims that his interpretation of it has been abandoned by Tony Blair.

The Nobel Peace Prize speech did nothing to burnish the perception of Trimble abroad. He was joint winner with SDLP leader John Hume, generally recognised as a major shaper of the agreement. Among both pro- and anti-Agreement unionists, resentment of the scale of Hume's international influence far outweighed appreciation of Trimble. In Northern Ireland as a whole, many believed Hume merited the prize on his own. Some thought Gerry Adams should have shared it with Hume and Trimble. Few saw Trimble as a credible peacemaker.

His own words suggest that nor did he see himself as such. The award in 1998 came too soon (eight months after the Agreement) for him to have worked out a comfortable or even coherent line. Straightforward celebration was impossible. He spoke after Hume in Oslo and made a singularly inappropriate and gauche reference to the other man, deriding those who believed vision in politics was desirable. Hume's citation had lauded his visionary quality and his speech characteristically celebrated the first steps away from violence, emphasised the possibility of betterment, even reconciliation. Much of Trimble's speech, by contrast, was emphatically downbeat, decrying vision in politics, with slightly embarrassing intellectual underpinning. The term 'peace process' was absent. But there were quotes from Edmund Burke, 'son of a Catholic mother and Protestant father', Amos Oz, George 'Keenan' for George Kennan.

In keeping with his preference for playing down significance, Trimble had turned up to receive a major honour with an acceptance speech in a resolutely minor key. It was a text devoid of any pretence at leadership, dark and pessimistic. A leading analyst, anxious to see idealism in Trimble at that point and generally optimistic about the potential of an imperfect peace, said sadly and with a degree of shock: 'He was preaching vigilance, caution and defensiveness, nervous mutton dressed up as philosophical lamb. There's no road ahead, either straight or potholed. It's one wee hill at a time with him peering trepidatiously round them.' The darkness of Trimble's language was striking. He reminded his audience six times that human nature is flawed. In the middle of the speech he made his single acknowledgement to date of the reality of Catholic grievance under Unionist rule. Unionists had perhaps 'built a cold house for Catholics'. Any warmth this might have generated dissipated in the chill of its surroundings, the shaken analyst noted. 'He had to twin it of course with the observation that unionists thought nationalists were trying to burn the house down.' Then there was all of this on one page alone: 'the flawed world, negative notes, false notion, spectres at the feast, fascist forces, dark fountain, terrorism'. It was a glimpse, he thought, 'into a psyche full of mistrust and dark shadows', and a psychologist might have had a field day with it.

Startled faces nearby suggested what some in the Oslo audience thought. Back home commentators noted that this was a politician who had come to the notion of accommodation late in his career and praised the 'cold house' gesture. The charge that Trimble has rocketed from extremism to moderation without time to think is not strictly fair. His days of Ulster Clubs agit-prop are almost two decades ago. There is a more recent and equally vivid hardline performance on the record.

The central town of his constituency is Portadown, Co. Armagh, known as the Orange Citadel because of the fervour and duration of local attachment to the Orange Order. Portadown is four-fifths Protestant. The Catholic minority have been complaining about Orange supremacism for well over a century. In July 1995, Trimble as an Orangeman since adolescence, and as local MP, argued forcefully with police that they must as usual allow a march from a little country church at Drumcree to pass the angry Catholic residents of Garvaghy Road. Contrary to every account Trimble has given of it since, trouble about Drumcree had been brewing for years. Mediators worked out a compromise with him and police; a small group of marchers might pass in silence.

As agreed, Trimble waited for the Orangemen in the town centre. Paisley lurked nearby, eager to outshine the younger man, ready as always to rail against any diminution of traditional Protestant 'rights' in a Protestant town. He moved in, teeth bared in characteristic snarling smile, as a reporter asked Trimble about the compromise with Garvaghy Road. There was no deal, Trimble snapped. In almost the same moment, Paisley seized his hand, swung it aloft and swept the much smaller younger man off in a victory parade. Even as a 70-year-old, Paisley had vigour and height enough to lift Trimble's heels off the ground. He walked as best he could, half on tiptoes, grinning uneasily. For a moment or two the unlikely couple performed an awkward minuet.

It was not a pretty sight. The cameras loved every moment. 'The Gay Wedding', the unkind called it. In every profile of Trimble the film clip became a fixture, the defining image of him for many Catholics. His tough stance on the march, however, gave him an edge a few months later, when Ulster Unionists came to elect a new leader to replace the elderly Jim Molyneaux. Trimble was seen as the most hardline of the candidates and won convincingly, the only occasion on which Paisley has made rather than destroyed a unionist leader.

As Drumcree became an annual stand-off between Orangemen, Catholics and the security forces, fresh Trimble images joined that of the Gay Wedding: the local MP, red-faced and furious, wagging his finger at police; in 1996, the revelation that he had engaged in talks in the Drumcree church hall, with the notorious loyalist paramilitary figure Billy Wright. He had talked to Wright to prevent violence, he said, then brought what he learned to the Secretary of State, Sir Patrick Mayhew. By then he was leader of the Ulster Unionists.

As tension grew throughout Northern Ireland in July 1996, with Orange blockades of towns and villages and the start of widespread rioting, a Catholic taxi-driver was found shot dead in his cab a few miles away from Drumcree. Police blamed Wright's gang, Mayhew and security forces huddled. Chief Constable Sir Hugh Annesley ordered a u-turn and forced the march down Garvaghy Road, police batoning Catholic protesters out of the way. Catholics, nationalists, some among unionists, the Dublin government, Labour in Opposition and a considerable section of British media opinion were aghast. Portadown Orangemen minted a medal commemorating the 1996 Drumcree siege and presented their MP with a special version: though they spelled it with the letters 'i' and 'e' reversed, which must have made the pedantic Trimble wince.

Years later, he was still being asked to explain the prance with Paisley. He deeply regrets it, the London cheerleaders claim. In 2001 he told a television documentary: 'If I'd any idea that it was going to be used, and misrepresented, in the way that it was, I would have taken great care not to have given that image. I was the Member for the area. Paisley was there as well, and I did not wish to see myself being upstaged by him.' An admirable admission of his own weakness, or evidence of crass insensitivity? He has made the admission about Paisley on several occasions. It has never occurred to him, or so it seems, that the offence lay first in his instantaneous and contemptuous repudiation of the compromise with Garvaghy Road. In 2001, he still could not bring himself to admit there had been a compromise. 'Discussion' took place, but his own role goes unmentioned except for the oddly phrased: 'It was quite clear to us that we were only going to resolve the matter with some degree of arrangement of that nature, but unfortunately it only turned out to be temporary.'

The people on Garvaghy Road are his constituents just as the Orangemen are. In his secret heart, Trimble must know that his repudiation of the compromise made them vow they would never consent to a march again. He also knows that there followed annual confrontation, widespread destruction and near-anarchy.

In spite of the visible distance Trimble has travelled to head a power-sharing administration at Stormont with the IRA's political wing, his most recent incarnation still has to contend in the public mind with the ill-tempered hardliner. The transformation is not gut-deep. It has been enough, however, to open him to constant abuse from bitter critics inside his own party, the worst slurs Paisley can think of, to threats scrawled on gable walls. Some of the marchers who gave him his medal have stoned his car while he electioneered. Letters to newspapers call him a traitor to the Order. He is still an Orangeman but he is no longer welcome in loyalist Portadown. A recent Twelfth of July, anniversary of the Battle of the Boyne when Orange King Billy defeated Papist King James, was spent in London.

When he signed unionism up for compromise on Good Friday '98, anti-Agreement graffiti artists dubbed him 'Purple Turtle', the illustration a clumsy overturned turtle of a deep-purple hue. The colour is wrong; the man who signed the Agreement and then oscillated between excitedly seizing the day and retreating in familiar tantrum mode used to turn bright red as soon as he lost his very short temper. For the past two years the temper flushes have scarcely appeared, at least in public. On recent occasions when past form would have seen him combust, Trimble has sounded almost sedated. In his gormless way, he confessed to the *Belfast Telegraph*'s Gail Walker (the sympathetic interviewer of his wife Daphne about the car park mob scene on the night of the election count) that he had thought of beta-blockers at one stage.

The old self still breaks through. Watching him on big occasions can be like watching one persona fighting the other, the physical fidgets an outward and irritating sign of a febrile political stance. An unremarkable physical appearance produces disproportionate unease in the onlooker. The bad old days may have gone, of storming out of a television interview without remembering to detach his mike, of turning on journalists in shuddering fury with what looked suspiciously like flecks of foam around the lips. But the memory lingers. A conflicted political personality glares through the gawky body language. In many eyes, some of them otherwise sympathetic to his painful political position, Trimble is above all a graceless man, his body ill at ease. 'He walks,' said a teenager watching him for the first time, 'like he has an itch he won't scratch.' Physical gracelessness is matched by, and may indeed reflect, considerable and unusual political gaucherie.

It has been played out in public. Many in Belfast's Odyssey centre in December 2000 and more watching on TV must have grimaced when Trimble first ostentatiously checked his watch then rose from his seat near Bill Clinton, while the American president was addressing a large audience during his last visit. As Clinton continued, Trimble left the stage. He had a plane to catch, he told aides, for a trip to Sicily to address an audience on anti-Mafia tactics. With embarrassment they relayed this explanation to reporters, who were already agreed on what had irked him in Clinton's text: a refusal to single out republicans for criticism, as Trimble had wanted, because the IRA had not begun decommissioning. Clearly long past trying to excuse Trimble's rudeness, an aide maintained that his boss simply would not have realised how his departure would look. It is a point that even his small fan club concedes. 'He has no manners,' one of the most loyal once sighed incautiosly among less smitten journalists.

The BBC's Belfast political correspondent Mark Simpson began a vivid report in June 2001 with a description of how David Trimble prepared to tell the Assembly that he had drafted a letter of resignation, the tactic he adopted to force the IRA to decommission. Simpson had been standing in the lobby at Stormont, he said, when a man sped past him and off down the long gilded corridor, 'running as fast as he possibly could'. The sprinter was the First Minister, hurtling towards the office of the Deputy First Minister, Seamus Mallon, with a copy of his letter before it became public. It later emerged that Downing Street had got ten minutes notice, the Northern Secretary seven, which suggested Trimble deliberately left it late to make his gesture to the touchy Mallon. As others in Stormont tiredly noted, the incident said much about the way Trimble does things: unexpectedly, without consultation, mishandling what would be better delegated.

His awkwardness, physical and political, was marked during the elaborate choreography necessary to secure the vote that reinstated him in late 2001, with a new Deputy First Minister, the SDLP's leader-in-waiting Mark Durkan. The resignation tactic was supposed to strengthen Trimble against internal critics. But he still lost the support of two of his own Assembly party members, and the first attempt to have him voted back in as First Minister ended swiftly in defeat. Mysteriously, he had been confident that he would be re-elected without much bother, certainly without the shenanigans it actually took. The delay and his miscalculation exasperated those already irked by Trimble's blitheness about pitching the process into crisis: republicans, nationalists, and by some accounts, Tony Blair and his man in Northern Ireland, John Reid. They were none of them mollified by his subsequent behaviour.

His successful reinstatement required a quantity of brazenness and a clumsy fix in the cause of preserving the institutions. It also took sustained effort by the government and by the small parties, the cross-community Alliance and one of the two Women's Coalition members who 'redesignated' themselves as 'unionist' to provide Trimble with the unionist votes he needed. As leader of the biggest unionist group in the Assembly by a slim margin, Trimble was essential to keep the structures up and running. Most came to do him honour, tongue in cheek.

The man at the centre of attention behaved as he tends to at his most stressed, ostentatiously not listening, tuned out so blatantly that watchers are forced to notice. Earlier he had spoken dismissively about the concept of redesignation, the likelihood of his survival depending on the Alliance party and Women's Coalition. As one speaker after another waded through the technicalities on his behalf, establishing how the rules would be bent, doggedly defending the manoeuvre against the filibustering and fake-scandalised wrath of Paisley and the multiple anti-Agreement splinters, Trimble flicked through a pocket diary so small that the uncharitable speculated it could only be useful to a person with no engagements.

The tension broke when the vote finished. Trimble bounced to his feet, recited the pledge of office with a beam of apparent warmth for Durkan and then rushed from the chamber tugging the much larger SDLP man along, in a vain attempt to outrun the Paisley forces and announce themselves to the press unheckled. Any pretence of dignity and decorum to lift the tone of the occasion evaporated, as the Paisleyites moved from procedural trench warfare to physical combat.

There followed what the giddier media called 'The Brawl in the Hall', a scrum as Paisley underlings tried to elbow closer to the newly elected duo and chanted 'traitor, cheat' at Trimble, with SDLP and Sinn Féiners wedged between and pushing back. A yelp called attention to a sixtyish Ulster Unionist Assembly woman, who almost toppled. Waiting while Trimble said his piece, Durkan glowered at the fray and Trimble's loyal Chief Whip Jim Wilson began to shepherd the two to one side, urging his leader 'just don't look at them'.

In Trimble's place, only the most stolid and unfeeling person could have found this anything but gruelling, and he is the opposite of stolid. Becoming one of the most despised species in the Paisleyite bestiary takes its toll. Trimble is a prize specimen, hardliner turned collaborator. Paisley's followers are world-class hecklers. The constant taunt of 'traitor, betrayer, Lundy, cheat' was deafening, the scrum buckling in hand-to-hand tussles as proximity and pressure played on tempers frayed for the previous few days, the whole thing fed by inter-party tensions and the underlying loathing between unionist and republican.

Later the cameras trucked in to be shown Trimble and Durkan having rewarding tea and biscuits, like newly delivered mothers, though in high-backed formal chairs. Watching the tea ceremony should have been soothing, except that for some a cloud passed over the sky. Cup in one hand, biscuit in the other, head down without reference to where his companion might be, Trimble's single-minded journey towards a seat took him at full tilt past the bigger man, between table and both chairs. There was an instant, before he made it to his own chair, when it seemed he was about to sit on Durkan's knee. Some observers foretold another less than mutually respectful and productive partnership.

Durkan's predecessor Seamus Mallon, also holder of the thankless post of deputy SDLP leader, only too clearly chafed under what he took to be daily slights. 'Deputy First Minister' is a cumbersome title for a job whose description and status the SDLP negotiated inadequately. The intention as per the Agreement's basic premise, to give nationalists 'parity of esteem' with unionists, was undercut by draughtsmanship that emphasised the 'deputy' tag, weakened the joint nature of the appointment and encouraged Trimble to posture as though he were Prime Minister of a single-party government. Though he plainly savours calling himself 'First Minister', he has never been known to talk seriously in public about the meaning and constraints of a joint office. At the start he was given to mentioning his 'deputy', with an inflection that very much suggested a humble assistant in his own party.

As a one-time close associate ruefully conceded, the SDLP 'deputy

First' became 'a chronic grump'. It began to be said by functionaries that the most difficult man in Stormont to deal with was not the ill-tempered Trimble, but an irascible Mallon. Those who inquired further discovered that Mallon got the label because Trimble spent as little time as possible in Belfast. 'He's bored stiff,' one insider sighed. 'I don't think he had any idea what devolved government was going to mean. Stormont just doesn't interest him.'

In mid-2001, when Trimble had made good his threat to resign and seemed in danger of failing to make it back into office, the improbable story began to circulate that the Ulster Unionist leader was in discussion with the Tory party – a shattered hulk without the ability to save itself – about the possibility of a 'safe' Westminster seat becoming available to him, plus a possible post in the Shadow Cabinet. A close acquaintance declined to shoot the story down: 'Of course, he hates this place. I don't doubt part of him would love to be off tomorrow if he could.'

Trimble saw himself as potentially a major player on the wider British stage, it was said, and was so regarded by some senior Conservatives. In the context of Conservative meltdown, with the untried and unimpressive Ian Duncan Smith recently elected leader, this estimate seemed less unlikely than the rest of the scenario. But as a 57 year old in 2001, Trimble must have faced the fact that he could be almost 70 before the next Conservative government arrived. During a stressful summer he might nonetheless have entertained daydreams of being treated respectfully in a more exotic place. As the story among some reasonably well-informed associates went, he dreamed of serving in London's heaven rather than continuing to struggle in what must have intermittently seemed like hell in Belfast.

Praise from the outside world is much needed. Once it was SDLP leader John Hume's ceaseless globetrotting that drew mockery. Few crises are reported without the now hackneyed observation that what Trimble fears about them most is missing an opera performance in London. No matter if invitations abroad clash with important business at home, off Trimble goes. Clinton scarcely noticed when Trimble walked out on him mid-speech, but others have been more put out. The relegation of political duty when it clashes with a private whim sparks unaffectionate anecdotes. His preference for jaunts over political engagement is a slightly tired joke among other politicians. A piquant moment is recalled by several people from the talks chaired by former US senator George Mitchell in autumn 1999, a final attempt to bridge the impasse over decommissioning. At one point the American ambassador is said to have asked Mitchell to come to London for dinner. 'I can't,' Mitchell supposedly said, 'I've got to chair these talks,' to which the ambassador allegedly replied: 'Well, David Trimble's coming.'

Mitchell and Clinton

An observer who has followed the careers of both Trimble and Hume says, 'It's a bit of a bad joke that just when his leadership looks weakest Trimble's got the taste for jetting off to tell the world about his achievements.' He adds sourly: 'At least Hume's achievements were real.' The sourness springs from the observation that Trimble accepts prizes and congratulations abroad for compromises that dare not speak their name at home. Invitations come in on the back of the Nobel Peace Prize from colleges and institutions throughout the world. Trimble is asked to speak as the unionist leader who made peace, joint prize-winner with Hume the nationalist. But joint appearances with Hume are avoided. Trimble gives speeches across

Europe and in the US, the contents of which swing between the liberal version of his political preferences, the preference for pluralism which he largely keeps for abroad, and his even odder version of the Good Friday Agreement. This bears little resemblance to the Agreement as interpreted by nationalists and republicans, or indeed the two governments. According to Trimble, nationalist acceptance of the principle that only a majority vote can take Northern Ireland out of the UK equals nationalist acceptance that since Northern Ireland remains in the UK, official symbols must reflect the British identity alone. The substance of his speeches elsewhere is often contentious – but he often speaks as though he led a united community.

Receiving the Legion d'honneur award in 1999 in Paris, he concluded ringingly: 'On behalf of all the people of Northern Ireland, I accept this, the supreme honour of the French Republic. It marks another step on the path to peace, pluralism and to the creation of that which France has always cherished, a sense of a common homeland, a sense of *patrie*.' Earlier he told the audience that the 'eruption of violence in Northern Ireland' coincided with the events in Paris in 1968, but the long-term results of each were very different.

He continued: 'If the civil rights movement had been left to carry on peacefully, who is to argue that reforms would not have come about without bloodshed? Sadly, however, the hijacking of civil rights, first by student activists and then by terrorists, was an unmitigated disaster.' The implication of possible merit in the civil rights movement is not one Trimble makes at home; this was for Paris consumption. But his version of the state of Northern Ireland in the '60s and the genesis of the Troubles is one only unionists would accept, an example of what may be Trimble's governing obsession, the need to exculpate his own political tradition.

His reactions to the Nobel Prize were characteristically contorted. Travelling in America when the award was due to be announced, he famously asked the aides with him not to waken him if news came through during the night. The party's annual conference soon afterwards studiously avoided mention of the award, to the amazement of visiting journalists. Obviously it was a liability to be twinned in the world's eyes, even (or perhaps especially) for praise, with nationalist leader John Hume, and for an Agreement about which his party was unenthusiastic.

In unionist eyes, one of Hume's chief sins is that he so successfully internationalised consideration of the Northern Ireland question, in the teeth of traditional unionist insistence that it was solely a British concern. Now he had inspired the suspect 'peace process' and elevated their own leader by association. For once Northern Ireland's Protestants had a potential star on the world stage, drenched in praise. Ulster Unionist party handlers, strongly influenced on this occasion by Trimble's own attitude, were having nothing to do with it. It was a very odd conference.

The man initially so dubious about international acclaim is now as taken as Hume with the idea of a grander stage. But Trimble's idea of his own role there is unfathomable. He may enjoy the company of right-wing Tory leader-writers, who none too discreetly see him and disgruntled unionism as a propaganda tool against the Blair government and Irish nationalism. There is a more innocent and childlike aspect of the London Trimble. Late in 2001, just ahead of yet another meeting of the troublesome and dissident-ridden policy-making Unionist Council, a photographer caught him sitting on the ground beside his little daughter in a Royal Opera House workshop, in shirtsleeves and with shoes off but tie still knotted, tired face awaiting instructions. Stories are legion of his touching pleasure in escaping Westminster to browse record and book shops, delighted at the freedom from his police guard. A House of Commons assistant describes him wandering back to his flat late at night via the tube and dodgy underpasses, green overcoat pockets crammed with newly bought paperbacks and Elvis CDs, briefcase clanking with the evening's bottles of German red wine. Might as well have 'mug me' written on his back, the assistant mused. He must have been greatly relieved when Trimble as First Minister on tour began using an official car.

The picture of a Pooterish innocent abroad emerges from a sympathetic biography by Henry McDonald, *Trimble*. It came from a named aide, yet another in the series of close associates, including his wife Daphne, who in describing Trimble's personality and behaviour leave him open to ridicule. Yet Daphne keeps on doing it, with the revelation that she had got a microwave for a Christmas present, the years he forgot presents but the children understood, how he comes home to sit and listen to his favourite operas and sip wine but not to talk, so she empathises from another room, how he hasn't any manners but she thinks he's improved a little.

Whatever else Trimble may be, he is clearly not a domestic ogre. But then, he offers anecdotes himself with a similar flavour: the beta blockers tale, the loving descriptions of his favourite mode of holiday, which involves driving the entire family without stopping for long hours across Europe to Germany or Austria. Perhaps because he hears nothing unflattering in such accounts, he seems equable about the tales others tell. For such an ill-tempered man, Trimble appears to harbour no resentment against the friends who point out his weaknesses. More than that, he seems not to notice.

The weird thing is that so many who mean him well and who exaggerate his stature as political leader also repeatedly expose his inadequacy and limitations, surely a unique phenomenon in the history of flattery. Is it subconscious awareness that the over-promotion is cruel, that the Trimble they have confected is painfully over-stretched by the role they claim he fills so well? In some, a patronising thread runs through otherwise fulsome praise. Queen's University historian Paul Bew, who has made a speciality out of interpreting Trimble, paints him as exemplar of the singular high-mindedness of unionism, distressed by the 'moral deficit' in peace process manoeuvres, possessor, like his people, of a laudable if 'provincial' moral seriousness.

'Moral seriousness' was not what came to mind when Trimble, speaking as First Minister, issued an immediate comment on the death of a young Catholic shot in Antrim in July 2001. Local police and other loyalists called it a sectarian assassination by the loyalist fringe group, the LVF. Loyalists steadily killed far more victims throughout 2001 than republicans, a fact unionist politicians seemed to find disorienting, presumably because throughout the Troubles most had claimed that loyalist violence was essentially reactive to that of republicans. In general they said little or nothing about the trend. But immediately after the Antrim killing, Trimble, who likes to claim inside security forces-type knowledge on republican and loyalist paramilitary matters, made a public statement to declare that contrary to general assumptions his information suggested the killers were the IRA in their anti-drug-dealer guise.

Another politician, hearing how distressed the bereaved family were by the implicit slur, asked the First Minister for an equally public retraction. A somewhat lame one emerged next day, but Trimble associates plugged away at the tale for some time. It later emerged that loyalists were indeed responsible. When the killing happened, Trimble's mind must have been busy with consideration of his own political future. His resignation threat took effect in July. The election experience left scars: losing more than 10 per cent of his vote to a DUP newcomer, knowing that unionists who refused to vote for him had come out to vote for Ian Paisley's untried candidate, plus the indignity of the car park ordeal on live television. The prospect of losing in the next election must have suddenly become very real.

Associates confided that during the campaign Trimble had been treated civilly only in Catholic parts of his constituency, despite lingering resentment there of his record on Drumcree. As the car park crowd chanted, the one-time Orange hero was now a Lundy, a traitor. Small wonder if he dreamed of escape and a future on the Conservative benches, however unlikely that might be. Everything about his Northern Ireland career must have seemed arduous, or at least unrewarding. One acquaintance over a long period says: 'You have to remember he didn't want an executive in the first place. None of this was his idea. And boy, does he hate his party.'

Is it hatred, disdain or near-despair that he feels? There are repeated accounts of internal meetings when in the face of opposition 'David didn't make any argument' or allowed the opposition case to go unchallenged. John Major's memoirs record how Trimble, a more flexible and adept leader than he had expected, had agonised about going into talks with republicans. Then came the ordeal of negotiations, the late last push for agreement inside his own delegation, the split, and ever after, a party divided down the middle, dissidents coming back again and again for another crack at him, with no end in sight.

Some sense a fatalism in him at big moments. Others think he knows his limits as an advocate. Indeed, he has said so publicly. It is hard to avoid the conclusion that he also lacks respect for his own grass-roots, middle-ranking apparatchiks and senior colleagues. A Westminster official saw the relationship in close-up, back in 1990 when Trimble was first elected. 'When he arrived at Westminster first the other Ulster Unionist MPs weren't delighted to see him. His record went before him. But he made it even harder for himself. The first thing he did was criticise their grammar in meetings; he'd correct someone in mid-sentence! These were all people who'd been MPs for years and in the party years longer than him.' It's a staple of every profile to record that in the leadership contest Trimble received the vote of only one Westminster MP, himself. He fought and defeated four of the other MPs for the post.

As the summer of 2001 wore on and the stories of an English career tailed away, he told a favoured journalist that he could not leave Northern Ireland politics, because he 'had no one to pass the baton to'. It is not hard to imagine how this sounded to his executive colleagues, ministers Sir Reg Empey and Michael McGimpsey, both ambitious men and already, according to insider accounts, part of a floating group engaged in discussion of what should come after Trimble.

'That was the penalty of the resignation tactic,' says someone who describes himself as a friend. 'Announcing it in advance probably saved him from electoral meltdown in the election. But it also made life without David thinkable to Reg and the rest: there's a floating cabal now.' Sir Reg became Acting First Minister. A Trimble aide commented on how fast Seamus Mallon had arranged for new notepaper with his own and Empey's names at the top. Trimble was allegedly wounded by this – but then Trimble's distaste for Mallon was no secret. Did he not realise he had slighted Empey?

To have a cabal discussing his succession in a sense merely formalised the war of attrition David Trimble had withstood since the Agreement: the repeated Ulster Unionist Council meetings at which his margin of victory steadily decreased, the certainty after each that no relaxation was possible. It has been the same story for over 40 years. Trimble's predecessors who attempted reform faced the same fate of death by a thousand motions. 'They are quite stunningly disloyal,' a long-time party insider remarks. 'But why wouldn't they be? There are no penalties, no sanctions. You lose a vote against the leader, but you go out immediately and start planning another Council trial for him.'

The central conundrum is that the party has no centre, or not one with organisational clout, no power to punish, limited patronage. Constituencies select election candidates, and delegates to the Council. The Council has final say on policy but with almost 900 people entitled to attend it is too big to be organised or coherent. The delegates tend to be elderly, male, sporadic activists, very conservative. They are not necessarily representative of the party as a whole, being more elderly on average than local councillors or the Assembly party. They have a fearsome reputation for consuming their leaders: O'Neill, James Chichester-Clark and Faulkner for turning reformer, but also the impeccably hardline Harry West, who presided over a loss of votes to Paisley, was swiftly dispatched and rarely heard from again.

A Trimble aide admitted, when the saga of challenges at meetings began in 1998, that it wasn't even possible to check that only signed-up Ulster Unionists attended. 'We know perfectly well there've been young DUP people there, passed off as Young Unionists.' To unmask them would mean stationing Trimble's scarce allies at the entrance doors, ready to challenge, but with a constituency officer for each constituency also present, since no ally could know every delegate's face. Trimble had insufficient support in the constituencies to run such checks.

Repeatedly Trimble says before Council meetings that no, he will not be lobbying by phone: 'Our people don't like to be bothered at home.' His enemies have no such scruples – they also have lists of likely delegates and until recently have had a posse of keen young lobbyists. Some of these have now defected to the DUP, where they will enjoy no such licence. Only 60 signatures are needed to force a Council meeting. Trimble's former allies, young lawyers with a passion for motions, meetings and amendments, made common cause with his older rivals to keep dragging him into the dock.

One-time Trimble lieutenant in negotiations, Jeffrey Donaldson, who walked out rather than sign up on Good Friday, has been a focus of discontent but never an open challenger for the top job. Behind him is the enigmatic figure of Trimble's predecessor, Molyneaux. It is a measure of the anti-Agreement argument inside Ulster Unionism that it has been largely incoherent and leaderless. Donaldson has raised dissident hopes and as often disappointed them. Those who hoped for a strong champion throughout the first years after the Agreement eventually began to drift away, some to the DUP, others to mutter off-stage. A possible alternative to Donaldson emerged when David Burnside was elected MP for South Antrim in June 2001. Once a Vanguard member like Trimble and Reg Empey and a spiky personality, he impressed some but was as strongly disliked by others, and, like Donaldson, criticised but chose to snipe rather than openly challenge.

The plea of the dissidents is that they merely want the party to stick to its pledge – no republicans in government until actual decommissioning began, was under way or complete, depending on the heat of the moment. But the charge-sheet expands or contracts at will to contain accusations of capitulation or simply a litany of complaint at changes made or pending, on the early release of prisoners, the reform of the RUC, the flying of the Union Flag, the mooted removal of 'the Crown insignia' from inside courtrooms. Everything that unionists do not like about the Agreement is attributed to the Trimble leadership. The most damaging charge is that he has lost votes to Paisley. Trimble's defence that the eternal wrangling makes the party less and less electable has had little impact, because it is put with only intermittent force.

Many who think Ulster Unionists unleadable also doubt whether Trimble has it in him to be a reconciler, because they think he not only lacks leadership ability but also conviction as a peace-maker. Some go on to insist that Trimble has come farther and managed better than they expected, several adding tiredly that the cost has often been nervous exhaustion for himself and frustration in others. The evidence stacks up, but on both sides.

After long and painful negotiation, and in spite of a last-minute walkout, he took most of his delegation with him to accept the Agreement. He then faltered under anti-Agreement fire and had to be rescued in advance of the referendum on the Agreement by a combination of cheerleading from Tony Blair, goodwill from abroad, nationalists and non-political groups of Protestants including clergy and business people. He went into government with Sinn Féin although there had been no start to IRA decommissioning, a major leap forward in his own terms. Again he was boosted from without and attacked from the same quarters. Then he began to set deadlines for decommissioning and to question republican sincerity, commenting that Sinn Féin people must be 'house-trained'.

Those who have always wanted him to be a straightforward persuader for the Agreement, and who have been repeatedly disappointed, watched with pride as he crossed the border into

Donegal for the funeral Mass of the three Buncrana children killed in the Real IRA bombing in Omagh in August 1998. He was welcomed from the altar, applauded by the congregation and greeted by the President of the Republic, Mary McAleese. For an Orangeman sworn never to enter a Catholic church, it was a considerable gesture. But he had to be coaxed every step of the way to attend the Belfast rally in January 2002 sparked by a loyalist killing of a young Catholic postman. He cannot bring himself to say that marchers should discuss parades with Catholics who live along their routes.

'If this thing falls to pieces I'll blame David Trimble to the end of my days,' said one prominent civic-spirited Protestant in 1999, as the process bogged down in the wrangle about decommissioning. 'What did he settle for if he couldn't bring himself to sell it?' The answer would seem to be that his intelligence settled, while his stomach stayed unsettled. The officials, journalists and observers in other parties as well as Trimble's who regard him with some sympathy as well as irritation, suspect that his party is indeed unleadable, 'a horror', as one puts it. Watching his behaviour up close, they conclude that his own simmering internal conflict leaches away his authority.

In the months after the Good Friday Agreement had been ratified by referendum, the other pro-Agreement parties hoped for progress but knew anti-Agreement pressure on Trimble was the most likely immediate obstacle. A comparatively sympathetic bystander in Stormont commented: 'He's so badly served by those around him. Up here there's hardly a well-known face. It's these infants. He spins and dithers. He probably imagines that way he risks less. But the man has enemies everywhere.'

He also has few friends, and those are badly treated, they might have added – a function of his own quirks and his party's failings. Ulster Unionists themselves say there is no party tradition of comradeship nor much social cohesion, compared to Sinn Féin's war-forged solidarity and discipline, the SDLP's relaxed and sometimes boozy camaraderie, eddying for years around their morose leader but sustained by successful strategy, the DUP's tight circle of defence against a corrupt and compromising outside world.

Among those who have seen the main players under pressure and at close range over several years, there lingers the memory of those last fraught weeks and days before the Agreement emerged. Only a week earlier, a unionist insider noted glumly that David Trimble had not prepared his people for compromise. Amid wide expectation that negotiations were headed for failure not success, he prophesied: 'If the British force Trimble to move now, they'll destroy him. They've left it too late. He's surrounded by enemies – and they're waiting for him like wolves.'

Trimble moved: the oldest and biggest wolf with the sharpest incisors chomped off a few chunks then continued to wait, licking his chops as unionist votes began to come his way. Paisley's menace, in most eyes, can destabilise any settled programme the Ulster Unionist leader might adopt. As Trimble pitched the Agreement's institutions into crisis in summer 2001, the insider who prophesied so darkly before the April '98 'breakthrough' remarked tartly that evidence still had not emerged of a thoughtful, deep-rooted, convincing Trimble conversion to compromise. In negotiations Trimble jumped, but not everyone jumped with him. The split has bedevilled him ever since. In this view, erratic progress at best, a series of jump-starts with the shortest periods of smooth running in between, was only to be expected.

'Up to the week before Good Friday, David's position was that there'd be a Welsh-type county council. No executive, no legislature. These were all key things. Out he comes with a legislature and an executive including the Shinners. When was that decided?'

When the deal emerged he lost the Young Unionist cadre of lawyers, originally Trimble fans who thought he would offer them promotion in place of ageing MPs. They ripped away in a sulk that many still maintain, and Jeffrey Donaldson took to lurking in the wings. The years since have been rocky, as they were bound to be. Trimble has limitations, but more realism and a better grasp of what was necessary and possible in negotiation than was obvious from his behaviour outside talks. One instinct urged him to sign up, another robbed him of energy and positiveness about what he had agreed.

'His brain tells him that for the future of unionism and his own reputation he has to deal. And his guts tell him they'll have him if he does,' commented an observer in the talks, more sympathetic than most to Trimble's plight. Struggling to weigh the 'rotten man management' he had seen with observation of the treachery Trimble rightly feared, he reckoned that the Ulster Unionist leader had shown more realism and more grasp of what might be salvaged for unionism than the other parties and the two governments had expected of him. This was also an official who said sadly of Trimble at the start of negotiations: 'No one goes to him for a wise judgement. He's not a sovereign being.'

For most of those who have seen him negotiate, or who have studied him at close quarters for any length of time, being fair to Trimble requires much weighing in the balance and the exercise of great forbearance. As a rule of thumb the closer observers get, the less admiration they have. The most positive home in on Good Friday, recalling the leap he made. They judge that he did it largely alone, dubious about the loyalty of some around him, reluctant to treat the most loyal as intellectual equals.

Often since, Trimble has sounded as though in denial. Nothing else explains the bland assertions that the Agreement is working, moments of apparent optimism, followed by what seems reflexive rubbishing of the outcome or exposition of an Agreement that no other party recognises. The repeated Council meetings would unnerve and exhaust someone with a settled centre of gravity, which Trimble so clearly lacks. But then, he makes a virtue out of having no strategy. None survives the battlefield, he likes to say, though in his mouth it sounds more alibi than mantra. It might be fatalistic recognition that unionism has a poor hand, or simply the way the man's mind works. Both in negotiations and the slack moments after resolution of a crisis, David Trimble has rarely spoken to a script agreed with colleagues or those across the table. 'He goes out there and says whatever he feels like,' says someone who has weathered the process. 'He's amazed and irritated that you're amazed.' If only anyone felt sure the leader ever saw farther than the next crisis, he sighs, or sat down and, with others, worked out a strategy and stuck to it.

Wearisomely often, the lumbering and undirectable Council is described as policy-making. It may have the power to make policy, but it has none of the necessary ability. What Ulster Unionism lacks is what the other main parties have so abundantly in their different ways, a committee to provide policy and direction, a central brain. The DUP, in Paisley, has had formidable political talents, supplemented by younger strategists of considerable agility and guile. Sinn Féin processes policy through endless debate, hammering out and refining lines to be taken until everyone knows them by heart. John Hume did much of the SDLP's thinking but always had bright people close by as sounding boards, Mark Durkan among them.

Unity of purpose is also something all three other parties share. Republican discipline has dark roots, SDLP admiration for Hume was like glue, and Paisley ran such a one-man empire that he could with impunity make jokes about being the Pope and appointing his cardinals as ministers. Ulster Unionists are spectacularly disunited. Often when David Trimble goes into negotiations he might as well be alone. Colleagues walk beside him; usually they will have had little or no preliminary discussion.

The apparent blitheness with which he has triggered crises, the misjudgements he has repeatedly made of what it would take to resolve them, has intrigued and often galled a wide audience of news-watchers, government officials, people in the other Stormont parties and some in his own party, whom outsiders might have imagined to be in his confidence. He neither trusts them nor rates their political intelligence. The confidants are elsewhere, on the other end of the phone or among the network of dilettantes in editorial offices. Some think Daphne might be a substantial influence. She did, after all, discover the 'Daphne Principle', that he would always secure a narrow enough majority in the party to stagger on. There is no real committee, policy-making or otherwise. 'There's not even a proper foursome sitting down to chew things over,' as one well-informed bystander puts it. 'He's awful at meetings and has too many of them. What he doesn't have are the meetings he really needs.'

Former Northern Ireland Secretary Peter Mandelson stays in touch, spinning his own silken agenda. Senior Ulster Unionists have been known to arrive in London for a working lunch with 'the leader' to find him, to their considerable distaste, in deep conversation with former IRA prisoner Sean O'Callaghan. The oddly assorted 'advisers' may sustain some of Trimble's wilder flights of fancy, but the tactics have the flavour of the man's own quirky personality. 'It's always the half-empty approach,' says one British ministerial assistant. 'For example, we offer him the prospect of handing back control of policing to the Assembly, to sweeten the Criminal Justice Review. He just ignores that. He snipes at the Review instead. Not Patten, he says condescendingly, not that atrocious, but it's not quite right.' To those who despair of Trimble, not because he signed the Agreement but because he has always refused to sell it with enthusiasm, the 'half-empty' tendency is the biggest irritant.

One political scientist says he thinks Trimble might be 'the perfect example' of a bad leader. 'Over and over you hear him set up objectives that he can't meet. Take the RUC. Why say we must keep the name when it had already gone? When the new service is already up and running, he starts in again on the badge.' A unionist who despite huge misgivings has clung to Trimble as the only hope for progress says: 'Why does he keep on agreeing to things he can't sell? Then everyone's supposed to rally round and save him from the antis.'

Rare glimpses of something like magnanimity and dexterity are followed swiftly for the observer by further bewilderment. After the IRA's start to decommissioning, in October 2001, the moment which eventually allowed him to return to office, Trimble managed to claim credit without sounding triumphalist. It was a rare example of him finding the right words, without eating them in the next five minutes. At his party conference a month later, when he should have bounded on full of proper pride in his own achievement, he sidled up to the podium like an awkward schoolboy in his first debate, and then muffed his big moment.

It did not help that Ulster Unionist conference management disdains warm-ups for the leader's speech, or that the leader arrived unheralded during the previous debate in the wake of the party's most prominent dissident, Jeffrey Donaldson. Regarded as too devious and opportunistic by many to be a credible alternative leader, Donaldson understands the media and is an adept poser. While he loitered intently near the bank of TV cameras, offering his 38-year-old profile from several angles against a flattering backdrop of grey and bald heads, Trimble sloped in unnoticed with his trademark armful of paper. The auditorium was three-fifths empty, the Donaldson faction's gambit of fixing a policy-making Council meeting for three weeks further on having undermined in advance much of the validation any annual conference could be expected to provide. Trimble's 'leader's speech' needed to stir and galvanise a muted, almost sullen audience.

The signs were that he had failed to galvanise himself. When he left the platform to cross the broad stage of the futuristic Waterfront hall, the long walk to the lectern looked stressful. The Trimble walk is quirky, half-scuttle, half-bounce. He edged into the light, low expectations written all over him. Glass lectern and see-through autocue gave no shelter. As he often does, Trimble looked like a singularly gawky teenager. It is as though he remembers occasionally with irritation that he must heave limbs around but resents the effort. Reasonable physical attributes become liabilities. As he read his speech with the lamest and sparsest of ad libs, two perfectly ordinary arms hung sausage-like, distracting the audience. The glittering backdrop of a futurist stage served only to highlight a drab performance to an audience that seemed tranquillised; high-tech meets duff technique and old tired party. 'I've been at livelier wakes than that thing,' one young reporter said later.

By any law of political management, Trimble should have been telling his people that this was a moment of triumph, that his stubborn insistence on IRA decommissioning after years of struggle had begun at last to bear fruit. Yet going by appearances, what he struggled with was the humiliating memory of the fix required to put him back into office. Thanks to the redesignation of Alliance as unionists, something he had pooh-poohed in advance, he won the vote. In his own head, he lost the struggle. To judge from his speech, he had allowed his critics' downplaying of the IRA move to diminish its significance, even for him.

Three and a half years after the Agreement and four years into the second IRA ceasefire, Trimble chose in November 2001 to proclaim the IRA anew as chief terrorist bogey. He could have kicked off his conference address on a resolute high note, celebrated his own reinstatement as First Minister. He should surely have declared the IRA a spent force, thanks to his persistence. Instead he insisted that history recognise violent republicanism as chief cause and perpetrator of the Troubles. It is a preoccupation many unionists share. Loyalist paramilitaries remain active, causing riots, pipe-bombing Catholic homes, killing Catholics and other loyalists. IRA violence by contrast is much diminished. At the end of a year in which loyalists had already killed a dozen people, the IRA two, here was the Ulster Unionist leader choosing to highlight the violence of republicans.

Those who had hopes of a new mood in unionism, once the IRA finally moved on arms, must have listened with dismay. In front of people whose insecurities and resentment sustain and are fuelled by his party critics, who brood fretfully on the paradox of hunted gunmen turned feted peacemakers and are destabilised by the spectacle of Ulster Unionists sharing power with the IRA's political front-men Sinn Féin, he renewed the sense of grievance. In the next breath, but with no sense of irony, he declared Sinn Féin and Ian Paisley's DUP to be parties which 'feed on grievance', while 'this party gives leadership'.

Bizarrely, he even conjured up the spectre of interning his Executive's minister for education, former IRA leader Martin McGuinness. 'I have written as First Minister to the Home Secretary,' he announced, blithely speaking as though he were in fact the prime minister of an orthodox government, with not the slightest care for what his new Deputy First Minister might think. He wanted the Home Secretary, said Trimble, to extend to Northern Ireland the emergency internment powers introduced during the Afghanistan war. This would be a useful tool against republican dissidents, he said, and also against the IRA, who remained a threat. In fact, the SDLP has always opposed internment. Mark Durkan should have been furious, but worryingly for those who fear he may be too modest and self-effacing as Trimble's nationalist counterpart, there were no reports of him calling Trimble to account.

When he should have been rallying support for the next Unionist Council ordeal a fortnight ahead, Trimble undermined himself and rekindled the most unhelpful emotions. As though unable to help himself, he returned to an obsessive theme, the need to revise the history of Northern Ireland so as to minimise or erase the record of nationalist grievance and present unionists as comparatively blameless. Before getting around to listing his leadership's achievements, Trimble turned back to a theme from his Nobel Prize speech and lectured on the IRA's immutable badness, their role as the prototype of 'Terrorism International, encouragement for terrorists globally'.

Many observers had concluded that the 11 September attacks in the US might not have produced the IRA move on decommissioning but had probably accelerated it, and that the 'war against terrorism' almost certainly sealed off any risk of mainstream republicanism turning back to full-scale violence. Trimble the amateur historian nibbled away at optimism and the historical record. At the moment when he could have claimed credit for shifting the IRA by his persistence, he chose to burrow back into apportioning guilt and blame, though he did not do it systematically, and nor did his journalist and academic supporters. 'There is no big speech in his history, is there, any more than in his politics,' says an irritated observer who has struggled to link up the articles and speeches. Trimble's clear preference is for rewriting history, rather than making it. When he finally mentioned the decommissioning move, his words were initially grudging, then breathtaking for the wrong reasons.

'It would have been hypocritical – and politically stupid – for us not to acknowledge the long-overdue contribution by republicans to the process. But we cannot allow the past to be rewritten. We do have to remember that in the '60s this society was evolving peacefully and positively. Problems could have been solved, a way of working together was emerging. Violence in pursuit of an unattainable united Ireland put back all that progress. We have now developed an honourable compromise. It would have come sooner but for the violence. The IRA campaign was for nothing. Worse, it has left a more divided people, with in places, greater sectarian bitterness than ever before. That is what republicans have yet to understand. That is why unionist people have cause to feel aggrieved.'

A fiction of considerable energy, this was delivered to an unresponsive hall, in a flattened voice with no oratorical flourish. At a stroke, out went the record of unionist resistance to civil rights demands which began the progressive collapse of the old unionist monolith. Away went the role of Trimble's own greatest rival, Ian Paisley, in fomenting grass-roots fury against any reform, away went Trimble's own wholehearted support for successive heaves against prime ministers trying to introduce reforms under pressure from London and harried by their own backbenchers, just like Trimble. Out went any recognition of nationalist grievance.

In came a totally fictional peaceful 'evolution' of a 'way of working together'. Many in front of him were veterans of anti-reform agitation in the late '60s and early '70s. Standing in the aisle as Trimble began was the flamboyant Lord Laird of Artigarvan, as plain John Laird the hardline tormentor of one unionist prime minister after another in the early Troubles. Many of those in the hall had spent their best years hounding Terence O'Neill, James Chichester-Clark and Brian Faulkner, and Trimble had supported them, in his pre-party-political shouting-at-the-television stage. Now he is similarly harassed for agreeing to a far more radical accommodation of nationalism than ever those premiers suggested or could have dreamt.

In the presence of fellow witnesses of unionism's long decline in the face of risen nationalism, the consequences of their refusal to contemplate reform, here was the new reforming leader tearing up the record. Then he went on to relaunch a defeated campaign: 'We will not give up until the hurt callously inflicted by Patten is addressed.' But recruits were already in training for the new policing service. It was another example of Trimble ensuring his own future humiliation. What must the party's rank and file think of him? To judge by the puzzled faces and silence, some are bemused by his contorted arguments.

Among people with a low opinion of their own political skills, frustrated and sometimes bedazzled by nationalism's ability to outflank unionism with apparent ease, Trimble's academic credentials and use of long words have gone a long way. But he refuses to use his superior vocabulary to talk them persuasively towards the future. As the party's vote erodes, a quantity of original admiration for the brainy leader has gone with it. 'You've got to keep close to your base,' said one party organiser, unconsciously using the term beloved of the republican party managers whom unionists watch with such appalled fascination. 'There's no point being a clever Johnny if your troops are all in the other field.'

Some are cynical. 'The perception is he doesn't much care about the RUC and it's all wind. Second, that he's culpable for not saying from outset the title's sacrosanct, which he didn't do.' The effect on the troops of being told they can recover what they have lost, while also hearing that the demons they now share government with are still demons, is something party activists – a comparatively tiny number – refuse to explicitly address. When asked, most openly sigh and roll their eyes, while others tend to close conversations.

It is left to outside observers to try counting the cost. 'He does everything arse about face,' one said, months before the Agreement was signed. 'It takes for ever, he creates obstacles so he can claim concessions. Who knows what that does to his community?' Having watched the consequences of what he deemed on balance an identical pattern of behaviour over the next four years, he is more depressed now than angry. The way Trimble spoke of decommissioning at the conference left him almost speechless. 'He just rubbished it. So much for how it was going to change the whole atmosphere.'

Insiders who have studied Trimble through the pre-Agreement negotiations into these first difficult years of the new era are convinced he had purely opportunistic reasons for pursuing decommissioning. 'He doesn't mean it. He doesn't need it as proof the war's over,' one says caustically. 'He demands it when he needs it to survive. It goes back all the way to Good Friday.' On this reading, trying to make sense of Trimble's tactics is hopeless. Indeed, though he has often questioned republican motivation, he has also as much as said publicly that he believes the IRA's war is over.

It came at a particularly strange moment, when the Colombian affair had made many angry at the cynicism of republicans and caused the most optimistic to question their behaviour. Trimble had just returned from a break; perhaps there was a touch of post-holiday dislocation. On early morning radio he clearly wanted to keep the focus on the damaging implication that the IRA was for unknown purposes sending emissaries to similar groups abroad, while refusing to begin decommissioning. But while he had been away the bulk of violence in Northern Ireland had been loyalist and the interviewer pushed him for a comment. Plainly irked, he replied: 'Well, of course most of these groups are mainly criminal, into drugs, and that brings us back to Colombia,' a splendid non-sequitur even by Trimble's standards. Then, as though to himself, he said: 'Of course, there are elements who just want to start the war again. I think they're mad.'

The twists and turns on decommissioning unsettle unionists as well as nationalists. What they never do is throw the wolves off the scent. Sniffing indecisiveness and lack of conviction, the anti-Agreement hunters continue to circle. During the 2001 election, a prominent Ulster Unionist told a reporter what he heard on the doorsteps: 'Decent ordinary Prods like it reasonably straightforward. They're saying Trimble changed – he said no guns, no government – and he didn't stick to that. And the DUP play on that. Everything from them is anti-Trimble. It's Trimble, Trimble, Trimble.'

When movement on IRA decommissioning arrived, it was too subtle by half to counter directly that suspicion. There was no film of what had happened, not even a description, no place, no time. Yet by the time another Council meeting was called in November to pummel

Trimble again, the sense of a broken taboo had seeped through. Enough republican unhappiness was visible to make the invisible start to decommissioning seem real at last. Trimble's opponents still demanded further movement, a timetable, a next step. But they broadened their focus to other gripes: symbols, the RUC badge, flying the flag. Decommissioning still niggled. There was no breakthrough or celebration, more a disgruntled shrug.

Immediately after the announcement in October that the de Chastelain commission had witnessed a decommissioning 'event', one of the most astute of experts assessed it from the vantage point of years of negotiation, drafting and advice to several of the main players. He thought it gave unionists 'a sense of victory of sorts'. With an optimism that seemed sadly misplaced even days later, he went on: 'Decommissioning has performed a very useful service . . . against a background where unionists felt, with some justification, that it was all downhill from the good old days, a great sense of loss of control and so on. I think the sense that they have carried a point on this very deep symbolic issue is probably going to be healthy.'

Perhaps so, but not for some time, to judge by the considered reaction of the Unionist leader most dependent on the de Chastelain mission. Expectations of a new unionist mood melted away when a chorus of 'bah, humbug' from dissident Ulster Unionists found an echo in David Trimble's refusal to enthuse his people. Not for the first time, he let the dissidents set the tone, incapable of being as upbeat as they are. Some listeners refused to take him too seriously. 'Isn't this what unionists always do after a big breakthrough?' said an analyst who saw the move as a convincing guarantee of republicans' commitment to turn away from violence. 'They run around like headless chickens for a while. When everyone's too fed up to give them any credit, they accept it and move sulkily on.'

From this perspective, Trimble's denigration of advance is the perfect reflection of a torn community. Observers are still scratching their heads about the man, and the politician. Efforts to 'help David' – though it had been a watchword during pre-Agreement negotiation and the next phase, when increasingly the helpers felt he could do more for himself – became exhausted. Nothing worked. He denounced the helpers and asked for more. Reinstated by the redesignation fix, his first reaction was to write to Tony Blair and John

Reid demanding that they now address the problem of unionist alienation. But when Reid began to think out loud on the subject of sad unionism, he disliked the result. 'Patronising', his aides said.

When Reid spoke publicly about the worrying extent of loyalist alienation and the lack of unionist confidence in contrast with the vibrancy of nationalism, apparently with the intention of sparking a debate inside unionism, he also said he wanted to see politicians jointly tackling the scourge of sectarianism. Trimble's reaction was to complain that, 'Reid seems to think only Protestants are sectarian.' Perhaps his revisionist conference speech was meant to be a refutation of Reid's boss, the British Prime Minister. Trimble had let it be known in London that he was furious at a passage in Tony Blair's speech to the 2001 Labour party conference: ' . . . in our own peace process, in Northern Ireland, there will be no unification of Ireland except by consent – and there will be no return to the days of unionist or Protestant supremacy because those days have no place in the modern world. So the unionists must accept justice and equality for nationalists. The republicans must show they have given up violence – not just a ceasefire but weapons beyond use. And not only the republicans, but those people who call themselves loyalists, but who, by acts of terrorism, sully the name of the United Kingdom.'

As an official noted dryly, 'David's problem was apparently the Protestant supremacy reference.' Aware that Trimble was permanently prey to Paisley, thanks to his own weakness and the nature of the party he leads, British government thinking publicly urged unionists to consider their political identity, and how best to preserve it. Behind the scenes, a harsher mood descended. The vogue for 'helping David' appeared to have passed. It was hard to tell whether his disposition to begin attacking Blair in public and to identify ever more openly with the Conservatives were factors in that government shift, or the product of Trimble's knowledge that he was out of favour. Support for Trimble was always the coldest of Blair's calculations in any case, outlined by a knowledgeable insider in late 1997: 'There is a recognition that he has moved and is displaying leadership skills. He is being treated as special . . . his stature has been deliberately built up by the government, but he'll be blamed if it doesn't work.'

If Trimble survived, well and good. If not, his successor, or the DUP if it were to become the largest force in unionism, would face the same situation – strong nationalists, intent on a deal at least as favourable as the Agreement. Either way, the implication came through strongly from both Reid's and Blair's speeches that unionists had better confront their past, assess their present and consider the likely future.

Trimble reacted to nudges towards working out an analysis for unionism by sounding more and more pro-Conservative and anti-Labour. Around his agitated, jerky figure, scribbling away at history's rough drafts and fidgeting with his diary, his own party began to think harder about the next leadership. The DUP counted off the days to the election when they would sweep into place as prime representatives of the unionist people, the role their leader had filled for so long.

Trimble has suffered a rough time in a tough position. 'If he had been in place a bit longer, if he hadn't been a latecomer to a process already begun, who knows?' says one close observer.

Instead, Trimble was bequeathed a rudderless and clumsy galleon by Jim, now Lord, Molyneaux, who has watched his struggles with an unhelpful eye and encouraged his internal opponents. Molyneaux's role in Ulster Unionist dissidence may not be as substantial as Trimble's friends often suggest, but his enmity to the Agreement is clear enough.

David Trimble was undoubtedly swept into the play of negotiation with the worst of hands. 'Look what he faced,' as the sympathetic observer says. 'British government joined at the hip to the Irish, the SDLP about to be nudged out of the way by the Shinners but still united, led by a man on his way out but whose grand plan they were largely working to. And then republicans, a formidable force, moving swiftly to jettison huge chunks of their own theology – and some of their most unpleasant aspects – under a commanding leadership.'

A loner in an atomised political culture, David Trimble has perhaps done as well as he possibly could. Against the odds, he has kept Ulster Unionists in the game and in the new arrangements. In the last weeks of 2001, with a challenge for the leadership possible in the March 2002 fixed annual meeting of the party Council, he was relaxed enough to talk about the possible extension of the remit of North/South bodies. This was progressing nicely, he said, thanks to careful negotiation of their powers. It might be time now to loosen the restrictions. When

Paisley's party lashed him for proposing stronger links, a swift Ulster Unionist statement denied there was any such intent.

Fussiness and anxiety about remaining in control are not the most likeable qualities, but hardly surprising in a man for ever running at full tilt to stay on top of a spinning world. David Trimble represents people who find little joy in what he agreed on their behalf, and his awkward personality has too often seemed the perfect reflection of dysfunctional present-day unionism. 'Still unloved', a Trimble aide lamented recently of unionists. 'You could almost feel sorry for Trimble,' said the sympathetic observer. 'But he's a hard man to like.'

There is also a positive perspective, always true in this process. Trimble exasperated many people during the pre-Agreement talks, including some in his own delegation. Even at his most irritating, another point had to be made about him; four years later it was still true. 'Bit by bit, with a lot of pressure, he's moved in the right direction. And he's still in there.'

IN SEARCH OF IDENTITY

Many Protestants and most unionist politicians are still struggling to regain their balance, their world-view tipped off its axis. Contemplating the IRA governing Northern Ireland, in the person of Martin McGuinness, is bound to be a lasting shock to individuals and to an entire community who have yet to look hard at themselves and the course of recent history. As one reporter who witnessed all but the first years says, 'They didn't know why the Troubles started, and they don't know why it stopped.' Or as another puts it, an exhausted outsider waiting impatiently now to sign off on the story: 'Oh, God, have we got to wait 20 years now for the Prods to catch up? Look how long it took the Provos to catch on that killing people wasn't the way to unite Ireland.'

To this way of thinking, unionist fixation on the IRA is not just a natural, human reaction to what looks like a victory for ruthless enemies, facilitated at every turn by the British government in liaison with the government of the south. It also represents a failure of political intelligence and a refusal to face facts. The problem the unionist community faces is that this unkind assessment is widely shared among the media, foreign academics, opinion-formers in London and Washington, politicians and political advisers to the three governments, British, Irish and American. Where some hold back from saying it directly because they fear being accused of partiality, they whisper it behind hands, an even less respectful approach.

This might seem unfair, given that 'the Provos' have moved smoothly into political power, negotiated a substantial amnesty along the way and are still demanding satisfaction for a whole range of alleged security force misdeeds. It certainly seems unfair to many Protestants that the world prefers the story Catholic nationalists tell, that being unionist, Protestant, is seen as being intransigent, bigoted, politically inept, supremacist in past times, grudging about the changed present. An entire community is lumped into one political grouping. This is not true of me, say individual Protestants. Many who have Catholic colleagues and neighbours insist that they have good relationships with them, and are wounded by being depicted as politically intransigent and inept. Some add that the hostility of this portrait only makes it more likely that liberal unionists will opt out of the effort to build a new political identity. Some Catholics similarly disclaim the label 'nationalist'. Voting patterns suggest that the overwhelming bulk of Catholics vote for the SDLP and Sinn Féin, the majority of Protestants for unionists. No significant number breaks the pattern.

The exhausted 'middle ground' of cross-community politics has failed to produce an alternative to the old blocs. From the tiny and fractured Left comes a thin wail of mourning for their own irrelevance. The 'new' politics, they say, is rigged to perpetuate the sectarian divide. Like the genteel intellectuals of unionism, too delicate to be party activists but too conflicted by their own origins to offer the rigorous criticism unionism needs, they attribute purely sectarian and tribal motives to the makers of the Agreement, and have no practical alternative to suggest.

Conviction that they are harshly judged is a stance that unites unionist hardliners, comparative moderates and individuals now otherwise estranged from the old political family. It is a belief born of refusal to admit publicly what many admit only privately, that unionists are not blameless victims and that the political violence had long and tangled roots.

Some years ago one of the most thoughtful and liberal of the political unionists, Fermanagh man Raymond Ferguson wrote in a review of a book of interviews with border unionists and nationalists, that they contained 'no hint of the hurt and bewilderment felt by a group who still wonder what they did wrong, what great sins they perpetrated that provoked so vicious a backlash from their nationalist neighbours'. Ferguson's point was well made, at least superficially. By far the bulk of killings in Fermanagh have been of Protestants by the IRA, with a negligible rate of detection and arrest. The genocide claim has a resonance there that it lacks elsewhere.

In a thoughtful and low-key way, Ferguson voiced a suspicion and resentment shared by many Protestants. 'How much do nationalists know of the activities of the organisation that likes to regard itself as the "cutting edge" of their community? How much support is tacit, how much active?' Those questions will fester for years, like their equivalents in Catholic nationalist minds. The big difference is that nationalists have found a way to forge on despite unresolved issues, logging them and demanding action but tackling a wider agenda at the same time. Another difference is that nationalists and republicans – in the persons of Hume and Adams – set about changing policies by facing their community with what had worked and what had not: the realities of a brutal and pointless war, the shifting attitudes in Dublin and London.

It was a painful business, which meant that both faced attack and denigration inside and outside their respective political spheres, Hume from as far back as the early '60s when he first argued that the nationalist minority must find a part to play inside Northern Ireland. Though there were no guarantees, and huge obstacles to shift, the dynamism in the nationalist process over recent years has been fed by the belief that progress was possible, the epic tale of mountains already climbed, coming out of the old swamp of despair, and loyalty from their own grass-roots. Each step onward boosted people with real leadership talent and made reverses surmountable.

The picture inside unionism is very different. As the twenty first century begins, unionists as a group have talked themselves into a prolonged bout of self-pity, instead of clinging to the obvious, and consoling themselves that the IRA has turned itself inside out. It is easy to see why Protestants find it hard to face their own community with similarly sharp questions to those posed by Hume and Adams, and why unionist politicians have grown faint at the prospect. It is difficult to present the passage from one-party government to today's shared government with republicans as other than a story of loss, without a touch of visionary eloquence or a dash of magnanimity and humility. Those are not qualities prized in unionist political culture, nor are nationalists noted for their modesty, or republicans for magnanimity.

The most formidable leader unionism has produced is a man whose career was built on the destruction of anyone who proposed compromise and accommodation with nationalism. The complement to Ian Paisley's long dominance is a pervasive political timidity. The communal penalties for proposing that Protestants must deal or perish have been multiple and frightening, involving all the loyalist paramilitary groups at various times. They range from the comparatively mild but debilitating tactic of freezing someone out of the golf club to the systematic scarifying that starts with silent phone calls in the middle of the night, and ends in hoax or real bombs under cars. A sizeable number, including clerics, have been forced out of public life by abuse.

Nationalism too has employed communal sanctions against mavericks or challengers. SDLP-founder-members, Paddy Devlin and Gerry Fitt, even Hume, have suffered republican attacks on their homes and families, mobs shouting abuse outside and, in Fitt's case, bursting into the house. The opposition between 'physical force republicanism' and 'constitutional nationalism', communal respect for both, shared purpose and growing self-confidence have managed nonetheless to sustain an immeasurably more lively and more open political debate than inside unionism.

Both nationalists and unionists in Northern Ireland have to silence a subconscious protest when they accept blame and propose lowering barriers. It takes the form of an imagined outcry from some ancient of the tribe, howling, 'If you admit our faults or tell our gang to put down their guns, you justify attacks on us and leave us defenceless.' In essence, that has been the argument against IRA decommissioning. It is perhaps also the explanation for an odd and disappointing failure in unionist thinking.

Protestants who take strong and unpopular positions are often unwilling to admit the abuse they take, very much like whistle-blowers in any society. These are people effectively blowing the whistle on what their community deems to have been a society largely created in their own image. They often make criticisms that their families and closest friends strongly resent. The extra twist is that many find themselves effectively stranded in terms of political thought and affinity in the camp of the other community, whom they still distrust and perhaps dislike. Few get the credit they deserve from nationalists, sometimes out of the knowledge that praise from nationalists will only make their lives harder, more often from sheer lack of generosity and imagination.

The former Ulster Unionist MP Ken Maginnis has consistently denounced loyalist violence with a forthrightness none of his former colleagues shared, usually a nationalist benchmark of non-sectarianism. But because of other statements he has made, often intemperate and even insulting because he was an outspoken defender and former member of the Ulster Defence Regiment, and before that of the B Specials, the unequivocal nature of his condemnation was not a quality many nationalists were disposed to praise. Nor did many seem to have regard for the well-known fact that he had been repeatedly targeted by the IRA. At one point upward of 12 IRA suspects had been either questioned or charged with attempts to kill him.

Sir Bob Cooper has yet to write a memoir but could certainly provide a vivid picture of the huge shifts over the past 40 years. A crusading O'Neillite young unionist first, he gave up on the old party and joined Alliance, then took another step away from the past essentially to police unionist misbehaviour, by heading the anti-discrimination machinery set up in the late '70s. The very concept of compulsory 'fair employment' fired unionist resentment from the outset. As late as 1994, Ian Paisley's deputy Peter Robinson was accusing the Fair Employment Commission, successor to the initial Fair Employment Agency, of trying to make life 'economically difficult' for Protestants who wanted to stay in Northern Ireland. This was an attempt at ethnic cleansing, he said. In the brisk, dismissive style Cooper patented, the Commission said the claim was unworthy of comment. In speeches, in newspaper letters pages, on radio, by Ian Paisley from the pulpit of the Martyrs Memorial, Cooper was described in often scurrilous terms as a lackey of British policy and of nationalism.

Those who have taken high-profile roles in structures set up to implement the Agreement or in enterprises that flow from it include the former Presbyterian Moderator Dr John Dunlop, the senior Ulster Unionist Peter Smyth, a QC, and the academic Dr Desmond Rea. John Dunlop sat on the North Commission, the body set up to find a way of dealing with contentious Orange Order and other marches, Peter Smyth on the Patten commission, which proposed the transformation of the RUC into the Police Service for Northern Ireland. Desmond Rea now chairs the new Policing Board.

These are all people with rare qualities of determination and self-assurance. They stand out from a class and a social world which prefers to stay well away from the difficulty that political involvement inevitably brings any unionist, the necessity to admit the need for reform. Middle unionism has as little as possible to do with politics. They vote, but in steadily falling numbers. Many mock the leaders of the two main unionist parties or silently disdain them as extremist – they failed to write or phone in sufficient numbers with encouragement when David Trimble decided to go into government with Sinn Féin. The affluent middle-aged discourage their well-educated children from becoming politically active. The result is disastrous. The most visible of contemporary Protestant unionist behaviour does not fit with the self-portrait of an innocent and misunderstood people. Unionists are still paying the price for past faults, because most others do not believe their self-image of injured innocence.

A prime example has been television film of Catholic schoolgirls as young as four spat at and cursed by adults who say their grievance is that they are intimidated by republicans. Rumbling through 2001 into 2002, the Holy Cross school affair did more damage to Protestants as a community than many seemed to realise. A composite picture over months lacked any shades of grey to the outside world. Instead it showed brutish Protestants pitted against inoffensive Catholics: on one side small weeping children, a gentle-sounding and magnanimous priest spokesman, strained mothers, harassed by thugs shouting sectarian abuse like 'Fenian whore' and throwing balloons filled with urine and dog dirt. Local Protestants no doubt had genuine grievances about the behaviour of the larger number of Catholics surrounding them. Only the oddest mentality could have imagined that making small girls cry on their first day at school would do anything but shame Protestants as a whole.

But the communal unionist reaction was defensive and aggrieved rationalisation rather than unambiguous disgust. 'There are two victimised communities here,' wrote an elderly and conservative columnist in the *Belfast Telegraph*. Other columnists complained that the media ignored 'republican manipulation' of much sectarian violence. An editorial which made a straightforward appeal for an end to the 'protest' against the schoolchildren and their parents was followed by several much less clear-cut.

The paper is a good barometer of 'middle unionism', the band of Protestant opinion which considers itself moderate and imagines this description is accepted by Catholics. To judge from letters pages, columnists and the predominant tone of editorials, *Telegraph* readers and many of its writers massively resent nationalist/Catholic advances, not an attitude Catholics regard as moderate. The masthead proclaims the *Telegraph* 'the National paper of Northern Ireland', a concept which immediately alienates those who recognise no such 'nation'.

In ways the paper is a mini-version of other former bastions of the unionist establishment, acclimatising too slowly to a new world order: Queen's University, Belfast and the civil service. In all three cases the original stance was 'Who, us? It's offensive to call us unionist-dominated. We're not political in any way. No idea what you're talking about. We don't even ask our employees their religion so we can't say if we employ fairly.' In the case of Queen's and the civil service, rigorous official monitoring showed up serious imbalances. Queen's buckled and accepted their responsibilities only when Bob Cooper turned over the stone to expose many unpleasant truths, and a spate of cases forced them to pay considerable damages to aggrieved employees, and when their student body became majority Catholic.

The civil service has been turned around in part because successive British governments realised that as ultimate employer they must show an example. Monitoring and remedial action has changed the public face of the service. Having always denied that discrimination against Catholics existed, the unionist response to these changes has been to run a tireless campaign claiming that the emergence of Catholics in greater numbers especially at higher levels means that Protestants now suffer discrimination.

Unionist political reaction to Holy Cross mirrored that displayed by the *Belfast Telegraph*: confused, angry, disposed to blame republicans and at least by implication to play down the behaviour of the Protestant

Glenbryn residents. As with the Orange marches at Drumcree, the rest of unionism failed to send a clear message of disapproval. The resulting mess showed an entire political class in a highly unflattering light, a community casting around to shift or diffuse blame.

A series of Protestant clergymen made contact with the priest who chaired the Holy Cross governors to offer support but seemed unable to influence the behaviour of the protesters. Lord Mayor of Belfast Jim Rogers, a lightweight minor Ulster Unionist, arrived to 'do what he could to help restore order' and almost immediately lodged a formal complaint that police had jostled him. On the day that a pipe bomb, just off camera, was thrown towards the police lines beyond which the children and parents were walking to school, injuring a police officer, the loyalist fringe party spokesman Billy Hutchinson made an immediate emotional response. 'I'm ashamed to be Protestant,' he said into the cameras, 'that anyone could do this to little girls.' He would now re-examine his involvement, he said. It was the rarest and most striking of moments, bringing sad head-shaking from those who had admired Hutchinson's and his party's bravery in the past but who knew he was now essentially on his own in a very vulnerable position. Within hours the communal imperative had squeezed him back into place and he announced continuing support for the Glenbryn residents again on camera.

Answering questions from the trouble spot, newly elected DUP MP for the area Nigel Dodds clearly wished himself miles away, though he had allowed himself be filmed near the noisy protesters chatting to leading UDA figure John White. Unsurprisingly intent from the start on showing sympathy for Glenbryn, and adamant that there had been republican provocation, Dodds did seem primarily keen to end the incidents. Speaking of his efforts to broker peace with the chairman of the Holy Cross school governors, Father Troy, though, he repeatedly called him Mr Troy rather than Father, a title fundamentalist Protestantism abhors for priests. Perhaps the habits of a lifetime were just too strong.

'I had no idea there are people who won't call priests by the name they call themselves; it amazes me,' one academic said privately. The DUP man's language instantly offended Catholics and struck a number of Protestant listeners as 'outlandish'. Another, again new to the idea, called it 'grotesque bigotry'. Few Catholics by contrast voiced any surprise. It apparently took a direct question from a radio interviewer some time later to make Nigel Dodds reflect on what he had said. But change he did, on air and on the hoof, with no defence of his previous practice: 'I have no difficulty in saying [pause] Father Troy.' It was an example of the possibility of movement from the most hardline figures, a small light in the Holy Cross darkness.

The affair did considerable damage to Protestant credibility and perhaps to their self-respect. A senior British source talked angrily later about the effect on the IRA, at one stage under considerable international and domestic pressure to start decommissioning because of the Colombian arrests of republicans emerging from FARC guerrilla territory. 'It just banjaxed everything. Holy Cross let them off the hook.' But he was more appalled by the Glenbryn spokespeople. 'You try to understand their grievances and their fears but you have to tell them how this looks to the world. And do you know what they say? They don't care!'

Arguably, although working-class loyalists appeared thuggish and moronic, the more damaging message to nationalists and outsiders was that polite unionism could not face up to Holy Cross. The disarray of the politicians and church figures on the scene accurately reflected public opinion, torn but defensive rather than apologetic and openly ashamed. It also reflected a community which is as socially splintered as its politics. Many middle-class Protestants are horrified when forced to contemplate working-class loyalists, but as a group, with honourable exceptions, they are generally unwilling to take the risks and trouble involved in trying to win them away from violence. There are fewer useful cross-class family links than among Catholics. The Protestant middle class is bigger and longer established; it therefore has less sense of obligation to abandoned roots and much more sense of social distance.

Insistence by unionists that the world should recognise the IRA as the prime villain of the piece, against blatant evidence of active anti-Catholic bigotry and loyalist violence, has paradoxically helped the IRA's political voice to re-create itself in the public mind, particularly abroad.

Unionist politicians still maintain in public that they think Martin McGuinness has not changed his spots, that republicans are 'ministers by day and terrorists by night'. Yet in private they say no such thing. On the contrary, many leading figures in conversation with non-unionists, though rarely in the presence of journalists, agree that they think 'Adams and McGuinness are for real'. In public and on the record, the conviction fails to come across. A picture of continued doubt, fear and mistrust is purveyed instead, a fiction which serves to keep mistrust alive in the audience. Even those who have thrown in their lot with the daytime ministers slip from civil to offensive without apparent hesitation, as in David Trimble's aside that the Sinn Féin ministers 'need to be house-trained'. It is a pattern of presentation and behaviour that has damaged unionists internationally, spoiled their relationship with many in the media and, most importantly, limited their own chances of finding a healthy way forward. Ambivalence towards loyalist violence puts the icing on it.

IRA violence has faded away, at least in comparative terms, over a period during which loyalist paramilitaries have continued to kill and bomb. But the fact that for almost a decade loyalists have been killing more than the IRA apparently makes few Protestants consider the pressing need to bring loyalist paramilitaries into politics and away from violence. In Catholic nationalist minds, unionists are hypocritical when they keep on demanding that the IRA disarm and disband while saying little or nothing about loyalists, or when they announce that both sides must stop violence because 'one is as bad as the other'. Many unionists seem genuinely not to be aware of the hypocrisy.

If anything, the peace process, a process which many see as republicans' way to achieve their objectives by other means, might have intensified the unionist sense of being under attack. Now the enemy truly is everywhere, most gallingly in government departments and the devolved administration at Stormont, the centre of long-vanished unionist power.

In private, many leading unionists will admit they are less baffled about the offence unionism has caused. A prominent figure once volunteered that he had spent an evening coaxing a friend to admit the 'gross way her home town of Derry was gerrymandered', before the two of them discussed it at length. In public or on the record, neither of them would call the city Derry, much less admit the past. 'You daren't. You never recover from that sort of thing.' Even in private, some will at one moment confess that long ago they recognised how unequal the treatment of Catholics was under unionist rule, then contradict themselves moments later.

There probably was a siege mentality, the admission goes, a form of one-party rule that was inevitable but perhaps led to some unfairness. The retraction tends to be prefaced with an impassioned attack on the corruption and church domination of the Republic, the old-fashioned Catholicism that frightened Protestants into behaving badly. One of the more unlikely defences is that unionists behaved badly because nationalists failed to provide an effective opposition. In most unionist accounts of how the Troubles began, a warm-toned preface runs: 'The whole of society was getting on very well in the '60s. And then . . .'

In comes the devious John Hume, more dangerous than violent republicans because more subtle, or the Trojan horse of a bogus civil rights agitation concealing the ancient enemy, the IRA. The Progressive Unionist leader David Ervine, Billy Hutchinson's colleague, is unique in his frankness: 'We treated Catholics badly and nearly lost the state,' he says. His party has not prospered for many reasons, but willingness to apportion blame to unionism made him and his party few Protestant allies and many enemies. The general unionist disposition is to blame nationalists and then Britain for much of their woes, never themselves. Many must know that the pitch is counter-productive.

One of the most galling effects, again admitted by some off the record, is that constant unsympathetic complaint obscures the genuine loss and pain suffered by the Protestant unionist community. The IRA killed many; the chronicle *Lost Lives* lists 832 Protestant victims, 358 civilians, the others members of the security forces. It might not be at all surprising that Sinn Féin leaders attempt to sweep over all mention of the IRA's victims with a blithe 'we have all suffered, we have caused pain but we have our victims too'. It is equally unsurprising that this makes many Protestants burn with rage and an overpowering sense of injustice.

Some of the bereaved, relatives of police, soldiers or prison officers, feel betrayed by British governments and embittered by the conviction that theirs was a futile sacrifice. Some show almost supernatural generosity, expressing genuine forgiveness and urging reconciliation. Many suffer silently. Over the years reporters have been struck by the comparison between the sense of silent, almost secret mourning in many RUC and UDR funerals and the formalised but highly charged rites of IRA funerals, visibly and assertively part of their community as well as a skilled propaganda exercise.

In a small rural graveyard many years ago, the media covering the funeral of a Protestant civilian killed by republicans, one of three shot dead in the little church at Darkley, County Armagh, watched with awe as mourners turned the ceremony into a joyful celebration of the dead man's life and 'witness to God', with hymns and spontaneous eulogies. One of the most experienced among us commented that it was all very 'un-Protestant', though of course the language and style was thoroughly biblical. He meant the expressiveness, the outwardness. Like others present, he thought much Protestant mourning during the Troubles had been shut away in private, apparently almost wordless. Though many Catholic families have also been crushed into silence by grief and the relatives of those killed by soldiers or police often say they are disregarded, we agreed then Catholic/nationalist grief had a more public and certainly a more communal dimension than that of many Protestants. The long-running Saville inquiry into Bloody Sunday, the occasion when British soldiers shot and killed 14 people in Derry in 1972, was still years ahead.

Four years on from the Agreement, a culture of unionist complaint and depression sits opposite nationalist confidence. The contrast is sharp, a splintered political community on the one side with a leadership torn by mutual dislike and mistrust, up against a buoyant people, well led, though paradoxically divided down the middle between Sinn Féin and SDLP supporters. But the divide is only into two, not into a dozen pieces like unionism, and has produced more useful debate than weakness. Disconsolate unionists, convinced the momentum is all downhill, face nationalists who believe more improvements are necessary and inevitable.

Over time it has often been difficult to distinguish pro-Agreement unionists from antis – partly because the bulk of the antis were so firmly inside the tent, though still carping, but also because from the start some pros had sounded such hostile notes. Business and church leaders weighed in early to boost the Agreement and drum up support for the referendum that gave it communal validation. They were reviled by anti-Agreement politicians and held at arm's length by the rest. The narrow pro-Agreement unionist majority daunted the cheerleaders, and their efforts since have been almost as fitful as David Trimble's positiveness. As the programme of implementation revealed the series of 'concessions' to nationalism, business has fallen silent and church leaders have sounded confused and at cross-purposes. Off the record, many admit that their biggest worry is about the violence of loyalist paramilitaries. A few admit that the level of sectarian hatred in their own community frightens them. 'I don't think you realise what's out there,' one said a few years ago.

The series of confrontations between Orange marchers at Drumcree, outside Portadown, blocked by police from parading past Catholic residents, shook clerics in all the main churches. Some were belatedly stricken by the realisation that they had been providing chaplains to the Orange Order for more than a century, many of whom had been in the habit of making fiery anti-nationalist and sometimes anti-Catholic speeches from Twelfth of July platforms. Others were discouraged into silence by substantial Orange contingents in their congregations.

One ecumenically minded cleric eyed his fellows with coldness after the disastrous 1996 Twelfth, when the RUC and Northern Secretary Sir Patrick Mayhew agreed on a U-turn to force a march past Garvaghy Road Catholics after widespread loyalist violence. 'There's real distancing going on,' he said. He foresaw resignations from lodges, though not swiftly. 'There will be a slow critique,' he said dryly. 'People say we have let ourselves down a bagful.' One Orange chaplain volunteered that he and other older members felt it had all been 'an absolute disgrace'.

When the second IRA ceasefire took hold in 1997, some of the most public-spirited Protestant clergy launched themselves into an attempt to bring about decommissioning. Several had been involved for years in building contacts across the lines, hosting discussions. A group met leading republicans repeatedly as the pressure on David Trimble focused round the demand for decommissioning. They kept trying, despite what some of them began to consider a clash of cultures. Republicans made little of their arguments and appeared to think that unionists had no genuine feelings about decommissioning. It need not be a large initial gesture, one said, but a gesture must be made. 'It's just the test, what proves that they're for real. Otherwise unionists will think it's all a con.' Everything else, he maintained, was unimportant. He had begun to wonder if republicans were willing to let David Trimble be destroyed. Did they not realise that Trimble genuinely supported the Agreement?

Some months before the start of decommissioning in October 2001, the clergyman said sadly: 'We go back and forth fairly often but don't feel we've got anywhere. A lorry load of cement poured into those bunkers, they're already compromised, what's stopping them? It would mean so much, it would change everything.'

It failed to change anything much, certainly not immediately. Perhaps the trouble was that it was invisible. There were no live reports from the scene, not even film. The IRA terms had always been that they would deal with the Canadian general and his commission alone, and that the form of decommissioning agreed between them would require no public performance that could be construed as a form of surrender. David Trimble's initial positive response became muted within days, as criticism of what was alleged to be an IRA con job poured in from dissidents in his own party and the DUP. Support for Trimble in the subsequent meeting of the Ulster Unionists' supposedly policy-making Council went up from 53 per cent to 56 per cent, which, as one glum analyst noted, 'means that one and half per cent changed their minds because of it. That'd cheer you up, wouldn't it?'

Initially, the underwhelmed response from unionists across the board drained the little surge of new optimism from the atmosphere. Gradually, unionists seemed to absorb as fact that whatever de Chastelain had witnessed, republicans' refusal to decommission had indeed disappeared. A slow coming to terms is a familiar unionist reaction to each hotly contested reform so far. The issue of decommissioning lost some of its power to sharpen mutual mistrust, but the demand, and the eventual IRA response, uncomfortably resembled the caricature versions of each other both communities harbour. Stiff-necked, self-righteous Protestants wanted proper penitence with evidence, not words; smooth-talking dishonest Catholics delivered a pretence that fooled foreigners but not their hard-headed neighbours. Behaviour on both sides fed anxiety that the process cannot expect any easy passages. On the other hand, the more scholarly commentators on republicanism were convinced.

A start to IRA decommissioning was a singular leap forward, they said, signifying real commitment to peace, and would over time contribute to political stability by reducing pressure on David Trimble. The downside for Trimble was diminished sympathy in London and Dublin, in spite of intense awareness of the growing threat that Ian Paisley's DUP poses to pro-Agreement unionism. Pursuit of decommissioning in itself might not have damaged him, though it had been fairly clear from April 1998 on that neither government was passionate about pursuing it. But hostility to the underlying thrust of the Agreement inside the leadership of supposedly pro-Agreement unionism crystallised in front of both governments, in the early summer of 2001.

In negotiations at the stately home of Weston Park, which produced the package foreshadowing police reform, demilitarisation and a real move by the IRA, the unionist agenda shocked both British and Irish officials. 'It's not much of an argument to say that you don't like equality and you don't want police reform,' one noted. 'And it's not the best negotiating tactic in the world to come in telling everyone else there's only item on the agenda, decommissioning. Then we discovered that after all this time Trimble and company want to tear up policing reform.'

The analysis of politically tone-deaf unionists, undermined by an inability to hear themselves as outsiders do, has held since first Northern Ireland drew international attention in 1968. Changes made on foot in response to Catholic/nationalist complaint, no matter how well-founded many of these appeared to the world, have been routinely characterised as 'concessions to terrorism' by politicians and spokespeople across the range of Protestant/unionist opinion. The peace process was always 'alleged' or 'so-called'. Unionists initially pronounced the words with a wrapping of audible contempt, like verbal barbed wire. But they misread the mood on the ground. Although the republican and subsequent loyalist ceasefires produced no euphoria, they did gradually diffuse a sense of communal relief and relaxation. Those most derogatory about the 'so-called, alleged peace process' in time softened the harshness of their references, clearly at the suggestion of their grass-roots or with their approval. Several began to preface their criticism with careful assurances that, of course, they too wanted peace.

It has been a long, slow verbal adjustment, almost certainly some way ahead of adjustment in hearts and minds. Refusal to countenance reform runs deep. As the Agreement laboured towards its fourth anniversary in April 2002, supposedly pro-Agreement unionists were still opposing the policing reforms, still trying to fend off or dilute the introduction of human rights legislation and an overhaul of the criminal justice system.

Policing has been the most emotive and divisive issue, with long-running denunciation for proposals drafted originally by a commission set up under former Tory minister Chris Patten: the reforms are lumped together as 'Patten' in unionist criticism. Wholesale change to the Royal Ulster Constabulary, especially dropping the name for a deliberately neutral 'Police Service of Northern Ireland', unionists argued, was an insult to the 303 officers killed, almost all by republicans. The form of that change, they further argued, diminished their British identity.

In many minds, though rarely so frankly expressed, remaking the RUC as part of a peace process came uncomfortably close to awarding republicans victory in the undeclared war. Admitting the necessity of reform would validate nationalist and republican complaints against a police force always described by unionists, and by successive British governments, as the thin line of law and order between society and anarchy, without fault save for 'a few bad apples'. But in what some observers saw, even through irritation, as a response so unpolitical as to be pathetic, unionists rallied round the symbolism of the RUC: the title, the cap badge.

In Westminster, David Trimble's supporters in the House of Lords fought the programme for 50/50 Protestant/Catholic recruitment to the made-over Police Service, designed to eventually produce an even balance from what had been a 93 per cent Protestant RUC. Of course, said unionists, they wanted to see Catholics joining the police in considerable numbers, but the plan to recruit a Catholic for every Protestant was discriminatory and they could not be party to that. The argument sounded particularly hollow given that the recruiting age cohort is 50/50 Catholic/Protestant.

A lobby correspondent described the reaction to this particular stand among those who knew little about Northern Ireland. 'People rolled their eyes. One old guy said to me "If they still can't see that opposing proposals to even up a Protestant police force just sounds wrong, then they're stupider than I thought."'

The peace process brought a long catalogue of offence in its wake. In many Protestant eyes, the IRA ceasefire was hard-won by a deal with republicans, which produced endless 'concessions'. Ranking these in order of offensiveness has always been difficult. Perhaps the truth is that all have offended to an indistinguishable degree: Sinn Féin ministers sharing power at Stormont with unionists, particularly the former IRA leader Martin McGuinness in charge of education; the accelerated release scheme which freed hundreds of paramilitary prisoners; the amnesty for 'On the Runs', OTRs, most of them republican fugitives who fled ahead of arrest; proposals to reduce the flying of the Union flag and to strip courtrooms and court procedure of royal insignia and references to the Queen. So much offence: the Protestant community at times seemed in shock.

Because policing touches so many sensitivities, 'Patten' came to stand for everything that was outrageous in the new dispensation, a systematic assault on political and cultural identity inspired by the now triumphant and triumphalist murderers of the IRA. 'Policing for many Protestants just became the lightning conductor for all the rest,' says one academic monitor of the process. 'It's not that it's really the biggest grievance.'

Conviction that they are under attack as a political community unites people across a wide spectrum, though only against critics. Internally, the splintering continues. Six parties represent unionists inside the Stormont assembly, and the largest one has several distinct factions. As unionism steadily becomes more fractured, it is as if totems of the past develop more value and must be defended more stridently. The phalanx of angry defensiveness mustered around recurring contentious issues – marches, symbols, the meaning of loyalist violence – includes some who do not count themselves unionist, dislike unionist politicians, perhaps do not vote.

They may not want to march themselves, but they do not like Catholics, especially those they have convinced themselves are 'Provos', telling Orangemen where they may march and where they may not. Some certainly realised that at Drumcree unionism was diminished by its own central ritual to nothing more than insistence on marching past furious Catholics. The point was once put to Trimble at a semi-social gathering of politicians and media. Why did he not tell the Orangemen how much they damaged unionism, he was asked. He responded mildly enough: 'And if I did, would you find me another party to lead?' Condemnation of the marching phenomenon from outsiders stung, especially from Britain. Yet to judge by public reaction on the street, in phone-in programmes and newspaper letters pages, many Protestants defended marches in part because they resented the critics so much.

When pushed, some non-Orange Protestants say they are concerned about cultural rights. From people who stay well away from the booze and squalor of Eleventh Night bonfires and watch the parades from a sedate stretch of footpath in South Belfast or on television, this defence of cultural identity is unconvincing. One observer who has charted controversies over marches throughout the Troubles thinks Drumcree has 'finished off any case for Orangeism as a major part of Protestant culture'.

A dire pattern emerges of serial last stands, each selected less wisely than the one before. Drumcree, originally a platform of resurgence and reassertion, looks defeated and humiliated. What was billed as the start of the fight-back has taken its place, like the struggle for the RUC title, among the symbols of loss. At least in 1995 some of the world saw Drumcree as a battle of competing rights. It was an arguable case, but the Orangemen lost the argument. The hostile picket of the Harryville Catholic church in Ballymena had nothing to commend it, except that somehow the world scarcely noticed. Holy Cross could never have been anything but disastrous for Protestants, 100 per cent loss from the word go. This time there was no argument, no 'on the one hand and on the other', except from the silliest and least persuasive of muddled minds. Given apparent determination to keep on attacking the concepts of human rights and equality, it has begun to look as though unionists have become determined followers of lost causes, disciples of self-destruction.

Many Protestants still believe that the republican agenda is clear – and here they are joined by some Catholics – that republicans are pushing to erase signs of Britishness from public life in Northern Ireland, that 'Ulster' is being Catholicised, Irishised. But the successive Drumcree spectacles were a nasty shock. Complaints about television coverage, and to radio phone-in programmes, came from many who called themselves Protestant and said they were repelled by the entire marching phenomenon. It was as though they had only just seen it. Revulsion did not produce a new wave of articulate moderates. There was no influx of impatient sympathy for the peace process and the painful necessity of reform to give David Trimble's crabwise progress new momentum.

There is a market instead for anti-politics, for know-nothingism, similar in some ways to the old, sterile negativity of nationalists, always a part of Protestant society but one that the end of wholesale conflict might have been expected to reverse. When politics became less dangerous, surely the timid and unpolitical might have discovered their civic duty? In the new era, the *Belfast Telegraph*'s response has been to give space to columns of considerable banality with the general theme of 'plague on both their houses, one's as bad as the other, doesn't politics make you sick'. The BBC has invested heavily in a locally produced comedy series with the title *Give My Head Peace*, fondly parodying rather than satirising sectarianism.

Paisley's drift into an unacknowledged, graceless and often ill-tempered participation in the Agreement's structures mirrors a wider mood in unionism, no longer able to watch at an ambivalent distance the mayhem perpetrated in their names by Protestant paramilitaries. The process has put Paisley and his relationship to the community he comes from under a spotlight which flatters neither. Loyalist violence has gone through various phases since the Agreement. Internal feuding soaks up considerable energy, as does criminality, and the majority of those killed by loyalists are other loyalists. It long ago became clear that no concerted and effective paramilitary onslaught on the peace process would emerge. After the brief bright promise of the Progressive Unionists and a flicker or two of political thinking from the UDA, much of the loyalist paramilitary world has lapsed back into gangsterism and chaos.

A clash of expectations has by and large succeeded the clash of weapons, though for isolated Catholics in Protestant towns or districts and across the peacelines of North Belfast, the static of low-level but widespread violence continues to crackle. The British government response has been slow, confused, but mainly intent on inserting the new devolved Stormont government into the breach. The two main local communities, the theme goes, must take responsibility for their own bad relationship. A basic imbalance makes that unlikely. Unionists have failed to take responsibility for their own political welfare, preferring self-pity and the pleasure of blaming others. Resentment of nationalism has been a costly waste of time and energy.

The victory for republicans has been to make defeat look like triumph. Unionists have helped them enormously, by complaining every step of the way that each republican advance was a 'concession', a diminution of Britishness, a defeat for unionists. Even the unhappiest republican supporters, watching their leaders advancing into Stormont and taking seats in the parliament of a partitioned Northern Ireland, began to realise that they were in the process of changing the place and the political system. The secret weapon was self-belief, borne aloft with commitment to just enough of the old republican theology to maintain distinctiveness. Republicans' insistence on an honoured place for Irish in the new dispensation irritates many other nationalists and induces rage in unionists. But it is a potent symbol, which instantly and permanently changes the Stormont atmosphere far more pervasively than any flag.

As they jib at Bairbre de Brún's fluency in Irish, some unionists must have the occasional uneasy secret thought. Beside the two skilled Irish translators in Stormont sits another functionary, there to provide services in another language, Ulster Scots. There are few calls on his services, since the language does not exist. When respectful treatment and support for Irish was stitched into the Agreement, Ulster Unionist negotiators insisted on parity of esteem: for Ulster Scots, at best a lively and colourful dialect in most linguists' estimate, not a fully formed language. The outcome is a farce, blinked at in public by many nationalists attached to the conservation of Irish.

Easily the most laughable aspect of the Agreement's implementation has been the financial and administrative support for Ulster Scots. Many Protestants, including some senior Unionists, are embarrassed by official approval for a recent invention which is supposed to be a vital part of their identity. They say little, even when advertisements appear in all the local papers in three versions: English, Irish and Ulster Scots. The new Equality Agency tried this strained silence to the utmost when its initial recruitment campaign began. Equality translated as 'Eeksie-Peeksie'.

A starting point for unionists in the quest for a political analysis built on realism and honesty might be the quiet abandonment of their own most recently acquired theological dogma. Republicans have prospered by shedding dogma cheerfully. Unionists could let Ulster Scots go, as wordlessly as it arrived. Self-respect is surely essential to any sense of identity.

5

DEMOGRAPHY, SEPARATION, FEAR AND LOATHING

Inside Northern Ireland, many people are as far apart as ever, the places they live in and their mindsets as separate. Where they live side-by-side, 'mixing' more often than not is artificial, constrained. Apart from pockets of resolutely integrationist non-conformism, principally those in 'mixed marriages', conversation and social contact across the political and religious divide are made careful and superficial by the knowledge of deep and potentially fractious difference.

In spite of the existence for the first time of a power-sharing government representing hardline opinion among both nationalists and unionists, reconciliation is still spoken of only in whispers, as a distant and desirable vision. The Protestant majority is slender to vanishing point; the power of demography has a new pull, and the whole question of numbers has become electric. It does not and will not make for easier community relations.

Where once the demographic balance convinced Catholics that political organisation for nationalism was pointless against an overwhelming unionist veto, many now see a different prospect ever more clearly. There may never be a Catholic majority: then again there may be, and inside the next decade. The largely segregated school-age population is already more Catholic than Protestant. Statistics for 2001 showed 173,000 Catholic schoolchildren, 146,000 Protestants, 22,000 others. In another few years the Protestant majority may have gone. An unaligned sector is slowly growing and may account for 4 per cent of the total: Chinese and Indian communities, plus a number who class themselves as neither Catholic nor Protestant, some the children of mixed marriages. Add to that a Catholic community that probably now makes up 46 per cent at least of the total population, and the Protestant share falls to 50 per cent.

Increasing convergence in the size of the two groups is at least as likely to heighten tensions as to resolve them. The signs are that increased tension will bear most heavily on Catholic individuals, at least where they live in small communities. But beyond the guarantee that Northern Ireland stays in the UK while a majority wishes it, a Protestant, unionist majority will never again dictate the shape of Northern Ireland's politics, and both communities know it. That is the message the Blair government delivered by opting for the Good Friday Agreement and the peace process. Unionists are still struggling with the message, their political leaders pretending that they signed a different Agreement.

On a miserably wet day in January 2002, thousands turned out for rallies throughout Northern Ireland to protest against the loyalist killing of a young Catholic postman in North Belfast, and against all violence in the name of politics. Tacit agreement between the trade unions and politicians kept the politicians off the platforms, because their presence would have destroyed the effect of unity. It would also have underlined the absence of some unionist ministers, and the presence of the two republican ministers might have brought boos rather than cheers from parts of the crowd. Unionist feelings were torn about the protest. 'It's a segregated rally,' one of the organisers admitted later. 'There are people who won't stand near other people and others won't come. What they say is why were there no rallies for Protestants killed by the IRA? Why now?'

Ulster Unionist Sir Reg Empey found a more graceful formula at Belfast's City Hall, when asked why his party leader David Trimble and the SDLP leader Mark Durkan, near him in the crowd, were not on the platform as First and Deputy First Ministers of the Executive: 'The strength of this,' he said, 'is that it's not led by politicians. We have baggage, we have pasts, we have made mistakes.' It was a deft side-step, the sort of remark that makes some think Empey, pragmatic and business-minded, might make a better job of selling change than Trimble. The presence of Trimble in the crowd did something to restore stubbornly optimistic observers, jarred originally to learn that only sustained persuasion had got him there. The DUP's two ministers stayed away but in another frail sign of progress, the party issued no denunciation of the rallies. Peter Robinson and Nigel Dodds instead made carefully bland remarks about ministerial duties: Dodds expressed recognition that others wanted to protest.

No one could have supposed that any peace process in the short term would substantially undo the segregation of decades and replace it with visibly developing harmony. The hope behind the Agreement is at best that if the new style of government takes root and the soil around it is not poisoned by the dregs of violence, then inside and outside politics in time people might begin to trust each other. In turn, that might lead them to live together. It is a modest hope, born of daunting experience.

The argument has to struggle against the risks and damage inherent in continuing friction between people trapped at the sharpest points of the divide. Sectarian clashes date back to the seventeenth century, long pre-dating the foundation of Northern Ireland. For the entire history of both communities, Protestants and Catholics in the north of the island have lived separately for the most part, though often in groups, side by side and with civility. Unguarded everyday speech reveals more than people might sometimes wish. 'That's one black hole,' a Catholic will say, pointing to some tiny village with a population almost 100 per cent Protestant. 'There's wee nest of Fenians over there,' a Protestant will say, pointing to a rural district almost 100 per cent Catholic. Neither, of course, would say any such thing to a member of the other religion: that would be bad manners, like open argument about the affairs of the day.

When it comes to how and where people live and what their living patterns say about their relationship, there is nothing new under the sun. The segregation of most of Northern Ireland is periodically rediscovered by academics and statisticians, but many live with it resignedly, sometimes almost unthinkingly, as a legacy of history. For many, indeed, it is desirable. There is genuine danger in 'mixing'.

In areas where Protestants have lost dominance, Catholics in the past few years have come under more frequent attack. There have also been more attacks in areas where Protestants still dominate, but where Catholic numbers have increased. The link, in some minds, is the general picture: that Catholics have increased in number in proportion to Protestants, while prospering economically and politically.

Mutual suspicion and the wish to preserve distinctiveness are the preservatives of segregation.

The real fear for many is that mixing means assimilation. The loudest voices in each of the two main groups have always told the weakest that they risk destruction from 'the other side', destruction meaning loss of identity. Some in the rural and urban borderlands, the most undesirable and dangerous places, have always lashed out at the nearest 'others'. The term 'sectarian' is used as an umbrella for this behaviour, though a word which originally meant bitter theological difference between small sects hardly seems adequate to carry the freight of bitterness about competition for territory and political dominance.

Peacelines of one kind or another, physical or mental, have been drawn and redrawn over centuries as political arrangements are made and remade. Violence routinely accompanies the draughtsmanship. The Good Friday Agreement in the eyes of both communities largely recast the arrangement since partition and the formation of a unionist state: like most such paper deals, in essence it reflected an already recognised reality. Even before it, Protestants increasingly felt that Northern Ireland was no longer a unionist place. They saw it all around them, in the shape of more, insistently visible, high-profile Catholics. Control had gone; power had gone. How could they share power, their political representatives pleaded, when they no longer had any? Refusal to negotiate in any meaningful way with moderate nationalism merely sped the process along, and widened it. The Agreement, and the arrival of republicans in open, overt power at Stormont, albeit shared and limited, was a sickening final jolt to unionists, to many Protestants, who had only ever dared look at their situation through half-open eyes.

Many find it hard to acknowledge that it is loyalists, not republicans, who are now responsible for most of the aggression. Yet loyalist violence of recent years has followed familiar patterns, occasionally more than one at once: targeting isolated Catholics in strong Protestant districts, a small community beginning to make an impact in a previously Protestant place, or most often and most sharply, where segregated communities find themselves locked in competition for territory.

North Belfast is the arena with most potential for disaster. Always a patchwork of borderlines, a blaze in one patch sets alight the next, sending sparks flying several patches away. Protestants and Catholics elsewhere are inflamed, terrified or shamed at the sight. No solution seems possible: 'containment' by policing or rehousing works for limited periods only; housing is a major factor in the problem.

As a parliamentary constituency North Belfast was once largely Protestant and unionist dominated. It is now increasingly Catholic, with a growing nationalist and in particular republican representation. Without the sprawling hardline loyalist estates of Rathcoole, a solidly Protestant suburb decanted from old red-brick streets, the constituency would already have a nationalist majority. In many ways, this place is the Northern Ireland problem in miniature: Catholics more assertive with the dismantling of each grievance, developing an affluent middle class, increasingly powerful and coherent while Protestants lash out in ill-directed anger, as the last vestige of their former supremacy and political hegemony visibly crumbles. More and more to many people, it looks like a one-way process: loss for them, an unstoppable rise for 'the other side'.

Sharp and bitter running battles throughout 2001 and into 2002 replayed scenes from 1969 and many of the following years. But the settings were also flashbacks to the riots of the 1920s and 1930s and to the previous century. Such clashes have often been sparked by the most apparently trivial of causes, though they have usually been at their worst when the precarious balance of the wider population is disturbed or somehow threatened. The new needle this time is the unnerving contrast in the psychological state of the two communities, between confident Catholics and downhearted Protestants. The bitter twist is that on past experience, the most vulnerable at such moments of heightened feeling are likely to be Catholics, living or working close to or among Protestants – like Danny McColgan, the 20-year-old postman whose death brought about those mass rallies, shot by two men who came out of the darkness pulling on balaclavas at 4.30 in the morning, as he arrived to pick up his mailbag in the centre of loyalist, UDA-dominated Rathcoole.

He was one of half a dozen Catholics working in the Rathcoole postal depot. His passion was DJing in a disco in central Belfast. He was the father of a baby girl and had been a pupil at North Belfast's one integrated secondary school, Hazelwood, perched precariously on one of the most incendiary peacelines of recent times. Soon after he died his partner Lindsay registered their little dauhter Bethany as a future Hazelwood pupil. Like many others, Danny McColgan led as unsegregated a life in North Belfast as he could.

The pattern of violence in Northern Ireland is tightly woven. Killings usually have a context of connections to previous incidents, gruesome cross-references to at least one other death. Sectarian confrontation of one kind or another bubbled and hissed in much of North Belfast for the previous year or more. But the bitterness crystallised, in the eyes of the world, in the mainly working-class sprawl of Catholic Ardoyne. This is where the Troubles originated, in a series of increasingly violent clashes through early 1969, which exploded in August that year, at the same time as an eruption between the Shankill and the Falls. The present President of the Irish Republic, former law professor Mary McAleese, has spoken about her memories as a school-leaver in August 1969, when she watched police stand by as loyalist mobs attacked Catholic homes, helped by some members of the part-time militia, the B Specials. The experience, she said, forced her to choose between a career as a lawyer and joining the IRA.

August 1969 in Ardoyne and the Falls revived much of the horror of the '20s and '30s, when the same flashpoints saw a large share of Belfast's seemingly endemic sectarian violence. Harsh experience of partial policing and forced migration in 1969 fuelled much subsequent violence. The events and legends of that period gave birth to the modern IRA and eventually the UDA, and regenerated the UVF after a burst of violent activity a few years earlier. A sixth of all deaths in the Troubles happened in North Belfast; both communities produced ruthless killers. One stretch was known as Murder Mile because so many people were shot dead there from passing cars, or dragged into black taxis to be found dumped in alleyways or by the roadside where the city peters out into scrubby hillside.

The shift in power, influence and numbers from unionist to nationalist in North Belfast has been gradual but traumatic. In the first years of the Troubles IRA bombs on the Shankill killed several children and elderly people. Ian Paisley formally launched the DUP in the emotional wake of one bombing, while Billy Hutchinson joined the UVF. In the years with the highest death toll many North Belfast victims were Catholic, when loyalist paramilitaries, including the UVF Shankill Butchers gang, inflamed by IRA bombings and the dissolution of the old Unionist Stormont parliament, went out to kill at random. They attacked where they thought they would find Catholics, in pubs, workplaces, walking or driving home, in districts once largely Protestant but even then beginning to change identity. The fringes of Ardoyne were a favourite target.

Ardoyne's people have suffered much, and some have generated considerable suffering. They do not look meek, and they do not look like an oppressed minority. When they move up a socio-economic bracket, some, unsurprisingly, take their district's assertiveness with them. A loyalist attempt to kill a man driving through the spread of more upmarket housing on the hills above the old streets failed when the driver heaved a concrete block out the window at the gunman. The gang found another victim and beat him to death: he was a Protestant, mistaken for a Catholic.

Late at night or on winter evenings the north side is still a chilling part of the city. Outsiders are unnerved by the rapid shifts in social and sectarian make-up. To the unfamiliar eye, even to visitors who return at intervals of a few years, the patchwork seems to change with lightning speed within short distances and sometimes within months. Protestant housing adjoins Catholic housing, comfortable middle-class dwellings sit beside graffiti-covered public housing where only one paramilitary group holds sway, and daubs the walls to say so. A fragmentation process has diminished one population, ending the dominance of decades.

Drive up the Antrim Road and the overwhelming impression is of bustle: young people in cars, children shouting and running, a string of takeaways selling fish and chips and pizza, pubs. Drive down crowded New Lodge and turn onto the Protestant Shore Road and the bustle stops. A line of pensioners' bungalows looks sideways at the bottom of the New Lodge. Once a unionist stronghold with clusters of solid bourgeois Protestant housing, a large working-class Protestant population and a Catholic minority, which in the main was markedly poorer, North Belfast now looks very different. Affluent Protestants began to flee in the early Troubles years. Many less well-off Protestants also moved out of Belfast, leaving an underclass behind. The big old red-brick villas of the Cavehill and Antrim Roads now house Catholic

lawyers and doctors or their offices. The worst Catholic districts have
been substantially rebuilt.

For decades Ardoyne, the small Bone district of the Oldpark Road
and the New Lodge, feared being overrun by their neighbours in the
much bigger Protestant heartlands of York Road, Crumlin Road and
Shankill. Now York Road is a sad straggle out of the city, long stretches
bricked up, the rest populated by those too old, poor or disheartened
to move to the suburbs. The Shankill is shrunken, torn by the inter-
loyalist feuding which in late 2000 uprooted several hundred people.
It is also haunted by the 1993 IRA bombing which killed ten people
inside and just outside a fish shop, including two children, a family of
three and one of the bombers. He was from Ardoyne, a 21-year-old,
Thomas 'Bootsie' Begley. He was trying to kill local UDA leaders
whose headquarters was above the fish shop. When he carried a bomb
in, it exploded in his hands. The shop was crowded, but there was no
one upstairs. A second IRA man survived, badly injured, to stand trial:
Sean Kelly aged 21.

The shop collapsed. People clawed at the rubble to reach the
injured and the dead, crying and cursing. The bombing came during
the meetings between John Hume and Gerry Adams that led to the
IRA ceasefire and, eventually, the peace process. When Adams helped
to carry Begley's coffin there was widespread Protestant outrage at
Hume for lending Adams political cover, and at their nerve in talking
about peace while the IRA went on waging war. Hume defended
Adams on the grounds that he could not disown a dead IRA man
without forfeiting his status as leader and therefore his ability to
negotiate a peace. From one perspective, Adams would be carrying the
coffin of a murderous bomber for their shared violent cause. From
another, he was attempting to bury the past and showing respect for a
fallen comrade, in order to carry his organisation with him. The point
was taken in the White House and eventually, though tacitly, among
British ministers. But fury lingered on the Shankill and farther afield.

For almost the entire length of the Crumlin Road, there are no
longer any Protestant homes, and the jail and courthouse which bore
its name are closed and increasingly derelict. A handful of rundown
Protestant streets straggle away from the road towards what remains of
the Shankill, once a street full of lively shopping, popular with Falls
Road Catholics. Now the streets between are bleak and bare, many

houses bricked up, the only flashes of colour from loyalist graffiti. The sense of lost territory is overpowering. Where the Troubles started around the top of the Crumlin Road is what the authorities at one point called 'sterilised ground': no houses, tastefully sloping brick walls, a triangular grassy patch. Nothing looks as it did in 1969. Houses have been cleared, rebuilt, streets broken up by bollards and peacelines. Belfast is now in part a walled city. Other cities cherish ancient walls as tourist attractions; Belfast is still building them.

Protestants are dotted in much smaller numbers now around the better streets they once monopolised, a Catholic river bursting out of the Ardoyne that grew from the ashes of 1969, a steady stream pouring up the hillside into newly built fake Georgian housing, over the hill into what was formerly solidly Protestant middle-class Glengormley. Catholics are sandwiched between Protestants at several points, but have by far the bigger overall numbers. Once an isolated Catholic district surrounded by strong loyalist streets, 'the Bone' is scruffy but bustling, small cheap shops and a huge pub clustered near a solid old church. It reaches out brashly now towards nearby Ardoyne, and Ardoyne strains at the seams, walls covered in graffiti, rundown shops, population young and growing, houses jammed up against the 1969 peacelines. The sectarian breakdown at the top of the Crumlin Road is a recipe for maximum edginess.

Have Protestants moved out of North Belfast because of intimidation or because they lose interest in living in a district once it is no longer primarily Protestant? There are a number of reasons, observers believe. 'A bit of aggro, claims by politicians on both sides that the paramilitaries on the other are whipping it up, then the numbers tilt a bit more,' says one local, 'and then more people start to say "ah to hell with it", and away they go out to Carrick.' The largely Protestant County Antrim town of Carrickfergus has developed a growing fringe of housing, and aggro of its own: 'Belfast brings its history with it, unfortunately,' says one local representative, although Carrick was never known for inter-communal harmony.

Housing managers know that on the Catholic side of peacelines in North Belfast there is a chronic housing shortage, with empty houses on the Protestant side. Any attempt to redraw boundaries to take account of changing housing needs is met with an anger verging on hysteria from a range of unionist opinion, from mainstream politicians to loyalist paramilitaries. It is one of the points where hardliners and the most moderate overlap.

About 14 years ago, in the midst of sectarian clashes in North Belfast and standing on a peaceline, a television reporter on camera put it to Chris McGimpsey, an otherwise deft and articulate unionist on the liberal end of the spectrum, that aggression had come first from the Protestant side. McGimpsey said paramilitary anger was inflamed by 'encroachment' on districts which had always been Protestant. The shift was already underway. For some time afterwards he complained that a report quoting his use of the word 'encroachment' also said it echoed a paramilitary justification of violence. He had been made to 'sound like a hardliner', he said.

In recent years, as Orange marching routes increasingly became the focus of controversy, several leading unionists have denounced what they called attempts to 'ghettoise' roads or districts. They mean that Catholics must not be allowed to define districts as theirs, then deny Orangemen the right to march through. There is little awareness of how this sounds to non-unionist ears. Some have always insisted that no part of Northern Ireland may be defined as nationalist, since the place is constitutionally British and therefore unionist. Ian Paisley said it in 1959, insisting that Orangemen must be allowed to carry the Union Jack through the mainly Catholic town of Dungiven: 'There are no nationalist areas in Northern Ireland. Ulster is Ulster.' As the Drumcree dispute gained steam, a leading Orangeman said: 'There are no nationalist areas of Northern Ireland, only places temporarily occupied.' Claims and assertions about territory come from several different voices, some more conscious and aggressive than others.

Soon after the Agreement, David Trimble told a television crew on the walls above Derry's Bogside, lightly, almost flippantly, that the entirely Catholic and emphatically nationalist district below them was now as British as Bangor or Bournemouth, because nationalists had agreed that Northern Ireland should stay in the UK while a majority wished it. In the last election, republicans talked airily about 'greening' the west and took two seats west of the River Bann. Large parts of Northern Ireland are now predominantly nationalist in terms of political representation, and Sinn Féin look forwards to taking the mayoral chain in Belfast. The electoral and demographic balance in the city, some reckon, is changing by the month.

A fear of an unstoppable green tide helped drive the residents of the small Protestant district on the edge of Ardoyne into the most self-destructive of actions. What came to be called the Holy Cross dispute, but which was originally more an accident than a dispute, was a squalid demonstration of futility and the hopelessly unpolitical nature of loyalism. This should be the last such loyalist dispute about territory if the loyalists cared what the world thought of them. But then if they knew how to appeal to the wider audience, Holy Cross would never have happened.

In early June 2001, Catholic protests at an Orange march known as the Tour of the North produced flurries of stoning and bad-tempered shouting back and forth as marchers passed the end of Ardoyne Road and the line of shops between that and the Crumlin. Against the altered demographic tide, Orangemen insist on marching. The Tour is a major effort every two years, more restricted on the interim year. This was a restricted year, limited further by direction of the Parades Commission, the official body set up to arbitrate on disputed routes and marching etiquette. The marchers and their supporters were resentful as always at the Commission's orders for quieter bands, smaller numbers, while Ardoyne Catholics were angry that the marchers still insisted on parading though a district that is no longer mainly Protestant.

The major clash pitted adults against children. As the dust settled, just before the end of the school term, Protestants began to attack children and their parents going to and coming from a Catholic girls' primary school, children aged 4 to 11, with a scattering of fathers but mainly young mothers, often with prams and holding on to toddlers. For months there were scenes many considered revolting. Police efforts to protect the Catholics were at first ineffectual, then intensive. In return they were stoned and occasionally petrol-bombed in nightly riots from both sides. Although attempts were made to shift blame, principally to suggest the scenes at the school were being manipulated and orchestrated by republicans, it was Protestants who came out looking worse, as they were bound to do.

The school was Holy Cross, which has been in the same place for 34 years with Protestant housing between it and the bulk of Catholic Ardoyne a few hundred yards away. It was opened on Ardoyne Road in 1967 to replace a dilapidated Victorian building at the top of the

Crumlin. The nearest houses were Protestant Glenbryn, but with green space around both school and houses. Now the space is a constrained box of new Protestant housing, the people of Glenbryn increasingly outnumbered and permanently off-balance. Some claim to be under constant attack from Ardoyne and argue for more houses. The demand in reality is for security in numbers no longer there.

In the midst of the Holy Cross furore a reporter interviewed one of the Glenbryn spokespeople in his home, his wife sitting beside him. She interrupted to say that Protestants were allocated inferior houses. What was wrong with her house, the reporter asked. There was nothing wrong with it, she replied angrily, but 'the others' had better houses. How were they better? 'They're big three-storey houses down there on Ardoyne Road, so they can pack more of them into them,' she said.

Complaints and incidents of aggression in Glenbryn increased with the arrival of new residents, families forced out of the Shankill Road during the feud between the UDA and UVF. The district's fragile paramilitary ecology was disturbed. As usual in such circumstances flags erupted first: a rash of UDA flags on lamp-posts, to tell the UVF and the nearby Catholics that the UDA now ruled Glenbryn.

During the three decades of the Catholic school's existence, there had often been arson attacks on the school buildings, taunts as children passed, but never a sustained campaign of hostility. The fact that the pupils were girls, the oldest 11, probably always reduced temperatures. As they stood around behind police lines in June 2001, some of the mothers said they knew Glenbryn faces to say hello to, from the shops at Ardoyne, the post office. A few said they remembered as pupils sometimes being shouted at, but nothing like this.

The behaviour that began in the last week of term was different, bound to make the perpetrators look ugly, moronic and mindlessly aggressive, never likely to bring anything but shame on the attackers and the wider Protestant/unionist community. A local observer with experience of the entire Troubles period sniffed despair and self-hatred. 'Glenbryn are lost souls. Other Protestants don't want to live there. Only the Shankill refugees with no choice came to it, gearing up the local UVF against the UDA, the two of them vying to be the hardest.'

The muttered rationale in the first disorganised Ardoyne picket line was 'we'll stop them getting to their school if they stop our marches'.

But when television cameras highlighted tearful Holy Cross children and muscled young men with paramilitary tattoos among the crowd facing them, condemnation poured in. The protesters hastily produced a list of justificatory grievances, headed by claims that the Protestant houses nearest Catholic Ardoyne were being attacked nightly.

As a defence, this lacked credibility. For months the most serious and visible intimidation had been loyalist. The chief loyalist paramilitary influence on the protesters, it was clear, was the UDA, the bigger and more incoherent of the two main groups. When the spokesman for the tiny Progressive Unionists, the political voice of the UVF, Billy Hutchinson, first turned up at the school in June, he stayed physically separate from the Glenbryn group, talking earnestly to police officers within yards of the stalled Catholic parents, working to reduce the tension. At one point he began to drive towards the Catholic group, apparently expecting them to be moved to let him pass. After a prolonged conversation with the officer in charge, he shook his head and slowly reversed away, a picture of frustration. Later, he told reporters that Sinn Féin had stage-managed the scenes at Holy Cross to create nationalist martyrs. To hear him make excuses for a sectarianism he had long before rejected was a measure of the communal pressure he clearly faced.

Hutchinson is incoherent and inconsistent, not through lack of intelligence or integrity, but because he has no solid, continuous internal support. Watching his performance compared to that of local Sinn Féin Assembly member and would-be MP Gerry Kelly was instructive. Kelly, who served a long sentence for bombing the Old Bailey in 1973, is one of the more abrasive republican front-men – he has steadily become more adept. As one analyst said, 'It's not that Kelly's a gem, but he has the team thinking behind him. Billy's on his own, with God knows what kind of backing from the UVF and the UDA barging around throwing pipe bombs.' Kelly also had the better case. No matter how many versions Glenbryn produced, the wider world declined to accept that republicans were responsible for them shouting obscenities.

In the end, the best account of how the Holy Cross saga began came from an American reporter with the fresh eye, patience and initial privilege accorded to an outsider to stand around in Glenbryn long enough to ask questions locals backed away from. A *Boston Globe* story began: 'It was in June when a Roman Catholic taxi driver on his way to the Holy Cross Catholic School swerved into a stepladder, injuring a Protestant baker who had been tying a tattered British flag to a wooden telephone pole.' The American reporter found the baker: 'James McLean stands holding his two-year-old son on his shoulders along the sidewalk in the Protestant section of the Ardoyne Road, where he and 100 other young men, many with the loyalist trademark shaved head and tattoos, spat out epithets against the frightened Catholic schoolgirls as they walked by with their parents.'

Hutchison and Ervine

The reporter said he had found two witnesses, one Catholic and one Protestant, who both asked not to be identified and said the story was less dramatic than McLean's version. The car swerved and hit the ladder, but McLean was not on it. He fell trying to get out of the way. McLean told varying stories about what happened next, agreed only on blaming Ardoyne Catholics for starting the trouble. 'They had knives and bats. What do they need those for if they were just picking up a kid at school? he said. 'They just want to kill us.' His father was introduced as a former loyalist paramilitary prisoner. 'When they tried to kill my son it was the straw that broke the camel's back,' he said. 'You have to stand up for your rights. We're being pushed aside here.

They want to come down and move into these homes.' McLean added, 'This peace process is one-sided, and it is not going to work. We won't let it work; not while Sinn Féin gets everything it wants.' The *Globe* concluded: 'For McLean and his friends it is increasingly difficult to define exactly what they're loyal to.'

A Glenbryn community worker attempting to justify the attacks in the early days gestured down the road towards Ardoyne. 'Look at this place,' she said, '1,000 of us and 7,000 of them! This is a small community that's under attack the whole time.' The media who turned up to watch a daily school run with a nasty difference were told by police that most provocation came from loyalists, probably the UDA. Several of the first Catholic mothers to speak to the cameras received death threats. Foreign journalists were baffled by the self-destructiveness they saw. In the eyes of the most experienced local observers the explanation was clear enough. Protestants were indeed suffering most in North Belfast and lashing out in response, but their suffering was primarily psychological, or political.

'The real objection in Glenbryn is that the Catholics they see every day behave as if they own the place,' said one veteran. 'They see expansion as a political act; being a Catholic is a political act, having loads of kids, Celtic jerseys, littering the place with dogs and babies and prams and slogans on the walls in Irish – it's all Catholic, all political, and it all offends them.'

The protesters raised a banner emblazoned with the words 'The Walk of Shame', but in the world's eyes the shame was all theirs. 'It doesn't make any sense,' the veteran sighed. 'It's Glenbryn's attempt to draw a territorial line like their politicians try to draw the line politically – this far and no further.' With a backdrop of riots that harked back to 1969, summer 2001 left many feeling hopeless. After the Colombian arrests and 11 September Sinn Féin began to flounder, the smugness evident after the election results suddenly gone. But Holy Cross, renewed after a break while the schools shut for summer, took the uncomfortable spotlight off them and played it on a scene at least as damaging for loyalists. Republicans did not have to manipulate Holy Cross; they only had to milk it. Condemnation of loyalists mentality and sympathy for the Catholic parents poured in.

The two communities came close to being locked into confrontation, mutual offence rubbed raw by the line-ups on both sides. Billy Hutchinson, who had served his time for the murder of two young Catholics, was visible from the outset. There were frequent visits from prominent UDA spokesman John White, jailed for the murder of two Catholics early in the Troubles, one an SDLP politician. But Glenbryn spokespeople complained that they had seen the Shankill bomber Sean Kelly among the parents, and that it was provocative and offensive when an ex-IRA prisoner, Brendan Mailey, became the parents' main spokesman. As a teenager, Mailey had been convicted for the murder of a young off-duty policeman, shot dead on the forecourt of a service station. From the start, Glenbryn had also complained about the presence of Sinn Féin's Gerry Kelly, as another ex-prisoner.

Kelly usually managed to stay some distance from the protesters, but was always there to brief the media. He linked Holy Cross to famous instances of injustice and bigotry elsewhere, with the help of constant messages from abroad. The Belfast Catholic morning paper the *Irish News* devoted its entire letters page on several days to e-mailed international outrage. The correspondence included a letter from the aged Rosa Parks, who sparked the anti-segregation protests in Alabama. Comparison with the forced integration of schools in the deep south of America must have puzzled some of the small children on Ardoyne Road. A gable wall got a new mural of little black girls under the words 'Arkansas 1957', little white girls under 'Ardoyne 2001'.

Northern Ireland Protestants were torn between offence at the sight of republicans occupying the moral high ground and excruciating embarrassment at the behaviour of people from their own community. Some, including politicians, tried to deny any moral argument, depicting the Catholic parents as fanatics subjecting their children to trauma for propaganda purposes – as though the trauma had been dreamed up by the parents – and pleading the pressures on a small Protestant community. The indefensibility of the Glenbryn behaviour was what struck people elsewhere.

On the second day of the renewed protest, 5 September, as the Catholics passed, someone threw a pipe bomb towards them. It exploded beside the police line, injuring a policeman in the leg. Children and adults screamed and ran in panic. Shortly afterwards, a 14-year-old Protestant boy was knocked off his bike and killed by a car almost two miles away from Holy Cross, in an area which had just erupted in rioting. Even the shocking death of a young Protestant could not turn the tide.

The Catholic group walked in silence to the school and prayed for the boy. Loyalists broke off their protest for the boy's funeral, but swiftly resumed it. Rioting spread through North Belfast, with nationalist youths attacking police and several attacks on Protestant homes. School buses were stoned. The lingering impression was that of thugs bullying harmless families. Glenbryn produced several spokespersons, one of whom was arrested with a number of others for disorderly behaviour; some were more articulate than others, but none made a reasonable case. A bespectacled, youngish man who joined Hutchinson's Progressive Unionists soon afterwards wondered on air if the Holy Cross principal had had scientific tests done, before deciding urine had been thrown at children who arrived in school with damp, foul-smelling outer clothes. It was more likely to have been stale tea, he maintained.

For one observer from the Republic with little instinctive sympathy for republicans or for Ardoyne Catholics, always too abrasive for southern sensibilities, a few mornings struggling to make notes in the noisy space between the school group and hissing, spitting protesters made the difference. Close up, she found the 'protesters' seriously offensive, their grievances unconvincing. That they took the heat off increasingly arrogant republicans in an increasingly tight spot was their most serious offence, she thought: 'Isn't it this lot's real sin, that they make the Provos look good?'

Mainstream unionist politicians have belatedly begun to take note of Protestant working-class alienation, as it is now routinely called. Few accept that this is the sharpest manifestation of a discontent and identity crisis some of them have themselves fed, by endless complaint about 'concessions to nationalists'. Those who do accept it make the admission privately. 'We should have been telling people from the start that this was a good thing for all of us, not a sell-out, or a not very nice thing,' said one Ulster Unionist a year after the Agreement. 'No wonder support for it's slipping away. We've confused and depressed people.'

Unionist politicians also tend towards incoherence on the subject because of reluctance to ascribe any credit to republican or nationalist leaders, because they still refuse to admit that systematic discrimination against Catholics ever existed, and because they reject the analysis of the newer breed of Protestant representative. Loyalist fringe spokesmen like Hutchinson and Ervine throughout their short history have pinpointed lack of interest in education as the factor which most damaged working-class people. They highlighted the low pass rates for the Eleven Plus exam in the Shankill, which means local children rarely go to grammar school and have little chance of higher, third-level education.

But there is a deliberate lack of clarity even in this comparatively forthright observation, perhaps understandably. A middle-class Protestant observer, an educationalist, has no doubt that Catholic attitudes to education have been and remain different: 'A Catholic friend, who runs one of the toughest schools in a tough spot, has told me it's tough all right but his parents still believe fundamentally that education's worthwhile. Whereas the Prods . . .'

He also recognises a fundamental cause of contemporary Protestant working-class depression as something no unionist political representative dare articulate. He was depressed himself, he said, having watched a locally made television documentary in which the presenter met only anger when he tried in vain to discover from people in a loyalist district the substance of their 'loss' from the Good Friday Agreement. 'This guy says to him "Are you a Protestant? You tell me that and I'll give you my fucking answer." I asked a friend brought up in one of the toughest loyalist districts what the loss was and he said jobs, not that the Catholics took them, but because they'd gone. It was the sense of it being their country that had gone, he said: "We are the people, and we can look down on the other lot."'

John Hume often attributed his own success and the success of other poor Catholics, and their positive politicisation, to the Eleven Plus and a good secondary education. But more nationalists than unionists now reject selective education as unfair, arguing for an improved and widely accessible comprehensive system, whereas unionists in Stormont have united to object to Martin McGuinness' proposal for an end to selection – some largely because it comes from McGuinness, most, avowedly, because they believe the Northern Ireland grammar school system is academically superior.

The PUP pair have frequently commented that Catholics use

education as a ladder out of poverty, where Protestants traditionally relied for unqualified work on defunct traditional industries like light engineering. They suggested this was because those jobs were preserved for Protestants. Other unionists resist the comparison. The theory is overplayed, one of the mainstream politicians most involved in a working-class district has said. Chris McGimpsey, an Ulster Unionist councillor on the crime- and drug-ridden Shankill, told the *Irish Times* in January 2002: 'I haven't come up with another explanation. All I know is that our children are not genetically inferior.' Working-class Protestants believed they had been defeated; republicans behaved as if they had won. 'That isn't the case. Republicans lost the battle in Northern Ireland; they are just too cute to admit it. But it has caused Protestants to be despondent. They don't see the point of anything, including education.'

A new university college is being built between the Shankill and the Falls. Nearby Catholic districts were excited at the prospect, as McGimpsey admitted, while Protestants show little interest. 'On the Falls the parents say it will be wonderful for the kids to go to university on their own doorstep. On the Shankill they wonder if their daughter will get a job as a cleaner.' In one of the most vivid comparisons yet made between the communities, he added: 'One community foresees its youth getting honours degrees; the other looks to its young people washing floors.' Yet his party supports an educational system many believe to be in clear need of overhaul, apparently to preserve advantages which have failed to filter down in quantity to less affluent Protestants.

The street violence in North Belfast followed more than two years of intermittent loyalist attack in other parts of Northern Ireland on Catholic property, churches, communal social premises like the busy clubs of the GAA (Gaelic Athletics Association) and individuals, generally those outnumbered in mainly Protestant towns. None of this was new, like attacks down the years by Catholics, whether republican or not, on Orange halls in mainly Catholic districts or isolated rural spots, and less often on churches and on Protestant homes and businesses. Like punishment shootings, paramilitary kneecappings and worse, this low-level violence began to capture more attention because the rate of lethal violence had diminished. Compared to drive-by shootings and sledgehammers through doors in the night, attacks on isolated 'others', like rioting across urban interfaces is the small change of sectarianism, a staple of centuries with a seasonal rhythm.

Increased loyalist attacks are a continuation of violence that predated the IRA ceasefire, fed by the controversies over Orange marches, fuelled before that again by the common Protestant belief that the security forces were not allowed to fight the IRA sufficiently strongly, that loyalist terror could compel Catholics to make the IRA stop. The standard unionist explanation for loyalist violence has always been that it is retaliation against the IRA. Unionist politicians still tend too often to react with direct or oblique justification and excuse, as once Sinn Féin routinely explained away IRA attacks. That has sounded increasingly feeble during these recent years while the level of IRA violence has stayed well below that of loyalists. The more recent variation is that republicans provoke loyalists by triumphalist or intimidatory behaviour.

But in 2001, police said loyalist pipe-bomb attacks, the crudest kind of device, had been running at a rate of almost one a day for over a year. Paramilitary-style 'punishment attacks' had gone up by a quarter from the previous year, with one on average almost every day. Loyalists were blamed for almost two-thirds of the 331 attacks and republicans, including the IRA, for the rest. When two loyalist youths died when bombs they were either holding or throwing exploded, unionist reaction was a study. One of these deaths occurred in North Belfast, and the explanation at first in the area, was that the dead youth was a hero defending the area, who was throwing a republican missile back when it exploded. The second was in Coleraine, a largely Protestant town in the now increasingly Catholic north-west. The town elected its first SDLP mayor in the bad summer of 2000. Here, some observers have begun to attribute a pattern of increased loyalist violence in part to resentment of the increased nationalist political representation. Commenting on the death of the youth, the newly elected DUP MP Gregory Campbell said republicans had shown young loyalists that violence paid.

The shift of power in Northern Ireland has been a painful business. There has been real suffering on both sides all along the way, real people behind the statistics, taking the strain. As Holy Cross dragged on, an elderly republican confessed in private that there was no enthusiasm among local Catholics for keeping going. They thought they had no choice, but they wanted it to be over: 'This is killing people, their nerves are wrecked. The doctor's surgery's full: kids bed-wetting, the parents in for stuff to get them to sleep. '69 was bad, but at least it only lasted a few weeks.' An experienced community worker thought 'the other side's in the same state. Apart from UDA types, who wants to get up in the morning to that? With the world mocking you?'

The parents who ducked the howling, spitting mob on the direct route to Holy Cross and instead took their children to the school's back gate, as unionists demanded, followed a route along the upper Crumlin Road past Protestant houses on the right, Catholic on the left. Both have decent gardens, fairly new cars, a step up from Ardoyne. Few of the Catholic residents have been there for more than ten years. In the early '90s, as the neighbourhood changed complexion, loyalist paramilitaries killed several Catholics in their homes there and wounded others.

It is a pattern familiar across Belfast, and to a lesser extent across Northern Ireland. Catholics move in, Protestants move out, and loyalist paramilitaries attack individuals, businesses, sports facilities. In the North Belfast suburb of Glengormley, once largely Protestant, now increasingly Catholic, loyalists shot and killed 18-year-old Protestant Gavin Brett in July 2001 as he chatted to a Catholic friend outside a Gaelic Athletic Association club. It seemed clear they hoped to kill a Catholic. The boy who was killed was the child of a mixed marriage, mother Protestant, father Catholic. He was the fourth person killed near the club or involved with it; the previous victim was the Protestant beaten to death nearby in mistake for a Catholic. The club had been attacked numerous times, notably on one occasion by seeding a pitch with broken glass.

In another district not far from Belfast, a sizeable Catholic population has settled happily, many of them young commuters, some with small children. The area is still described as Protestant. 'For God's sake don't draw attention to us,' a man pleaded recently, only slightly humorously. 'We've had no trouble yet because we're all of us out most of the time.' A few miles away, another similar commuter community has begun to 'have trouble'. Their mistake was to use a rented field as a makeshift pitch for children to play Gaelic football, while negotiating to buy. Cars have had tyres slashed. The owner of the field has been threatened. It sounds like the first move in a familiar pattern.

As the political geography of Northern Ireland changes, a range of
Protestant behaviour is observable. Only a fraction is violent, as many
would be quick to point out. By far the most common reaction is
flight – Catholics move into an area and Protestants move out. But this
is not admitted either. 'South Belfast is North Belfast, except for the
violence,' one sharp-eyed commentator says. He means that the area
has also changed complexion – once solidly Protestant and unionist,
Catholics are now highly visible and increasingly influential.

South Belfast was once home to the city's old money, the district
where judges, lawyers, doctors, professors and a smattering of senior
civil servants and unionist politicians, the professional classes, lived in
large red-brick villas with handsome gardens. New apartment blocks
spring up where villas have sold off large gardens. Many of the others
are still home to lawyers and doctors. But instead of McCracken
Memorial Presbyterian or St John's Church of Ireland, these
professionals attend the big new Catholic church, which replaced a
much smaller one, built originally by philanthropic employers in the
big houses for their Catholic 'domestics' and at that time called 'the
Maids' church'. A growing number send their children first to St
Bride's Primary, beside that expansive new church, then to Methodist
College or Victoria College, like the children of those Protestants who
still live beside them. There are quite a number of children in many of
the four-wheel drives on the Malone Road now, more per family, a
wholly unscientific straw poll would suggest, than in the large cars of
the remaining Protestants. Social scientists said recently that the
Catholic birth-rate has fallen quite dramatically. 'Not that we've
noticed,' says a cheerful mother of four, 'lots of babies around.'

The Protestants who left, and are still leaving, South Belfast were
not threatened by the IRA or by the wealthy Catholics who now live
on the Malone Road. They have not given their reasons for leaving in
public, but it is fairly obvious that intimidation was not responsible;
unionist politicians could have been relied on to spread the word. The
Protestants who left were not threatened by anyone, except, some
suspect, by the prevalence on their tree-lined streets of little and big
Deirdres and Niamhs and Ciaras and Liams, perhaps most of all by the
Liams and the Fintans, 'and maybe the occasional appearance of a kid
with a hurley-stick', says a new resident dryly.

Methodist College, Methody, is very keen on its rugby team. The team won its first schools final in ten years in 2001. Many in the large crowd noted the names of players and made their own calculation; just under half the team-squad was Catholic. Rugby was once a passport into Northern Ireland's upper middle-class world, played only in the state; effectively Protestant schools which catered for the more affluent, the game for professionals at a time when many professions were dominated by Protestants and a tough proposition for Catholics above a certain level. Now the law is increasingly a Catholic world, at all but the very highest level, and the law has arguably been the greatest generator of new wealth in the past 15 years apart from property speculation. Not long ago two barristers succeeded in overturning the requirement to swear allegiance to the Queen for new QCs, pleading that the requirement denied respect for their Irish political identity.

The newly rich Catholic does not necessarily abandon any aspect of Irishness or traditional identity. Once it might have been so, but once this was a smaller and less confident group. On weekend mornings at the affluent end of South Belfast about 120 boys aged 6 to 16 regularly trot off to a playing field once owned by a venerable Protestant grammar, but they are going for Gaelic football practice. The Catholic upper middle class knows the value of various sports. For many, there is considerable sport in subverting the establishment by joining it.

The SDLP despair of them. The party's few activists in recent years have complained that the number of upwardly mobile and affluent Catholics willing to enter politics must be almost as low as in the famously apathetic and anti-political Protestant middle class. Some have clearly found ways to change the face of the society they live in which are more congenial than the tiring, costly, even dangerous, game of politics – taking over the courts, buying up property, expanding the traditional Catholic business of selling drink into a series of empires. But they have not abandoned politics entirely. While party membership withers, the SDLP's vote has climbed steadily in the South Belfast Westminster constituency. More slowly and more recently, so has that of Sinn Féin.

For some Protestants in mixed middle-class Belfast, the immediate future is not terrifying, but clearly not inviting either. 'They're a shower,' says a newly affluent Protestant married to a Catholic, a position that affords a useful, if not infallible, perspective on the sociological shifts of the times. 'They're abandoning Belfast to the

Taigs and you know why? Because they don't like it now they have to live beside Catholics. After all those years bad-mouthing wee working-class bigots on the Shankill.' Another observer, a Catholic, has watched the Malone change hands with mixed emotions. It was his ambition to bring up his family in a mixed area. But as soon as they moved in, he realised his neighbours were in the process of moving out. He takes it almost as a personal slight. 'What do they do when South Belfast goes green? They head off down the coast to Bangor and North Down, as close as they can get to Scotland. The same thing's been happening steadily for the last ten years in the leafy parts of North Belfast.' Like the disapproving Protestant in a mixed marriage, this man sees Protestant middle-class flight as a failure of leadership. Where is the voice crying stop, hold fast, learn to mix? 'They fight it in North Belfast, they flee South Belfast,' says the first man with a hint of sadness. 'Or they hide out in East Belfast, where there's nothing but Protestants as far as the sea, and they whinge about concessions to the IRA, when they mean reforms that should have happened years ago. And these are the people with all the advantages.'

In information derived from the census of 1999, middle-class South Belfast stood out as the only part of Northern Ireland where the mix of population resembled that of the population as a whole. In other words, the numbers of Catholics and Protestants in these leafy streets were beginning to match each other, although more anecdotal evidence, standing in for scientific fact while the 2001 census is slowly number-crunched, indicates that this ideal state may never be reached. Census questions have been phrased and returns pored over by statisticians and sociologists who themselves on occasion have had the sharpest of axes to grind. The finer details of what is no doubt a complicated and protracted phenomenon may be imperfectly understood on the ground. Some effects or interrelated developments are glaringly obvious and predict more dramatic outcomes, at least to the ordinary citizen. It seems plain that the nationalist vote has grown because the drift of politics has energised more Catholics to cast their votes, and because there have been more young Catholics on the register at each recent election. When Sinn Féin edged out the moderate SDLP to become the major nationalist party, it also became apparent that the political geography had changed. Local government and Westminster results confirmed that unionism was in retreat west of the Bann, with one MP left in East Londonderry, and no unionist councillors from the west side of Derry city. The unionist vote has fallen as Protestants see politics slipping away from them and as unionism disintegrates further. In each case, the process feeds on itself.

Over the past two decades nationalist political leaders, once crushed and passive, have steadily outflanked unionists. As if that were not depressing enough, Protestant unionists also see a numbers game playing out in distinctly discouraging style. Their general response to this and to the political picture looks likely to influence the outcome in a way even less pleasant to contemplate. Young middle-class Protestants have increasingly left Northern Ireland for higher education and stayed away on graduation. It is not yet clear whether the new political situation is likely to entice a significant number to reverse this trend. If the unionist mood hardens into pessimism about the future, a reversal seems highly unlikely. In this scenario, the opposing trend of falling Catholic births might not be enough to again increase the margin of Protestant numbers over Catholic. Doubts, fears and speculation surround the entire question.

The drift and dimensions of demographic change has become a live political issue, a hot potato tossed back and forth on the assumption that whatever the finer points, there is an underlying trend away from a clear unionist majority towards growing balance in the numbers of the two communities. This is an assumption some unionists still strongly reject, while others take it as encouragement or terrible warning, to dig in more intransigently rather than to deal.

Sectarian violence in North Belfast diminished for a time after the rallies of January 2002. There was a widespread stubborn insistence, voiced in letters columns and radio and television discussions, that sectarianism must not be allowed to derail a process that had already delivered an imperfect but substantial peace. The problem is that no one knows how to turn a communal wish for peace into reality, except by the slow workings of political institutions on a wing and a prayer. The forces ranged against peace are powerful, sometimes all the more so because of their inarticulacy. In places like North Belfast, the fight for expression becomes murderous, although often there seems little to voice beyond a yell of anger.

The minds of the Protestant, unionist community were not changed by years of bombs and bullets from the IRA, and the rise of the Catholic, nationalist community will not be stopped by loyalist violence. Even if peace does put down roots, some fear it might take another 30 years to move minds closer together, longer again to see people willing to deal with each other with open minds and hearts. But a cautious, segregated peace rally was better than none.

The challenge for those who want the peace to work is to show hopeless, self-hating Protestant youth a way to broaden their lives through training and education, investment in their battered community, and example. For the Catholics in North Belfast, any comfort in their new-found numbers is spoiled by the knowledge that co-religionists scattered in smaller numbers nearby are likely to face increasing attack. The best they can do is to hold their nerve, build their lives and their community and stay well clear of claiming victories.

Protestants have had no victories for a long time, 'except the Good Friday Agreement, but they're determined not to admit it', as one frustrated bystander says. Their political leaders may be edging around to more positive positions, eyeing each other as they manoeuvre. In time that might produce a willingness to start telling their people that security cannot rest in numbers alone, that it needs cooperation and a civic spirit. In much of Northern Ireland, where the numbers game has brought nothing but fear and loathing, that would be a flying start to normality, and another step towards peace.

6

PROSPECTS

This far down the line, what are the chances of a stable peace emerging in Northern Ireland? The various players are more clearly in view, habits recognisable, form recorded. For all that, pitfalls are easy to predict and intermittent crises are sure to arise, a sense has edged into the open of a process with its own life, sturdy and resourceful.

Almost every participant, though for different reasons, wants to see the institutions of the Good Friday Agreement survive. There have been many twists in the path since the emergence eight years ago of a process intended to bring unionists and loyalists, republicans and the rest of nationalism into some kind of accommodation under the stewardship of the British and Irish governments. The course of events has been erratic and sometimes bewildering, occasionally tragic. When Irish National Liberation Army (INLA) prisoners shot and killed the loyalist leader Billy Wright inside the Maze prison, two days after Christmas in 1997, the killing launched a brutal cycle of revenge and put enormous pressure on negotiations at a crucial stage. By contrast, the Omagh bombing in August 1998, only months after the successful referendums on the Agreement, so horrified opinion generally that it produced renewed determination to make the peace work.

In public reaction across Northern Ireland, among both Protestants and Catholics, there was a recognition that the dissident republican bombing was directed against the fledgling settlement and the new majority who had voted for the Agreement. A dry political compromise developed a life of its own. Anti-Agreement unionists who initially tried to turn public outrage about the bombing against mainstream republicans faltered and went quiet in the weeks after Omagh, in the face of a steely popular will to protect the progress made so painfully.

No matter how confidently anyone claims to have mapped out the prospects, much of the path was unforeseeable. One prediction has come true. Republicans have become major players, as some foretold from the start. But the rest of the argument claimed that an imperfect peace had been bought at the IRA's price. The most striking fact about the process has been the way the Sinn Féin leadership successfully sold a major climb-down as victory. Only in a political world already turned upside-down could Sinn Féin taking offices in Westminster be seen as a triumph for an organisation once sworn to 'end the British connection'.

The bulk of the Good Friday Agreement most resembles the prescription put forward over years by moderate nationalism: power-sharing in Northern Ireland, a programme to achieve equality and deliver institutions of state capable of attracting the allegiance of both nationalists and unionists, the Britishness and Irishness of the two main traditions recognised in concrete form by links with both London and Dublin, and by cross-border institutions. That programme bears no resemblance to the traditional demands of republicans for British withdrawal, Brits out, the unification of Ireland. Nor is it a programme that lifts unionist hearts. That was never likely. The process was intended to end the violence by drawing republicans into politics and putting nationalists and republicans into government, and by establishing new political arrangements to transform those established when Northern Ireland was set up. Since those arrangements were largely tailored to unionist wishes, it was unlikely that unionists would greet their replacement with pleasure.

Unionist politicians come close at times to suggesting that the peace process has meant a deterioration, rather than a better quality of life for large numbers of people. Northern Ireland was an unsatisfactory society before 1969, not the Utopia some occasionally profess to recall. There followed the kind of violence that made already existing bitterness much deeper. Nobody should pretend that the Good Friday Agreement can magic it all away. There are no guarantees, but in spite of bad periods and recurring crises anyone who remembers what life was like before the ceasefires of 1994 knows the improvement.

Grim statistics say much. The first IRA ceasefire was on 31 August 1994, followed on 13 October by a loyalist ceasefire. In the seven full years before 1994 and the eight months of the year before the IRA move, the death toll was 724. In the remaining months of the year and seven subsequent years to the end of 2001, the toll was 159. Many thousands of people will grieve for the dead of the Troubles for the rest of their lives; many thousands will deal with physical or mental pain from their injuries every day until they die. The release from a dragging, miserable conflict is still tangible, the blessings of relative peace worth counting.

The line-up of players has big weaknesses, and prompts basic questions. In the short term the two governments can be expected to continue their close cooperation, but with different emphases. Tony Blair's government is still keenly aware of the difficulties to be resolved and the potential for collapse. In another few years Northern Ireland may well slip down Blair's list of priorities, but only if political progress stabilises. The leader of an almost entirely supportive party with huge majorities and time in hand, Blair was able to push on a process already cautiously begun by his predecessor, John Major, leading a minority government and a hostile party. Having followed an untried route away from the Troubles this far, a British Prime Minister with the strongest of parliamentary hands will surely not be inclined to turn back.

There are thorny decisions still to be made, particularly on policing. It has been the most barbed of issues, the sorest remaining point of political conflict between unionists and nationalists. Responsibility for policing rests with London, as it has for the past 30 years. The practice of setting one community to police the other bred a culture in turn arrogantly dismissive, then defensive about complaints, bolstered by reluctance to investigate or censure. It could still undermine progress. But the record suggests Blair understands what needs to be done. He must see the potential for damage if policing is hobbled by the snares of the past.

Decommissioning, the second issue most focused on by unionists, has dogged the process. The SDLP once struggled to be heard above the sound of gunfire as a convincing and reasonable nationalist voice in London and in Dublin. They have had to struggle to stay relevant again as republicans arm-wrestle the British over decommissioning. Blair has not helped by creating the impression that guns might be bartered for proper policing, as well as for the tidying up of the loose ends involved in demilitarisation and some form of amnesty.

Dublin's level of interest is harder to predict than London's. The Republic obviously has a serious and lasting interest in seeing peace bed down. Successive Taoiseachs have invested vast effort, but throughout this recent phase of development there has been no personal commitment at the top equivalent to that of Blair, and a layer of talented officialdom may not have been adequately replaced. Bertie Ahern has neither an instinctive feel for developments in Northern Ireland nor discernible passion about the outcome. His amiability and comparative lack of ego may have eased negotiations at difficult points, and his reputed talent for deviousness may have had its uses. But dependence for advice on Sinn Féin as senior northern nationalist voice is a different proposition to guidance from John Hume – and even Hume's advice was occasionally unwelcome.

While Blair takes the strain, some think the disposition in Dublin is to switch off between crises. This makes for wry faces, given that Dublin pushed London in the first place to establish a peace process. Self-interest requires fundamental Dublin commitment to the process, but self-interest has been steadily more coloured by party political interest as the extent of Sinn Féin's southern political ambitions becomes more evident and realistic. There is an argument that since decision-making remains British and nationalists look positive, a more overt Dublin role is unnecessary and might be counter-productive, further annoying unionists without assisting nationalists. A decisive and influential Sinn Féin 'independents' bloc in the Dail might well trump that argument.

Unionists and nationalists look to London and Dublin with very different attitudes. From unionists most effort still goes into complaint about the outworking of the Good Friday Agreement, while from nationalists the main impression is of an almost dismissive briskness, a confident 'let's get on with it'. The mismatch between expectations is increasingly obvious, a constant niggle at hopefulness. But one underlying premise of the Agreement was that trying to manage Northern Ireland within the parameters of what unionists wanted did not work. There will be no disposition in either government to tear up a deep-rooted partnership, or to rethink that guideline.

Sustaining progress in a process meant to deliver equality is bound to be difficult, with supposed partners of glaringly disparate commitment. There was an unfocused but widespread desire in both communities to see the back of the Troubles, but no consensus on what basis that could be achieved. Going back is unthinkable, but this has never provided any guarantee that the peace process will go forward. War-weariness and something like shame at the duration of the violence did not translate directly into political dynamism. They did contribute some impetus, however, boosting the efforts of John Hume and Gerry Adams and helping to muffle nationalist scepticism.

Among unionists, the most dynamic effect was evident among loyalist paramilitaries. Those in the unionist community who did most of the killing saw the potential of peace, and of getting out of jail, where many others saw only danger. When David Ervine, Billy Hutchinson, Gary

McMichael and David Adams at one point voiced honestly the need to compromise and the possibilities they saw of improvement for all, many Protestants felt real warmth and liking for them, and some pride. But too much of loyalism had no real commitment, and the short-lived fringe parties lacked the respectability and influence in their own communities that republicans built up over decades of genuine involvement in every aspect of theirs. Frequent and consistent criminality has helped to destroy districts where loyalist paramilitaries hold sway, driving out jobs, businesses, the most able and independent. Republican dominance also has a dark and intimidating side, but not a history of embedded and blatant criminality. Sitting in on small local festivals is a genuine interest for Adams. Johnny Adair, the tattooed and muscled UDA overlord in the Shankill, is a very different figure in his community.

The sector least affected by the Troubles, mainstream unionism, was least persuaded and most resistant to the idea of any new deal. Their unhappiness is more malaise than focused political discontent. Six months after the first IRA ceasefire any sense of momentum had already disappeared as discussion bogged down on the issue of decommissioning. One inside observer of the British response and the interplay between British ministers and unionists said at the time, 'I think the Protestant community is very frightened by the apparent end of violence, because it betokens their need to address a political agenda they don't want to address. There's fear about that, and anger at the fact that that bastard Adams has got away with it.' That anger still chokes off potential tendencies in unionism to talk up the possibilities of peace rather than do them down.

Looked at in the harshest light, a sea of green met a tide of begrudgery, the last vestige of Protestant, unionist superiority swept away by the IRA's most cunning manoeuvre; their cessation of military operations, what unionists damned as a 'pan-nationalist peace process'. The slowly dawning awareness of continuing, and in some cases increased, loyalist violence as republican violence ebbed has been much resisted.

Unionists, many suspicious of all change, never produced ideas for a settlement sufficiently imaginative to attract respect in governments, let alone among nationalists. Unionism had been buffeted by events and forces much more powerful than itself. It won and retained power in Stormont in the 1920s by force of arms, of numbers, the weakness of the south, the weakness of northern nationalists, British and international indifference. There is no tradition of negotiation, no recognition that compromise might be essential to conserve essentials. This unbending approach has left unionists leaden-footed and vulnerable, weighed down by the most rigid of slogans: no surrender, not an inch, what we have we hold. They lost direct political power in 1972 but preserved the illusion of superiority by using their numbers to wreck the 1974 Workers Strike, then stalled and refused to engage in real negotiations. 'Ulster Says No' banners, to protest at the 1985 Anglo-Irish Agreement's ratification of liaison between Dublin and London, yellowed with age as the alliance grew stronger.

The 1998 Agreement was in many ways a top–down remedy, negotiated under heavy pressure from external forces: three governments pushing both sides to compromise. The product was not everything nationalists wanted. In some respects, notably the north/south institutions, it fell far short of both SDLP and Sinn Féin hopes. But nationalists, for whom the Troubles began as they came out of a long political sleep, emerged seeing possibility. Unionists, including the entire political leadership, saw only loss, cumulative and very painful, in increments through years of violence and turmoil, then in a solid tranche. They lost a sense of control and a society which reflected their image of themselves: dominance of a civil service, a judicial system, a police force.

The political leaders of unionism have by far the harder task and meet it in poor shape, inherent ability and intelligence inhibited by present division and the weight of their own history. The long-established leaderships of the SDLP and Sinn Féin were either enthusiastic or ready to profess enthusiasm. Between them they carried the peace process through their entire community to all but die-hard republican purists. Ulster Unionists, with a comparatively recent and insecure leader, were half-convinced and carried an accordingly muddled message to half the unionist community. The DUP refused to take part in negotiations, were totally unconvinced and carried that message convincingly to the other half of the unionist community. Where republicans and nationalists look on their respective leaders as having advanced their interests, the only unionist voice capable of enthusing is that of Paisley, and his message, or at least the message he has yet to disavow, is that Ulster has been sold.

In nationalism there is no clarity on the detail of the political way forward. The communal feeling is perhaps not quite the march of a nation, but there is a widespread sense of a people on the rise, sure that the wind is at their back. It is a relatively recent experience among the Catholics of Northern Ireland and many patently relish it. The face of the society they live in, never one that reflected their own, is changing as they watch. Gerry Adams and Martin McGuinness make republicans proud of their capability and if IRA violence disappears will look increasingly more credible to other nationalists. Mark Durkan is not John Hume, but he may fill a new and valuable role. The made-over Stormont might tempt few to find out about the content of debates or the detail of inter-party dealings in committees, but the old ghosts are gone. To hear Adams say, 'I've now got a grudging admiration for the new northern institutions', and that, although the north/south arrangement should be more dynamic, the 'people of West Belfast' approved was one measure of how far the process has come.

Possibility is still an intoxicating novelty. For those Catholic nationalists whose political involvement does not extend beyond voting, the sense of possibility probably swamps unease that the party of John Hume, architect of a peaceful future, has been slighted in favour of Sinn Féin, built on the guns of the IRA. To know that for the first time they have the numbers not to be ignored or belittled is a reinforcement. Even the least triumphalist could not be expected to mourn for crestfallen unionists. To feel the world's approval is a bonus. Many believe the IRA is heading towards dissolution and most look forward with a good conscience, convinced that the settlement they envisage will do no one an injustice.

Unionism by contrast has become a byword for division, discontent and misery. It is enough to scan the faces of the political leaders: Trimble, Paisley, Robinson, Jeffrey Donaldson, Nigel Dodds. None of them inspires or encourages; most dislike and distrust each other. Recrimination about the way the conflict is ending and about the proposed path towards peace saps energies, and time and talent is dissipated in fighting each other. The sense of drift is mirrored in the continued, often internecine violence of the loyalist paramilitary world.

The majority is all but gone, leaving resentment and fear. Protestants have fled the western part of Northern Ireland to cluster in the coastal strip around Belfast and have largely regrouped to one side of the city itself. The grief of the bereaved and pain of the injured are voiced by politicians largely as a reason for refusing to implement the Agreement with enthusiasm. Protestants cannot even hold on to the notion that they are part of Britain in any way that most Britons would recognise. The knowledge that they are disliked, inside and outside the UK, is deeply painful for many, embittering for some. Repeated Drumcree confrontations, Holy Cross and loyalist violence reinforce the negative image but are prolonged, rather than limited. Many have turned away from politics and long ago abandoned the attempt to voice a more constructive vision for unionism. Frank public assertion that reforms were necessary is all but impossible.

Politicians tell them either that the peace process is a fraud but they will work inside its institutions to stymie it, or that it is dislikeable but the best they can do. The unionist community hears their leaders describe them as a direct and honest people, who like things said plainly. Yet there is an awareness that Ian Paisley's party is working the institutions, but not to destroy them, and that a section of David Trimble's party likes the Agreement much more than they admit. 'I was looking around earlier today and there are all these people with serviettes stuffing themselves,' said Trimble's deputy, Sir Reg Empey, in February 2002, referring to the DUP and other anti-Agreement unionists in Stormont. 'These are the people who are talking of this "great Satan" of an institution. They love it. They love it.' It was a vivid depiction of a clandestine pleasure, but Empey, the most enthusiastic of Trimble's associates, has rarely been as vivid in praise of the Agreement.

A comparison of the leaderships of the parties says much about the state of play in the two groups. Adams has led a movement in collegial style, a secretive collective working obsessively to preserve the unity they know is vital. Hume led a sometimes disgruntled party in a slapdash way, but given the status and influence he won for them, few seriously questioned his pre-eminence. Paisley has surfed charismatically and irresistibly at the head of a party and church of his own making, while Robinson has the inclination to work the Agreement but is limited by his leader's presence. Ulster Unionists are a party without a centre, difficult to lead but also impossible for the disaffected to hijack in a coherent way. Someone with remarkable personal and political qualities might have convinced them that peace would ease their insecurities: Trimble is not that person. An incoherent party unsurprisingly produced a leader with intelligence but no strategy, for ever playing it by ear, torn and uncertain. It is unlikely that any of his putative rivals could have done better.

Given the state of the Protestant community, they needed more leadership than Catholics did: they got less. It is also true that it would have been a much tougher proposition, in a culture which still sees all change as loss, for any unionist to sell the Agreement. The effort was not made. This has been a period during which power has passed from one group to another, probably finally, without any real contest. Effectively unionists have announced, by spreading blame rather than encouraging self-respect, that they are incapable of changing a debilitating frame of mind, and that someone else should do it for them. But unionism's problems cannot be solved from outside – for the sake of self-respect alone, unionists must help themselves. As John Reid discovered sharply when his effort to empathise and challenge sectarianism became grist to the mill of complaint rather than analysis, the outsider's effort is all too easily misunderstood or distorted.

In a new century, a positive way of judging political contributions in a traumatic period might be to ask who helped end the conflict. John Hume heads the list; that Gerry Adams is now taken seriously as a constructive political figure is in the first place due to Hume's tirelessness in broaching a peace process. Adams gets credit for helping to bring the Troubles to an end because he has sustained that process. He gets the benefit of the doubt, in the hope and growing conviction that he and those around him are sincere in turning away finally from violence, though there are still honeyed words to smooth over brutal inconsistencies or stalling on decommissioning, bad moments like Colombia, the deaths of people arrogantly disposed of as 'drug-dealers' or dissidents. There was a long and vicious war before this long and exhausting peace. A total of almost 1,780, 300 of those from their own organisation, died violently because IRA leaders and their followers believed they had the right to kill. The stark roll-call of the dead stays on the record, beside the judgement of the peace process that the leadership of Adams and those around him has finally done the decent thing, with skill and considerable courage.

However dispiriting the heedless ruthlessness of the IRA, leading nationalists has been in many ways a more rewarding task than leading unionists. Nationalists, as led by Hume, have for years seen the potential for progress all around them, if only the violence could be ended. Since the peace process, republicans to a great extent have seized that potential and begun redefining it.

Nationalists may never win the united Ireland they once aspired to, but they have certainly achieved a measure of control in a Northern Ireland that is no longer unionist or exclusively British, feet under the table now where once the complaint was alienation. The question is whether they will be satisfied to extend that transformation, or will push on towards some form of union with the Republic. Adams and Sinn Féin will try to maximise their potential by building up their vote in the Republic while using Westminster as a base within the old enemy's camp. Durkan will presumably build on the Hume legacy to maintain an SDLP line to the next Dublin government.

The nature of both SDLP and Sinn Féin and their relationship are liable to change as the process continues, since the distinction largely depended on one group waging war and the other reviling them. Is it to be steady and unadventurous driving round the block for nationalists, gentle acceleration or foot to the floor? Many might not be disposed to wait patiently while unionists shuffle forward, eying each other warily, especially if street clashes continue unabated with continuing evidence that they are propelled by the last but lingering remnants of loyalist paramilitarism. The death toll of 2001 showed that most killings by loyalists, which accounted for most of the tally, were the result of inter-loyalist feuding. If violence fades and unionists begin to sound more positive, both hefty suppositions, the prevailing inclination in the nationalist community might be to work the institutions as vigorously as possible while exploring the road ahead, steering around unionists where necessary.

Republicans are fond of announcing that their 'analysis' is superior to that of others, with the suggestion that their progress is entirely according to plan. Like many of their other pronouncements, this is less than the truth. They have had the chance to develop political confidence, and judgement, to a very large extent because of the efforts and the vision of John Hume. In the opinion of many observers, some impressed and others hostile, it was Hume who gave Adams the language to smooth over a rough passage, from making war to making peace. Many think a little warily that republicans are indeed transformed now, or in the middle of a transformation. There is also a widespread bitterness that so many died before republicans reached this point. In many minds, the success they now enjoy came only when their leaders absorbed at last and then recast for their own supporters the language of a thousand Hume speeches. 'It was denigrated as Hume-speak all those violent years, that people can live together, politics is the way ahead, violence only does damage, that there is hope,' says one expert, galled occasionally by what he hears as Sinn Féin's aggrandisement of their own political prowess. 'They seemed turgid speeches because they were repeated so often. But in the end that language provided an exit route from the Troubles.'

The SDLP's new leader must be even more galled. Mark Durkan faces the prospect of struggling to regenerate a party upstaged by the people his own mentor guided into first place. The twists in the path since have often given Adams and his colleagues bad moments, but most witnesses would agree that they make their own luck. Adams and McGuinness were never Hume puppets. As to where they go from here, the only certainty is that republicans will make the next bit of the journey in comparatively good shape.

But neat summaries now belie the spills along the way. In September 2001, before the first instalment of decommissioning and the stratagem that restored David Trimble as First Minister, there was widespread fear that the institutions might come tumbling down, leaving a dangerous vacuum. More tests lie ahead. For everyone involved, it has been a bone-shaking business. There must be senior republicans who behind professions of confidence whistle silently when they look back at the road. Soon after the first IRA ceasefire a leading republican figure confessed that 'the one big fear is that the Brits will sit on their hands and do nothing'. It was precisely what happened. The process thereafter has rarely been smooth for more than weeks at a time.

At dark moments, a sense of wonder is easy to misplace but should always be recoverable on examination of what has happened – Sinn Féin sharing the government of Northern Ireland with the DUP and evidently enjoying it, Peter Robinson and Martin McGuinness exercising power as ministers fairly and competently, without any believable claim of bias by either. The betting at Stormont is that a coalition of four disparate parties will not endure as a method of government, and that some more manageable model will emerge in time. Whether it will emerge before another election puts the DUP and Sinn Féin into the two top spots is another question. The emergence of Peter Robinson as leader of the DUP, problematic though his succession might be, would also change the dynamics. As his own man, it is just possible that Robinson would be a revelation. Few doubt that he would read republicans better than David Trimble. Even fewer would expect him to kick over the table and walk away.

The prospects of peace becoming more secure are uncertain and in a sense circular. If enough unionists are to be reconciled to the Good Friday Agreement to sustain the political institutions, power-sharing at Stormont needs a period of unbroken operation. If it is seen to work on the ground, hostility to it might be outweighed by approval clearly enough so that unionists inside Stormont would stop talking out of both sides of their mouths. In turn that would encourage more confidence and belief at the grass-roots. It is not impossible. Paisley, Robinson and the DUP come out of this stage of the process in a different mood to when they went in. Less than 20 years ago the DUP could not have been cajoled or forced into anything remotely like the current arrangement: now it is hard to imagine what would take them out. Only republicans have moved farther.

Cause for hope struggles with experience, but the shifts are real. The pragmatic loyalist voice has been lost for the moment in a wilderness of sectarianism and violence, but may recover. Theirs was the closest attempt to saying the unsayable, that a numerical majority is no longer a civic majority and can no longer be used as arbiter of political destiny. As that slow realisation works its way through an entire community, the bitter streets of North Belfast may well continue to claim innocent lives. Dissident republicans and loyalists with no more than the vestiges of direction will retain the capacity to cause mayhem for a considerable time. But when the IRA deliberately and in front of international witnesses put a quantity of their once-sacred store of arms beyond use, they broke a grim continuum as well as their own rules. In the minds of many, most importantly republicans who once revered the armed struggle and disparaged politics, this was a commitment to politics instead of violence.

In February 2002, in front of a New York audience and on a platform with David Trimble, Mark Durkan, David Ervine, the White House pointman Richard Haass and George Mitchell, Gerry Adams said: 'I don't think we can force on unionism an all-Ireland state that doesn't have their assent or consent.' Unionists would need to feel a 'sense of ownership' in a united Ireland. There was an admission that territory could be united only by winning minds. It was the language of political persuasion, Hume's language again, eight years on from that first Adams visit to New York, an early milestone on a long and bumpy road.

The peace process will stumble for years and may still periodically grind to a halt. Trust will not conquer mistrust for a long time, if ever, but trust is not essential to a peace process. Hatred and sectarian bigotry will take decades to fade, if it ever does. Many in Northern Ireland would settle for a society, at least initially, where people hated each other but stopped killing: a modest goal, but a kind of peace. That John Hume wrought the language of peace should be his political epitaph.

CHRONOLOGY OF A PEACE PROCESS

1990
FEBRUARY Sinn Féin vice-president Martin McGuinness said Peter Brooke was the first Northern Ireland Secretary 'with some understanding of Irish history'.

APRIL Gerry Adams, Sinn Féin president, said if Britain talked to Sinn Féin about eventual disengagement from Northern Ireland, there might be an unannounced IRA ceasefire.

JULY Tory MP Ian Gow was killed at his home in Sussex by an IRA booby-trap bomb.
   IRA bomb at London Stock Exchange.

SEPTEMBER An IRA spokesman dismissed speculation about ceasefires and said the only debate within the republican movement was 'on how to prosecute the war'.

NOVEMBER Peter Brooke said Britain had 'no selfish strategic or economic interest' in the union of Great Britain and Northern Ireland.

DECEMBER For the first time in 15 years the IRA declared a three-day Christmas ceasefire.

1991
FEBRUARY Gerry Adams called reports that he was preparing ceasefire proposals 'fictitious', but said Sinn Féin was ready to 'take political risks'.
   The IRA fired three mortars at 10 Downing Street.

SEPTEMBER Adams said he was prepared for 'open dialogue' and wanted to see all acts of violence end.

DECEMBER The IRA announced a three-day Christmas ceasefire.

1992

JANUARY Peter Brooke said Sinn Féin could only become involved in talks if there was a cessation of violence, not 'temporary ceasefires'.

Eight Protestant workers who had been repairing a police station were killed by an IRA landmine at Teebane Cross, Co. Tyrone.

FEBRUARY An IRA spokesman said its campaign would cease only when there was a British 'declaration of intent' to withdraw.

MARCH Gerry Adams said the slogan describing republicans with a ballot box in one hand and an Armalite rifle in the other was 'outdated'.

APRIL Presidential candidate Bill Clinton said that if elected he would lift the visa ban on Adams.

An IRA bomb wrecked the Baltic Exchange district in the City of London, killing three people and causing damage worth hundreds of millions of pounds.

OCTOBER A series of IRA bombs in London.

DECEMBER Further bomb attacks on London.

NI Secretary Sir Patrick Mayhew said in a speech at Coleraine that there were welcome signs of fresh thinking in some republican circles.

The IRA announced a three-day Christmas ceasefire.

1993

MARCH Two young boys were killed in an IRA explosion in Warrington.

APRIL When Gerry Adams was spotted entering John Hume's home it was revealed that Hume–Adams talks had been going on in secret.

Taoiseach Albert Reynolds said he was willing to talk to Sinn Féin if the IRA ended its violence.

In a joint statement Hume and Adams rejected any internal solution to the conflict in the north. They also said they accepted that the Irish people as a whole 'have the right to national self-determination'. They added, 'We both recognise that such a new agreement is only achievable and viable if it can earn and enjoy the allegiance of the different traditions on this island, by accommodating diversity and providing for national reconciliation.'

An IRA lorry bomb at Bishopsgate caused many millions of pounds' worth of damage in London. A journalist was killed trying to photograph the lorry.

MAY The IRA bombed several predominantly Protestant towns in Northern Ireland. Hume said he would continue to talk to Adams.

JULY Hume said he believed the IRA wanted to end its campaign. In September the IRA maintained an undeclared ceasefire for a week to coincide with trip to Northern Ireland by prominent Irish-Americans. Hume and Adams announced they had reached agreement and would pass their ideas to the Irish and British governments.

OCTOBER Sir Patrick Mayhew demanded an unconditional end to IRA violence and rejected the idea that Britain would 'persuade' Unionists to accept Irish unity.

An IRA attempt to bomb UDA HQ on Shankill Road killed nine Protestant civilians and one of the bombers. Gerry Adams was criticised for shouldering the coffin of Thomas Begley, the IRA member killed in the explosion.

Adams said that if the British responded positively to the Hume–Adams proposals, he would be able to persuade the IRA to end its campaign.

The UDA killed seven people in a pub at Greysteel, Co. Londonderry, bringing the number killed by loyalists since the Shankill bomb to 13.

In a joint communiqué, the British and Irish governments appeared to reject the Hume–Adams initiative and renewed support instead for inter-party talks begun under Northern Secretary Peter Brooke.

NOVEMBER John Major ruled out the Hume–Adams initiative.

Details emerged of extensive secret contacts between the British government and the IRA, despite strong British denials. Sir Patrick Mayhew said there had been 'communication' but not contact and claimed the IRA had sent a message saying that the 'conflict is over' and asking for British advice on how to 'bring it to a close'.

DECEMBER Adams said, 'The Six Counties cannot have a right to self-determination. That is a matter for the Irish people as a whole, to be exercised without impediment.'

Downing Street Declaration released in London by Major and Reynolds. Mayhew said any talks with Sinn Féin after an IRA ceasefire would have to address the surrender of IRA arms.

Adams called for 'clarification' of the Declaration from London. Major turned this down.

President Clinton welcomed the Declaration and said the question of a visa for Adams was being kept under review.

The IRA announced a three-day ceasefire.

1994
JANUARY Reynolds said he would clarify the Declaration.

Republic lifted the long-standing broadcasting ban on Sinn Féin.

Adams said he would not accept a ceasefire as precondition of involvement in talks.

Clinton granted Adams a three-day visa, and was condemned by Major. Adams visited New York.

MARCH IRA mortar attack on Heathrow Airport – none of the devices exploded.

The IRA called a three-day ceasefire: Adams said it 'did not come easily'.

JUNE Irish foreign minister Dick Spring said there would have to be a handover of IRA guns to verify ceasefire.

Six Catholics killed in a loyalist attack on a pub in Loughinisland, Co. Down.

JULY IRA killed three loyalists and bombed three Protestant pubs in Belfast.

AUGUST On 31 August the IRA called a 'complete cessation of military operations'. Major called for evidence that it was permanent. Reynolds said the campaign was over 'for good' and promised to swiftly recognise Sinn Féin's mandate.

SEPTEMBER Reynolds, Hume and Adams met in Dublin and shook hands in public.

Major said the IRA had to say it had abandoned violence 'for good'.

Clinton lifted White House ban on contact with Sinn Féin. Major said exploratory talks with Sinn Féin could begin around Christmas if republicans indicated they intended to give up violence for good. Mayhew said IRA arms would be part of the discussion.

OCTOBER Declaring the Union to be safe, loyalist paramilitary groups announced a ceasefire.

Speaking in Belfast, Major said it was now his government's 'working assumption' that the IRA intended the ceasefire to be permanent.

NOVEMBER The Clinton administration announced an aid package for Northern Ireland.

Newry post-office worker Frank Kerr killed by IRA during armed robbery. The IRA said its statement of 31 August stood, with Adams expressing 'shock and regret'. Reynolds resigned as Taoiseach and leader of Fianna Fail. Bertie Ahern was elected as new leader of Fianna Fail.

DECEMBER British Government announced that exploratory dialogue with Sinn Féin would begin on 7 December.

President Clinton appointed George Mitchell as his economic envoy to Northern Ireland.

Adams said it was 'unlikely' that weapons would he decommissioned 'short of a political settlement'. First official meeting between government officials and Sinn Féin. Decommissioning was identified as a stumbling block.

Major said a Sinn Féin promise on arms would not he enough: there had to be 'significant progress' before the British and other parties would join Sinn Féin at the table.

Fine Gael leader John Bruton was elected Taoiseach in a 'rainbow' coalition, involving Labour and Democratic Left.

Delegations from the loyalist fringe parties, the PUP and UDP met Stormont officials.

1995
JANUARY The Northern Ireland Office announced end of ban on ministers meeting Sinn Féin and political representatives of loyalist paramilitary groups.

FEBRUARY The document 'Frameworks for the Future' was released by the two governments.

MARCH Sir Patrick Mayhew outlined conditions for Sin Féin joining all-party talks, including 'actual decommissioning of some arms'.

MAY Mayhew met Adams in Washington, the first encounter between a republican representative and a government minister.

JULY RUC permitted Orange march through Garvaghy Road, Portadown. Paisley and Trimble celebrated by walking together through cheering supporters.

AUGUST Adams said republicans were ready to make 'critical compromises' to achieve peace.

James Molyneaux announced his resignation as leader of the Ulster Unionist party. Trimble was elected to succeed him.

SEPTEMBER Mayhew met UDP and PUP representatives.

OCTOBER Mayhew told the Conservative party conference that the governments were considering inviting an international commission to help resolve the decommissioning dispute.

NOVEMBER The government published a paper proposing all-party preparatory talks and an international body to consider decommissioning.

President Clinton shook hands with Gerry Adams during a visit to Belfast.

1996
JANUARY British and Irish ministers met Sinn Féin leaders at Stormont. The international commission arms, headed by George Mitchell, recommended that talks and decommissioning should occur in parallel. John Major announced plans for elections in Northern Ireland.

FEBRUARY IRA ceasefire ended after 18 months with the bombing of London's Canary Wharf district, killing two men and causing enormous damage.

John Major and Taoiseach John Bruton announced 10 June as start of talks to decide format of elections to a Northern Ireland Forum. Sinn Féin would be excluded in absence of an IRA ceasefire.

MAY Forum elections were held.

An IRA statement said there would be no decommissioning in advance of an overall political settlement.

JUNE Major and Bruton opened preliminary talks at Stormont, chaired by George Mitchell, but without Sinn Féin.

JULY Orangemen returning from Drumcree church were prevented from marching along Garvaghy Road. Four days of loyalist roadblocks and disturbances followed. A Catholic taxi driver was shot dead not far away, near Lurgan, County Armagh.

The UUP, DUP and others withdrew from talks in protest at the Drumcree ban.

The RUC reversed the ban and forced the march through, and sealed off the lower Ormeau Road to allow an Orange march there. Rioting in nationalist areas followed.

The SDLP said it would withdraw from the Northern Ireland Forum.

Mayhew announced a review of marches.

AUGUST Ronnie Flanagan succeeded Sir Hugh Annesley as RUC Chief Constable.

SEPTEMBER Loyalists began picketing Catholic services in retaliation for nationalist protests against Orange parades.

OCTOBER An IRA bomb attack on army headquarters in Lisburn, County Antrim fatally injured a soldier. It was the first IRA bomb in Northern Ireland since 1994.

NOVEMBER Loyalists attacked the congregation attending Mass at the Harryville church, Ballymena, County Antrim.

DECEMBER An RUC officer was shot and wounded by the IRA at the Royal Victoria Hospital, Belfast, as he protected DUP politician Nigel Dodds who was visiting his terminally ill son.

1997
FEBRUARY Bombardier Stephen Restorick was killed by the IRA in Newry, County Down.

MAY Labour won a general election and Tony Blair became prime minister.

Gerry Adams was returned as MP for West Belfast, Martin McGuinness as MP for Mid-Ulster.

Blair named Mo Mowlam as Northern Ireland Secretary and allowed exploratory contacts between officials and Sinn Féin.

JUNE Sinn Féin was barred from the resumed inter-party talks at Stormont.

An RUC officer was beaten to death by a loyalist mob in Ballymoney, County Antrim.

A general election in the Republic led to a coalition between Fianna Fail and the Progressive Democrats, headed by Taoiseach Bertie Ahern.

Two RUC officers were shot dead by the IRA in Lurgan.

JULY IRA announced new ceasefire.

The Rev. Ian Paisley's DUP withdrew from talks.

An RUC decision to force the march down Garvaghy Road led to days of nationalist rioting.

A teenage Catholic girl was shot dead at the home of her Protestant boyfriend in Aghalee, near Lurgan.

AUGUST Mo Mowlam met a Sinn Féin delegation.

Establishment of Independent Commission on Decommissioning, headed by Canadian General John de Chastelain, to oversee the weapons issue.

Mowlam declared the IRA ceasefire sufficient to allow Sinn Féin to join talks.

SEPTEMBER Sinn Féin signed up to the Mitchell Principles of non-violence and entered all-party talks. Two days later the IRA announced that it had 'problems' with the Principles.

David Trimble led the UUP into talks, walking in alongside representatives of loyalist paramilitary groups.

The governments agreed on the composition of the Decommissioning Body to be chaired by de Chastelain.

OCTOBER Martin McGuinness said Sinn Féin was 'going to the negotiating table to smash the Union'.

Negotiations began at Stormont with the participation of eight parties and the two governments. Sinn Féin leaders Adams and McGuinness met Blair for the first time at Stormont.

DECEMBER Adams and McGuinness made their first visit to Downing Street.

The Stormont talks adjourned for Christmas, the parties having failed to reach agreement even on an agenda. Ulster Unionist MP Jeffrey Donaldson said he was advising party leader David Trimble to withdraw from the talks because of the 'concessions train'.

Loyalist paramilitary leader Billy Wright was shot dead inside the Maze prison by members of a republican group, the Irish National Liberation Army.

1998

JANUARY Mowlam visited Maze prison to persuade loyalist inmates to back the peace process, following an upsurge of loyalist violence in the wake of the Wright killing.

FEBRUARY As the peace talks moved to Dublin Sinn Féin was suspended from the process because of IRA involvement in recent killings.

MARCH Two men were shot dead by the Loyalist Volunteer Force, an anti-ceasefire splinter, in a bar in Poyntzpass, County Armagh. The victims were friends, a Protestant and a Catholic.

An LVF statement said there would be more violence and threatened 'collaborators'.

David Trimble and Gerry Adams attended British Embassy lunch in Washington.

Adams said a deal was possible within three weeks and that he wanted Sinn Féin to be part of it. George Mitchell released paper on north–south relations. Talks resumed and Sinn Féin returned. Mitchell set deadline of 9 April for agreement.

APRIL Taoiseach Bertie Ahern said there were 'large disagreements' with London over the powers of cross-border bodies

Adams said in a newspaper article that history could be made but the deal would be 'transitional'.

On 7 April the UUP rejected as 'too green' a draft presented by George Mitchell, plunging the talks into crisis only 72 hours before a settlement was due.

Blair flew to Belfast to help rescue the deal. He said: 'I feel the hand of history upon our shoulders.' Throughout the night of 9 April, Clinton telephoned the participants at regular intervals.

At about 2 a.m. on 10 April the UUP and SDLP resolved their differences.

A letter was provided by Blair to reassure Unionist representatives on arms decommissioning, as requested by Trimble.

At 4.45 p.m. Trimble telephoned Blair and Mitchell to inform them his party would agree. Unionist MP Jeffrey Donaldson withdrew, leaving Stormont before the final speeches.

11 April: Trimble received the support of his party executive.

18 April: The Unionist party's ruling council supported the Agreement.

27 April: Chris Patten was named as Chairman of the Independent Commission on Policing set up under the Agreement.

30 April: The IRA said it had no plans to decommission.

MAY Strong support for the deal was expressed in referendums on both sides of the border.

JUNE Elections to new Northern Ireland Assembly. Supporters of the deal won 80 seats and opponents 28.

JULY Assembly met for first time. Trimble was elected First Minister designate, with the SDLP's Seamus Mallon as Deputy First Minister designate.

Days of rioting and widespread roadblocks followed ban on Drumcree march. In a loyalist arson attack in Ballymoney, Co. Antrim, three young Catholic boys were killed.

The legislation allowing for early release of prisoners came into being.

AUGUST A Real IRA car bomb in Omagh killed 29 people, in the single deadliest attack of the Troubles.

SEPTEMBER Sinn Féin said it considered violence to be a thing of the past.

Blair and Clinton visited Northern Ireland and travelled to Omagh to view the scene of the explosion and meet relatives of the dead. They also visited Stormont to meet Assembly members.

Trimble promised to create a 'pluralist parliament for a pluralist people'.

OCTOBER Trimble told his party conference that Sinn Féin could not join an executive without the IRA decommissioning.

NOVEMBER Hume said that decommissioning was not a precondition of the Agreement, but that it was the will of the people that it should take place.

DECEMBER Hume and Trimble jointly received the Nobel Peace Prize in Oslo.

Agreement was reached on the structure of the Executive and cross-border bodies.

1999

FEBRUARY Assembly voted to confirm the new government departments and cross-border bodies.

MARCH Tony Blair called for IRA decommissioning to begin if Sinn Féin were to join the executive.

The two governments signed treaties establishing the new north–south, British–Irish and inter-governmental arrangements.

APRIL Decommissioning talks ended in stalemate, but the governments produced a declaration calling for a collective act of reconciliation and the putting beyond use of some weapons on a voluntary basis.

JUNE A Blair deadline passed without agreement on decommissioning.

JULY Blair and Bertie Ahern set out a plan entitled 'The Way Forward' under which devolution would begin on 15 July. Decommissioning would begin within days, to be completed by May 2000.

The UUP rejected Blair's urging to join the devolved government before IRA started decommissioning. Mowlam called on the Assembly to meet on 15 July to nominate an Executive.

UUP members boycotted Stormont as the Executive was nominated, causing it to be declared invalid since it lacked sufficient cross-community membership. Mallon then resigned as Deputy First Minister, calling on Trimble to step down.

Blair and Ahern started review of peace process, with George Mitchell recalled in September as a facilitator.

SEPTEMBER Unionists reacted angrily to publication of the Patten Report which proposed changing the name of the RUC and far-reaching changes to policing.

OCTOBER Peter Mandelson replaced Mo Mowlam as Northern Ireland Secretary.

NOVEMBER Ulster Unionists and Sinn Féin expressed desire to set up inclusive Executive. Pressure mounted on Trimble from anti-Agreement Unionists.

IRA said it was ready to discuss decommissioning and would appoint a representative to the Decommissioning Body. Mitchell concluded his review saying that the basis existed for decommissioning and coalition government.

Mandelson told the Commons that he would freeze the workings of the Agreement if the IRA did not deliver on arms decommissioning.

The UUP ruling council voted to accept a leadership compromise paving the way for Assembly and Executive to operate.

Trimble said he had given a senior party official a post-dated letter of resignation as First Minister, to come into effect in the event of inadequate movement on arms.

The Executive was formed, with Trimble at its head and Mallon as deputy First Minister. Ten departmental ministers were appointed, two of them from Sinn Féin. The DUP said they would function as ministers but would not attend executive meetings.

DECEMBER

1 December: Devolution was restored at midnight.

2 December: Irish government signed away Articles 2 and 3 of the Irish constitution laying claim to Northern Ireland. IRA appointed an interlocutor to Decommissioning Body.

General de Chastelain issued an upbeat report saying that recent events and meetings 'provide the basis for an assessment that decommissioning will occur'.

The Irish cabinet met members of the Northern Ireland Executive in the first meeting of the north–south ministerial council.

2000

JANUARY De Chastelain met the governments to deliver a report on progress on decommissioning. Blair reported to the Commons that insufficient progress had been made.

Trimble made clear his intention to resign in the absence of progress on decommissioning in advance of his party council's meeting on 12 February.

FEBRUARY Mandelson announced the suspension of devolution and a return to direct rule. This led to many recriminations from nationalists and republicans. Sinn Fern claimed a major advance on decommissioning had been outlined in a new IRA statement, later withdrawn.

The government welcomed the IRA statement as significant.

MARCH In Washington for St Patrick's Day, Trimble told a press conference that the Executive might be re-formed without prior IRA decommissioning as long as there were firm guarantees of decommissioning. He was re-elected UUP leader, defeating challenger the Reverend Martin Smyth by a narrower margin than expected.

MAY Blair and Ahern spent two days at Hillsborough Castle meeting local parties, then announced a target date of 22 May for the return to devolution.

The IRA issued a statement saying that if the Good Friday Agreement was fully implemented they would 'completely and verifiably put IRA weapons beyond use'. They also agreed to a number of arms dumps being inspected by international figures.

Cyril Ramaphosa, former Secretary-General of the South African National Congress, and former Finnish President Martti Ahtisaari were named as monitors of the IRA dumps.

The Ulster Unionist Council approved the party rejoining the executive on the basis of the IRA arms offer.

At midnight on 29 May, devolution returned.

JUNE A number of IRA dumps were inspected.

JULY Before the Twelfth of July parades Portadown Orangemen announced plans to bring Northern Ireland to a halt. Released UDA prisoner Johnny Adair appeared with protesters at Drumcree. Scores of roads were blocked. Some violent clashes with security forces followed,

The final prisoner releases were made under the Good Friday Agreement.

AUGUST For the first time in two years troops returned to the streets of Belfast as a loyalist feud claimed more than a dozen lives. Loyalist leader Johnny Adair was returned to prison by Northern Ireland Secretary Peter Mandelson on security force advice in an attempt to calm the feud.

OCTOBER There was a second inspection of IRA arms dumps by the international monitors.

The UUP's ruling council narrowly supported David Trimble after he announced a plan to exclude Sinn Féin ministers from north–south ministerial meetings unless significant progress was made on decommissioning.

NOVEMBER More loyalist feud killings took place.

DECEMBER President Bill Clinton visited both parts of Ireland for the third time.

The loyalist feud was declared to be at an end.

The two Sinn Féin ministers initiated a legal challenge to their exclusion from north–south meetings. General de Chastelain issued a pessimistic report on the decommissioning process.

December 28: Ronnie Hill, in a coma since the IRA 1987 Enniskillen Remembrance Day bombing, died aged 68 in the nursing home his wife Noreen bought in Holywood, County Down, so that she could care for him herself. Ronnie Hill was principal of Enniskillen High School.

2001
JANUARY John Reid became Northern Ireland Secretary after the resignation of Peter Mandelson.

APRIL A further loyalist death brought the feud toll to 16 in 17 months.

A Catholic man was shot dead in Co. Londonderry by gunmen believed to be the IRA.

MAY Trimble wrote a letter of resignation for the second time. The resignation was to take effect on 1 July if there had not been significant progress on the decommissioning of IRA weapons.

A Catholic man was shot dead, apparently by the IRA, in West Belfast.

Bill Clinton, no longer president, made a fourth visit to Ireland.

The IRA announced that it had established regular contacts with de Chastelain.

JUNE In the general election and local elections Sinn Féin and the UDP made significant gains at the expense of the SDLP and the UUP.

In the aftermath of the election the UUP's ruling council met and re-elected Trimble as leader, though there were doubts about his continued survival.

JULY Trimble carried out his threat to resign as first minister.

AUGUST Intensive negotiations produced government movement on policing, followed by an announcement that the IRA had suggested an acceptable method for disposing of arms. Trimble said this was not enough and actual decommissioning was needed.

The government announced a one-day suspension of the Good Friday Agreement, in effect creating another six-week interval for further negotiations.

Sinn Féin and the IRA were pressed to explain what three Irish republicans were doing in the South American country of Colombia.

SEPTEMBER John Hume stepped down as SDLP leader on health grounds.

Worldwide publicity was given to a loyalist protest in Ardoyne, North Belfast, aimed at preventing Catholic schoolgirls and their parents from attending the Holy Cross primary school.

A 16-year-old Protestant youth was knocked down and killed by a car near Longlands Road in North Belfast.

A second one-day suspension was announced to allow another six-week extension for talks. Trimble threatened to withdraw the UUP ministers from the Executive.

The UUP and DUP nominated members to the new Policing Board.

Martin O'Hagan became the first journalist to be killed in the Troubles when he was shot by loyalists.

OCTOBER Northern Ireland Secretary John Reid declared that the UDA, UFF and LVF ceasefires were over.

The three Unionist Party ministers in the Executive resigned to put more pressure on the IRA on decommissioning. The unionist ministers resumed their positions after de Chastelain announced that the IRA had carried out 'a significant act of decommissioning'. Trimble announced that he was prepared to resume office.

NOVEMBER The RUC badge was removed from police stations as the force became the Police Service of Northern Ireland.

Trimble was re-elected first minister with the help of some members of the Women's Coalition and the Alliance Party who redesignated themselves as Unionists. Mark Durkan of the SDLP was elected deputy first minister. The election was followed by a scuffle involving assembly members.

Durkan was elected leader of the SDLP to succeed John Hume.

A Protestant teenager in North Belfast was killed when a bomb he was holding exploded. He belonged to the youth wing of the UDA.

The Holy Cross school confrontation appeared to be resolved.

DECEMBER Chief Constable Ronnie Flanagan announced that he would retire within months.

Police Ombudsman Nuala O'Loan published a highly critical report on the police investigation of the Omagh bombing.

William Stobie, the only person to stand trial in connection with the killing of lawyer Pat Finucane, was killed.

The Policing Board agreed a badge for the police service.

Amid criticism from Irish-American allies of republicanism, Adams visited Cuba and met Fidel Castro.

2002

JANUARY 19-year-old UDA member killed by his own bomb in Coleraine, County Londonderry.

Resumption of the Holy Cross disturbance. Other schools threatened. A loyalist gang, including at least one armed man, entered grounds of a Catholic girls' secondary near Holy Cross and damaged 17 teachers' cars.

Nationalist rioters in Ardoyne attacked police.

20-year-old Catholic postman shot dead in Rathcoole, Co. Antrim.

Bertie Ahern said two-thirds of attacks in North Belfast were by loyalists, with few arrests.

18 January: rallies across Northern Ireland to protest against loyalist threats to postal workers, school staff and to call for an end to all paramilitary violence.

More North Belfast violence: attacks on Protestant homes in White City, Whitewell Road. Attacks on Catholic homes in Newington.

19 January: David Trimble said he would take unspecified action if there was not further decommissioning by the IRA: 'Please carry out the promise you have made. Get on with the job and stop belly-aching about others.'

21 January: Sinn Féin's four MPs travelled to Westminster to take their offices in the House of Commons, with allowances and expenses expected to total £400,000.

30 January: Relatives and others gathered in the Bogside to mark the 30th anniversary of Bloody Sunday, when 13 people were shot dead and a 14th was fatally injured by paratroopers.

FEBRUARY Bloody Sunday inquiry resumed after adjournment for anniversary.

Gerry Adams said in New York that an all-Ireland state which did not have their assent or consent and did not 'reflect their sense of being comfortable' could not be forced on unionists.

The Policing Board proposed a compromise between Ombudsman Nuala O'Loan and Chief Constable Sir Ronnie Flanagan, that a senior officer from an English force would oversee the Omagh investigation.

Northern Ireland Secretary John Reid said in Washington that he was asking the US government and Irish-Americans to reach out to working-class Protestant communities. If the peace process was to work, both communities had to have a sense of ownership of it.

Reports said the results of the 2001 census would show a significant drop in Protestant numbers and continuing rise in the Catholic population.

11 February: An American group, the Lawyers' Committee for Human Rights, published a report into the death in February 1989 of the lawyer Pat Finucane, and claimed to have new evidence for allegations of collusion between security forces and the loyalist paramilitaries who killed him.

INDEX